Global Acquisitions

GLOBAL ACQUISITIONS

Strategic Integration and the Human Factor

Stan Lees

First published 2003 by
PALGRAVE MACMILLAN
Houndmills, Basingstoke, Hampshire RG21 6XS and
175 Fifth Avenue, New York, N.Y. 10010
Companies and representatives throughout the world

PALGRAVE MACMILLAN is the global academic imprint of the Palgrave
Macmillan division of St Martin's Press LLC and of Palgrave Macmillan Ltd.
Macmillan® is a registered trademark in the United States, United Kingdom
and other countries. Palgrave is a registered trademark in the European
Union and other countries.

ISBN 0–333–77629–1 hardback

This book is printed on paper suitable for recycling and made from fully
managed and sustained forest sources.

A catalogue record for this book is available from the British Library.

A catalogue record for this book is available from the Library of Congress.

10   9   8   7   6   5   4   3   2   1
12   11   10   09   08   07   06   05   04   03

Printed and bound in Great Britain by
Creative Print & Design (Wales), Ebbw Vale

To Laura,
who playfully taught her dad
the Game of Golden Lemon

Contents

List of Tables and Boxes

Tables

Boxes

List of Figures

Acknowledgements

A book that has been brewing away at the back of the mind for nearly a decade is influenced by many people, only some of whom can be mentioned. First and foremost is John Hunt at London Business School, with whom I worked in the late 1980s and who helped set in place the tentative foundations of the book. Also significant in taking my thoughts forward in those early days were the groups of acquisition managers on executive programmes at Stitching de Baak in the Netherlands and at City University Business School in London in the early 1990s.

Managers on Lancaster University's various MBA programmes brought experience and critical insight, especially those from Eastern Europe and the Far East. Their perspectives were different and enormously enriching. Companies I have been involved with on various aspects of merging and demerging remain confidential, but their contribution is also acknowledged.

A special word of thanks is extended to Stephen Rutt and the team at Palgrave Macmillan. They understood the reasons why at times deadlines had to be renegotiated and this was appreciated.

Every effort has been made to trace all the copyright holders but if any have been inadvertently overlooked the publishers will be pleased to make the necessary arrangements at the first opportunity.

Introduction

This book is about managing the post-deal integration stage of mergers and acquisitions (M&A). It addresses the question of how best to approach and manage the bringing together of two firms to achieve acquisition goals. It is not about identifying targets for takeover or conducting financial analyses or negotiating the deal, although each chapter has important implications for these and other pre-deal activities.

The book is aimed directly at those managers in a merger or acquisition who are charged with the complex task of interfacing and integrating the two very different sets of personnel, structures, systems and cultures from each side. The need being addressed is the now compelling evidence of under-performance in the majority of mergers and acquisitions.

For most firms, acquisitions are exceptional events in at least two respects. They happen infrequently, and when they do there are seldom any tried-and-tested procedures to guide action. It is common to read of acquisitions failing because the elements of the two organisations could not be combined into a coherent and functioning whole, or that integration styles destroyed those very qualities in a target that made it attractive in the first place.

Guidance on how to approach such matters is not always easy to find. There is a sizeable literature on the various parts of the acquisition cycle – some researched from different academic perspectives, some reporting particular case examples, some drawing upon the wisdom of experience – but all widespread and not always easy to access.

The material in this book is a selected blend of theory and practice, research and experience, woven together to provide some essential frameworks to guide the integration of mergers and acquisitions. It is intended as much for targets as for acquirers, not least because the target role in planning how to make acquisitions work is regularly overlooked. There is no shortage of prescriptions and recipes for bringing about changes in the target – some with a distinctly imperial flavour – but very little on how to use target expertise as an integration resource (and also as a check on possible acquirer misjudgement).

Some firms, of course, are fortunate. Those that acquire on a regular basis may already have a refined set of integration procedures that they can apply confidently to each situation they encounter. Their accumulated experience has been distilled into an organisational knowledge base that can give them a distinct competitive advantage over rivals. Most firms do not have this capability but appear to need it.

Two of the messages coming from decades of merger and acquisition research are difficult to dispute. The first is that the majority of firms seem unable to deliver the full value-added that their takeover calculations promise. The second is that the way in which firms implement their acquisitions is more likely to destroy shareholder value than add to it. These findings are as true for small national firms as for large global corporations.

Why this should be so and what firms can do to avoid value destruction will be examined in some detail in the following chapters.

Strategic Integration

Strategic integration in a merger context means the way acquiring and target firms are brought together must be finely tuned around the strategy driving the deal. That is the central message of this book. Acquisition strategies (i.e., external *market competition* strategies) and integration strategies (that is, internal *organisational cooperation* strategies) must go hand-in-hand. Each must inform and shape the other. Neither is of lesser significance.

Tight Integration is Essential to Avoid Value Destruction

Firms often value target companies in terms of synergy and efficiency gains without examining what the gains will cost to deliver.

A planned and detailed integration strategy is the only way to establish the true cost of realising synergy and how best to go about delivering it.

Tight Integration is Essential to Ensure Target Commitment

Commitment shapes performance. This is absolutely central to the psychology of takeovers. After a takeover, fear and uncertainty run through the acquired business and performance often drops. Managers and staff are expecting change and they want a clear picture of the future.

A carefully planned integration strategy helps build commitment to the new owners. It ensures that all functions and levels receive consistent and convincing information about new business directions, whether jobs are secure and where major changes are to occur.

Tight Integration is Essential for Bridging National Cultures

Globalisation has brought all firms onto the world stage. Companies from all corners of the world are stretching into countries where management thinking can be totally unfamiliar. This is as true for international corporations merging to become truly global players as it is for small firms making their first overseas acquisition.

An integration strategy built around a solid understanding of how national culture shapes management thinking is more likely to deliver value and minimise costly culture clashes.

Tight Integration Addresses a Recurring Criticism of Strategy in Practice

In the business world, strategy is all about competition; about how firms choose to pursue competitive advantage and profitability. But particularly in Western management thinking, the domain of strategy is usually confined to the *external* positioning of a company in relation to markets (usually financial and product markets). Strategy formulation often proceeds with insufficient regard to the *internal* organisational conditions necessary to make financial and commercial strategies 'happen'.

This is especially true in mergers and acquisitions. Decisions about how best to interface and integrate two companies are absolutely crucial for performance, yet such matters are frequently regarded as afterthoughts, as activities passed down the line for senior managers to get on with; certainly something less glamorous than 'the thrill of the chase'. It is still the exception rather than the rule to find implementation dynamics appearing as a central component in acquisition planning and negotiation.

Integration Strategies are Different

Integration strategies are different in substance from commercial strategies. The necessary mindsets and skills are very different. The typical merger planning scenario – with its finely refined calculations on target valuation, market shares, cash flows, tax synergies, price to earnings (P/E) ratios and similar – is very much a formula-driven, number-based endeavour. And when strategy is number-driven, managers can be lulled into a false sense of security. Numbers can suggest that 'right' and 'wrong' answers really do exist.

Integration strategies, in sharp contrast, do not have 'right' or 'wrong' answers. Decisions about how best to bring together two uniquely different firms draw heavily upon judgement, experience and 'best guess' choices. Change-management skills drive the agenda, not number-crunching proficiency. In cross-border deals, integration requires perceptive insight into how national culture and national 'business recipes' shape human behaviour. A deep understanding of human and organisational and cultural processes is the crucial capability, not financial and market knowledge.

This is not the language of deal-making. It is the language of trying to make deals work. And, as the following chapters will demonstrate, the integration agenda can be incorporated into every stage of acquisition planning and long before negotiations begin. Strategic integration is both an early and a critical pre-deal concern.

Source Material

The material in the following chapters is drawn from primary research, published sources and company practice. The primary research covers a twelve-year period from 1986 to 1998 and proceeded in three stages.

First was the study *Acquisitions – The Human Factor* (Hunt et al., 1987). This was the first known attempt to systematically explore the human factor in a large sample of acquisitions – in this case, 40 acquisitions made by major UK companies during the mid-1980s. The study examined how interpersonal and leadership factors influenced business and organisational decisions at key stages across each acquisition, from early planning through to at least two years of implementation.

Although the report had a limited circulation, some of the results were published (Hunt and Lees, 1987; Hunt, 1990; Lees, 1992). One important finding was the group of seven factors, seven aspects of acquirer behaviour, that had a direct impact upon commitment across all levels of a target company (see Chapter 13). But this was no more than a first cut at the database and was very much from a broad *psychological* perspective – mapping out in broad terms how senior people on each side acted and reacted at different stages of the process.

The second stage was to extend the human factor into the *organisational* determinants of acquisition behaviour. During 1991–93 the database was revisited with three broad questions in mind.

1. How did acquiring managers conceptualise the integration process (the strategic mindset question)?

2. What sorts of pre-deal decisions could compromise the value-creating potential of integration?

3. How did the dynamics of implementation and integration influence commitment and performance on target side?

Out of these broad questions arose the shape of the first integration frameworks. But at this stage they were highly tentative; especially given the limited size of the sample (40 acquisitions).

Then, over a five-year period, the frameworks were 'soft-tested' on acquiring and target managers from the UK and mainland Europe on a heuristic 'does this fit your experience?' basis. How useful were the frameworks for integration planning? Did they capture the important variables? Could they shed light on earlier successes and failures? Were they helpful for building up an organisational knowledge base on acquisition management?

Through this very exploratory research – hypothesis-building rather than hypothesis-testing – a process of continuous refining took place. In total, over 200 managers gave valuable feedback and insights from their own domestic and cross-border deals in the UK, mainland Europe, the Commonwealth of Independent States, Asia and the Far East. The feedback remains confidential but is gratefully acknowledged.

Another Source of Insight

Another source of insight – much more indirect – has to be mentioned. It concerns external advice given to acquiring companies. This usually is not easy to gauge given the secrecy that surrounds so much M&A practice. But over the years while the different parts of this book have been taking shape, it has been possible to gain an insight into some of the integration advice given to companies from a range of sources, including some high-profile establishments. Sadly, that advice appears not always to have been of a consistent quality.

The spread has ranged from sound and sensible through to simplistic and even misguided. Some advice showed a deep understanding of the issues, usually from advisers who had made the field their specialism. Other advice betrayed a naive understanding of how organisations actually function and only the dimmest appreciation of the realities of integration. Of course, the sample is tiny and one cannot generalise from hindsight judgements of managers – some of whom, after all, chose to follow the advice they were given.

However, if the examples are representative (and data on acquisition performance suggest they might be) then there are grounds for concern. It is worrying when managers are persuaded to follow advice that at times may be dubious. It is doubly worrying when they pay through the nose for the privilege.

This brings me to the reasons for writing the book. The dispassionate reason was to plug a hole in management understanding and to build bridges between strategy and the essentially human aspects of organisation and management. But the real motivation, the felt imperative, was to raise the quality of thinking about integration and to provide some benchmarks for practice where few currently exist. If advice from some of the world's highest profile consulting houses can be of variable quality, the reader is left to guess what the advice might look like further down the ladder.

The Structure of the Book

This is not a 'how to do it' book; it is a 'how to *think* about doing it' book. The difference is crucial. It is simply not credible to say 'This is how best to integrate an acquisition.' Every acquisition or merger is unique: different parties, different circumstances, different expectations. There is no single best way of bringing two firms together and it is dishonest to claim otherwise. However, there are some very helpful ways of *thinking* about how to do it – applicable to acquisitions, mergers, joint ventures and other strategic alliances – and that is what is offered here.

Each of the chapters will invite you to scrutinise your own M&A mindset and those in companies you are familiar with. No matter how elementary or sophisticated your mindset may be, you will be asked to look at received wisdom and to rethink some fundamentals. Remember also that although the chapters follow a time logic of pre-deal to post-deal and beyond, all the issues covered are essential components of acquisition planning. All need to be considered before a deal is completed.

The book is divided into five parts. The general approach is to start with theory and then move into practice, shifting from 'hard' knowledge to 'soft' knowledge along the way. However, the dynamics of integration are not entered into immediately.

Part 1 gives a brief overview of the acquisition field and explains some of the thinking behind the chapters. Concepts central to the book – especially strategic integration, the human factor and managerial mindsets – are all explained in detail.

Part 2 explores the backcloth to integration. Here we take a critical look – in a way that perhaps has not been done before – at some of the heavyweight 'taken for granted' assumptions that have driven acquisition activity across the twentieth century. The compelling research evidence on acquisition underperformance from finance, economics and strategy, the three major disciplines in the M&A field, is also examined.

One of the messages of Part 2 is that integration cannot deliver value if it is not there to start with or if pre-deal decisions have already destroyed much of that value. So, from the research evidence on acquisition underperformance, twelve of the most common ways in which managers can destroy acquisition value are identified.

Part 3 begins to examine the dynamics of integration through the eyes of an integration manager incorporated early into the acquisition planning process (see pages 85–7 for an overview of the integration agenda). It goes through the major 'hard' issues that have to be considered and the types of data needed to make informed choices. There is a chapter on due diligence that emphasises organisational and capability audits. There is a short chapter on the essential controls that have to be in place early. And there is a chapter on integrating structures that offers some frameworks for carefully bringing together two organisations around the business goals of an acquisition.

Part 4 concentrates on people. It examines typical human reactions in mergers and offers some frameworks for developing acquisition-specific Human Resource strategies. A three-stage model for building commitment to an acquisition from both an acquiring and acquired perspective is examined in depth.

Part 5 is predominantly about culture. It examines the culture concept and the dynamics of culture in some depth and identifies areas where culture clashes are likely in mergers. Some new frameworks for understanding national culture are then offered that are especially relevant to international mergers.

The final chapter examines some of the key issues in developing global integration managers.

Kurt Lewin, the father of social psychology, once remarked that there is nothing so practical as a good theory! There is, unfortunately, no theory of how to manage mergers and acquisitions, and it is important to underscore yet again that the book makes no such claim. There are few 'how to do it' pre-scriptions.

What the book does claim is this. When there is no theory to guide action, the next best things are some models and frameworks, some cognitive maps, which both sides can share to guide *thinking* about action. Models and frameworks on their own are no more than abstract mental maps, but when rooted in context and shared by both sides, they provide a focus that can be invaluable for planning and negotiation purposes.

- First-time acquirers with no experience of integration should be able to devise their own integration frameworks from the material in the book without the need for third-party intervention.

- Targets can use the frameworks to be more in control of the integration agenda.

- More active firms can build up an in-house knowledge base from the experience of earlier acquisitions. The frameworks can then develop into local, tentative theories-in-use – by no means perfect, but grounded in the specific culture and acquisition experience of each firm.

- Firms with refined implementation procedures should find the frameworks invaluable for reconsidering and perhaps improving what they already do well.

This is the spirit in which the book is offered. It is intended to help all firms move quickly up the integration learning curve from whatever position they find themselves. If that happens, it can go a long way towards reversing the view that mergers and acquisitions are one of the top ten ways of destroying shareholder value.

Part 1

Acquisitions in Perspective

Acquisitions: The Promise and the Problem

'Making an acquisition deliver ... that's what separates the men from the boys.'
(Chief Executive Officer, leisure)

Acquisitions and mergers[1] are about growth – often rapid growth. Of the three major routes (see Figure 1.1) a firm can choose if it wants to grow quickly, the growth-through-acquisitions route offers the greatest possibilities. **Organic** growth can be slow: market penetration can be difficult against established competitors and it can take many years for a company to reach any appreciable size. Growth through **innovation** can be costly: it carries a high risk of technical failure, and at the time of making the capital investment there is no certainty of demand for the capacity created.

But **acquiring** viable companies 'off the shelf' offers immediate access to their markets, technology, finance, management skills and much more. Firms can diversify quickly through acquisitions. Operating efficiencies can be improved. Greater size increases market power and protects against economic and market instability. And the downside is cushioned. If the purchase proves to be disappointing, usually it can be sold off to another buyer. From a strategic perspective it is easy to understand the attraction of acquisitions and why growth through acquisitions has become almost a generic strategy in many companies.

Testimony to the power of acquisitions and the economic concentration that follows is visible all around us. One glance at the economic and corporate landscape says it all. At the end of the nineteenth century, it was still a world of small-scale local enterprises. At the beginning of the twenty-first century, it is a world of corporate leviathans. The 100 largest companies in any industrialised country owe their size and power principally to a succession of acquisitions and mergers.

In the US, the 50 largest multinationals, each a product of multiple acquisitions, control well over 25% of total US corporate assets. These firms drive the global economy. They dominate world production and global markets. They transcend national boundaries, and often eclipse the autonomy of

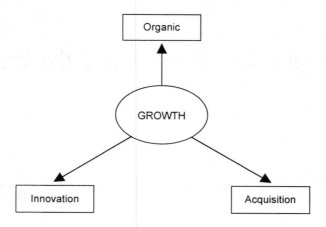

Figure 1.1　Three major routes to corporate growth

national governments (certainly in the spheres of economic and industrial policy). All of which sends out a very powerful message. Today, some of the biggest firms in the world have more economic power and influence than many United Nations member states. These firms seem to have become huge and successful by stacking acquisitions one on top of another. So, why not follow their example?

It is a challenge some firms would rise to. There is certainly no shortage of firms eager to follow the acquisition trail. The market for corporate control (Manne, 1965) grew exponentially during the last ten years of the twentieth century (see Figure 1.2).

Mega-deals and globalisation have been responsible for the sharp rise in both the number and the value of deals in the late 1990s. However, underneath the peak lie the solid mass of acquisitions pursued each year for the usual life-cycle reasons – just as they have always done across the decades:

- start-up firms seeking a specialised partner for growth

- expanding firms needing the marketing expertise of a larger firm

- mature firms finding it cheaper to buy in capabilities than to develop them in-house

- stagnant firms diversifying into new industries in the hope of rejuvenation

- declining firms in dying industries merging to reduce capacity and improve their survival chances.

In other words, companies grow by assimilation into others, and for all sorts of reasons. Then they mature, decline, go into liquidation or are taken over, and thus shape and grow into something else. Acquiring and being acquired are thus perfectly normal activities at different stages in the business life-cycle as environmental circumstances change.

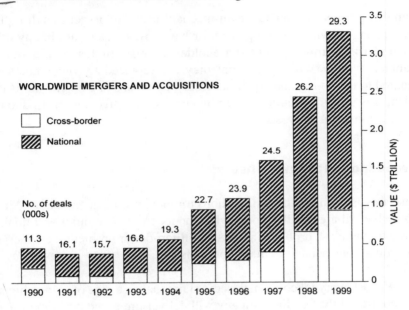

Figure 1.2   Global acquisition activity, 1990–99

Sources: © *The Economist* 9 January 1999; data for 1999 from *Acquisitions Monthly*

In fact, for all but the smallest companies, the probability of being acquired is higher than the probability of going into liquidation. Research has shown that if a company disappeared from UK stock exchange listings prior to 1950, the major reason was liquidation. Post-1950, it was attributable almost entirely to takeover or merger (Singh, 1975). If viable parts of a business can be saved in time, the acquisition process would seem a more efficient – and certainly a more socially responsible – alternative to bankruptcy or voluntary liquidation.

However, of all the justifications for acquisitions, the two which usually carry most weight are the claims that takeovers improve economic efficiency and protect investor interests. With shareholdings in most firms widely dispersed, corporate executives have broad discretion to act in ways that may benefit their own interests but not necessarily those of investors. The takeover mechanism, when operating efficiently, is argued to protect against this in two ways:

1. The act of takeover is said to replace underperforming managers with more able counterparts.

2. The possibility of takeover acts as a threat to *all* corporate managers who do not act on behalf of shareholders.

From this perspective, the takeover mechanism is said to act as a discipline upon managers who are complacent or have lost focus or are in any other way underperforming, to put shareholder interests first. If not, action by financial markets will ensure that they are replaced by other managers prepared to do so – ultimately, if necessary, by means of a hostile bid. All of which, it is argued, should keep companies competitive and profitable and safeguard investor interests.

How Sound is Takeover Theory?

These are just some of the justifications for mergers and acquisitions. All are impressive; all are solidly grounded in theory from economics and finance. However, there is a problem, a massive billion-dollar problem. Few mergers and acquisitions behave as theory predicts:

- Almost every takeover makes the claim that a change of ownership and control of the vendor company will deliver improved performance and better shareholder returns – except that the returns don't always materialise.

- Most acquisitions claim that greater size will bring higher levels of efficiency and improved competitiveness – but only sometimes.

- Synergies can be stubbornly elusive.

- Capability transfer often doesn't happen or transfers across to competitors.

- When poor results are announced, financial markets do not discipline as consistently as the efficient-market model predicts they should. In fact, the way in which financial markets interpret underperformance and the types of sanction they impose seem to vary across industries and countries, and also across time.

There is a wide gulf between what takeover theory predicts should happen and what actually happens in the post-acquisition period. This is not to deny that many firms have used the takeover route to grow successfully and profitably. Their acquisitions have delivered all that was expected of them; sometimes even more. But other firms, particularly those with over-optimistic expectations about the power of takeovers to deliver corporate growth and renewal, often have been bitterly disappointed. A range of studies has shown a consistent pattern of poor long-run performance in both acquiring firms and target firms.

But didn't big firms become large and successful by making acquisitions one after another? Yes, they did, but with this critical proviso: *those that survived* did it more efficiently than the rest. They acquired in a way that, on average, delivered performance and shareholder returns. In most instances, they managed their acquisitions in a way that delivered returns greater than the cost of buying and integrating the targets – or if not, they cut their losses and divested.

Big successful firms are the survivors in the acquisition game, the tip of an enormous iceberg. Underneath lie the remains of thousands of companies, large and small, that couldn't make their acquisitions deliver. Corporate history is littered with the names of companies that went on an acquisition spree with a bag of debt chasing poorly understood hope. They tried to be big but couldn't make it. A few years later, with their share price in tatters, they disappeared without trace, unable to manage successfully what they had bought.

Acquisition history tells us some stark truths:

- It is easy to buy market share, but much harder to retain and increase it.

- Getting hands on the cashflow is easy; making the cash flow faster is more difficult.

- Buying know-how is simple; knowing how to manage and develop it is far more complex.

- Taking a competitor out of the market only takes a day; turning a competitor into a collaborator can take years.

- Laptop computers can identify synergy potential; realising the synergy can defeat teams of world-class managers.

These lessons apply equally to acquisitions where there is a good strategic fit into existing businesses as it does to diversifications into new areas. But we don't know the reasons why. This is the central problem in acquisition performance. Takeover theory predicts synergy – that <u>two plus two can equal</u>

five. There are few definitive explanations as to why, post-deal, the majority of acquisitions struggle to get two plus two to equal four.

Value Destruction

Value-destruction and why it happens remains the biggest unresolved question in mergers and acquisitions. Some analysts blame rosy-eyed calculations or rushing the deal. Others blame flawed strategy. Business life-cycle reasons are also suggested. But increasingly the finger is being pointed at a fundamental weakness in both the theory and the practice of Western strategy.

> Strategic models offered to companies rarely specify the economic and organisational conditions necessary to make strategy 'happen'. And when top managers follow the models, they often compound the weakness by making strategic decisions in isolation from the senior executives who have to carry them out.

The effect in mergers and acquisitions is the all-too-familiar practice of strategy separated from implementation. Deal-makers rarely get involved in implementation, and implementation managers – whose job is to make acquisitions deliver their intended value – are rarely at the table when a deal is negotiated. Sometimes the first they know about a deal is when the implementation job lands on their desks. If they have never done the job before, or if they are already fully stretched, or if there is no knowledge base from the firm's earlier acquisitions to offer guidance – all very common occurrences – then implementation can be seriously handicapped.

At present, there is very little help available to companies on how to avoid value destruction. We know very little about how firms make their acquisition decisions or about how they select a particular style of implementation. The whole area remains an enormous and uncomfortable black hole in management understanding – uncomfortable because it puts the spotlight on how selective management research can be in terms of the inefficiencies it seeks to remedy.

For most of the twentieth century, armies of researchers have crawled all over workers on the factory floor to seek efficiency gains – which sometimes have amounted to no more than a few pennies. During the same period, countless thousands of mergers and acquisitions have taken place in every industrialised country. They were the most significant shapers of the corporate landscape as it evolved in the twentieth century, and their cumulative expenditure amounted to a truly astronomical figure. Yet it was

---

Box 1.1   Porter on paper synergy

If you believe the text of the countless corporate annual reports, just about anything is related to just about anything else! But imagined synergy is much more common than real synergy. General Motors' purchase of Hughes Aircraft simply because cars were going electronic and Hughes was an electronics concern, demonstrates the folly of paper synergy ...

It is all too easy to create a shallow corporate theme. CBS wanted to be an 'entertainment company', for example, and built a group of businesses around leisure time. It entered such industries as toys, crafts, musical instruments, sports teams and hi-fi retailing. While this corporate theme sounded good, close listening revealed its hollow ring.

None of these businesses had any significant opportunity to share activities or transfer skills among themselves or with CBS's traditional broadcasting and record businesses. They were all sold, often at significant losses, except for a few publishing-related units ... erod[ing] the shareholder value [CBS] created through its strong performance in broadcasting and records. (Porter, 1987)

---

not until around 1980 that *management* researchers began to pay serious attention to them.

It is a sobering thought that if twentieth-century management scholars had been more willing to challenge strategy at source and put boardroom ineffi-ciencies under the microscope, we would now have an acquisition knowledge base capable of delivering efficiency savings of huge proportions. We could have gathered invaluable insight and wisdom from the thousands of integration managers who had 'hands-on' experience of bringing together so many different companies across the decades. But most of that experience has been lost – gone with the managers to their graves.

That lost opportunity – given the number and size of current deals and the magnitude of underperformance – potentially is worth billions of pounds and dollars every year. Supposedly gilt-edged mergers and acquisitions are now going sour at a jaw-dropping rate.

- AT&T bought NCR in 1991 for $7 billion, then sold it for $3 billion in 1995. Culture clashes were blamed.

- Quaker Oats acquired Snapple, a US soft drinks manufacturer, for $1.7 billion in 1994 and then sold it for $300 million in 1997. Indecisive integration and a clash of management styles were reported.

- In 1999, SmithKline Beecham sold Diversified Pharmaceutical Services, a US pharmacy-benefits management firm, for a knockdown $700 million. It had been acquired in 1994 for $2.3 billion.

These were just some of the headline-grabbers in the 1990s. Choose another decade and the names would change, but not the message. Far less publicity is given to the thousands of smaller acquisitions that run into trouble. Their losses may not be as great, but cumulatively they also run into billions. Most have one problem in common – an inability to integrate two companies together to deliver value.

What help has been available to these companies? Up to now, very little. We are still pretty hopeless at explaining why one acquisition turns into gold and another into a lemon.

Integration: The Value-Creating Capability

In the twenty-first century, the critical economic resource will be knowledge, rather than capital or labour. Knowledge, we are repeatedly reminded, is the new engine of economic growth. This is especially true in mergers and acquisitions. Any two firms can merge using their shares as capital, but knowing how to combine the two firms to create value is the scarce resource. In today's flexible, globalised world, the ability to integrate acquisitions and alliances speedily and effectively is not just a strategic desirable. It is a competitive necessity.

Large corporations can no longer rely on their sheer size to act as a barrier against other companies entering and taking their markets. Increasingly, it is smaller companies that steal their market share, not other big companies. This is because smaller companies with state-of-the-art technology have learned something very important.

With traditional business boundaries and borders collapsing faster than ever before, smaller companies have learned that they can use acquisitions and collaborative ventures anywhere around the world to obtain and develop new technologies and bring them to market at speeds unimaginable a decade or so ago. *Provided they are nimble and are able to integrate together the various businesses and capabilities, smaller firms can beat the giants at their own game.* It is an example repeatedly demonstrated in the Tiger economies and now occurring on a global scale.

Nor can large corporations simply rely on a continuous supply of smaller companies for rejuvenation or to stave off competition. They can no longer just say: 'We're rich enough to buy whatever capabilities we need.' They also need the ability to integrate the purchased value quickly and effectively into their existing businesses. But the rigidity of large corporations often works against the more flexible and innovative character of smaller firms and can stifle capability transfer. In the knowledge sector especially, if acquired staff dislike the new style of management, value-purchased can simply walk out the door. And, if it doesn't, we know from research that 60% of all innovations are imitated within four years – and often from a lower cost base (Pfeffer, 1995).

Fast and effective integration – to ensure that value-purchased quickly becomes value-added and not value-lost. It is a capability that all firms will need if they are to compete successfully in the future. Mega-deals may grab the headlines but in the global economy of the twenty-first century firms of all sizes will need to become involved in acquisitions or mergers or joint ventures or some other form of strategic alliance simply to stand still. Firms that lack a capability will source it, worldwide if necessary. Firms with innovation, talent or ideas will be seized upon. The boundaries of firms, markets, even entire industries, as they have traditionally been conceived, are becoming increasingly fuzzy and unrecognisable.

Fast and effective – at **being** *integrated*. Both sides need to create the optimal conditions to make an acquisition or alliance work. Often target firms know how best to achieve value-added and increasingly they will drive the integration agenda in the future. The days when the larger or dominant partner dictated the style of post-deal management and integration are disappearing fast. Smaller firms joining global corporations are now resisting being gobbled up. They want to keep some measure of autonomy and independence, as much for performance reasons as for staff morale.

Hard bargaining in the future will be as much about price as about prospective management style. It will require a new breed of deal-makers able to operate at this level of subtlety and able to recognise the performance significance of values on each side. Global goliaths hoovering up smaller companies around the world will need to adopt multiple styles of integration, tailoring each to the circumstances of the target. Delivering results will require a new breed of integration manager.

At present, around 85% of integration managers have little or no experience of the task and do it as an addition to their main job. In the future they will be highly specialised; selected as much for their psychological disposition and Human Resource skills as for their business and technical acumen. An ability to be comfortable and effective interfacing across multiple boundaries will be essential. For example, in the knowledge sector, a typical integration task might centre on the development of an item of cutting-edge software. This could involve pulling together several different ventures from around the world, each with a different management style and different cultural expectations, with the driving impetus coming mostly from below, to deliver a 'product' which has no form, no weight and which owes no national allegiance. An example such as this may not be the easiest to grasp, but it does illustrate very clearly that managing in the dot.com 'weightless' economy requires mindsets that have evolved significantly from the traditional factory model of management.

Fast and effective integration – not just of firms and their structures but also systems, processes, cultures, and right down to individuals and their motivation and commitment. That can be one of the hardest things to achieve. Talk to any managers with acquisition and merger experience and they will tell you that structuring the deal is usually straightforward. It is afterwards that the really intractable problems arise.

Go further and ask them what, with hindsight, they would do differently, and two answers are always consistent. One is that they wish they had known more about the reasons why acquisitions (and other collaborative ventures) underperform *before* they entered into negotiations. The other is that they wish they had devoted far more time and effort to planning the implementation and integration *before* the deal was signed.

The following chapters should go a long way towards meeting these wishes.

CHAPTER 2

The Human Factor and Strategic Integration

'If I can't figure out how a company thinks, I won't go after it.'
(Managing Director, electronics)

The human factor is a broad term and it is important to clarify what it is intended to cover. This chapter goes into detail on how the term is used here and also explains some of the thinking that lies behind the book. It should not be skipped even though it is conceptual. It goes straight to the heart of the current critique of strategy.

The human factor can be considered at several levels. At a straightforward level, it is about *bringing together two different sets of people from each firm and managing their reactions and uncertainties*. Or it is about *handling any closures, redundancies, redeployments or relocations that become necessary after an acquisition.*

At a slightly deeper level, it is about *dovetailing two different personnel/ Human Resource Management (HRM) systems and their respective practices* – reward systems, selection methods, appraisal and development systems, employee relations procedures, and so on. These are important considerations but not primarily what the book is about.

Moving deeper still, the human factor is about *bringing together the major influences that shape people's behaviour and performance, their thinking and their actions, on each side.* Chief among these influences are the different structures, systems, controls and procedures, the management styles, and the values and beliefs on each side. *In international mergers, the human factor extends into national culture* and includes the task of interfacing the sometimes very different management styles and workplace expectations in different countries. And in all acquisitions the human factor includes *power and politics* on each side and the way these sometimes pull in different directions to influence both the style and the effectiveness of post-deal management (see Figure 2.1).

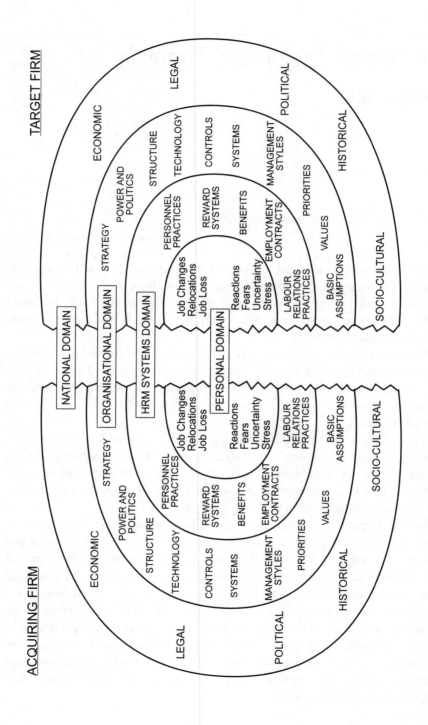

Figure 2.1 Domains of the human factor in acquisition integration

We know from acquisition history that the way in which these variables are brought together and managed can make or break an acquisition. All too often, inappropriate or bungled integration has destroyed the most promising of acquisition strategies and grounded the strategic intentions of some of the world's most powerful business leaders. We also know that at present there is very little guidance available to managers on how best to proceed. Which aspects should be changed on the target side and which should be left alone? When is full merging appropriate and when not? What type of interfacing is most effective for commitment and performance? How fast should it all happen? Later chapters will address these practical questions in more detail and suggest how they might be approached in different acquisition contexts. At this stage, it is more appropriate to note two points:

1. Most people regard integration as predominantly a technical matter – with perhaps a human edge. Few regard integration as fundamentally a human matter with technical dimensions.

2. Integration in practice acts as a mirror upon strategy. Weaknesses in strategic thinking are mirrored and writ large in the way that firms approach integration.

If we combine these two observations, we will see that there is even more to the human factor than the issues outlined above.

The term 'human factor' as used here is not a derivative, an afterthought, of strategy. Nor is it some lesser consideration to the technical aspects of integration. It is a central and fundamental component of *both*. The term as used here captures what is currently missing in so much of strategic thinking. It is a counterpoint to depersonalised and rational-numerical approaches to strategy.

In acquisitions, for example, the vast bulk of strategic planning is formula-driven with the emphasis almost exclusively upon financial and economic and commercial considerations. These, as we know only too well, provide the *necessary* but *not sufficient* preconditions for a successful acquisition. Rarely is detailed consideration given to planning the human and organisational conditions necessary to make strategy 'happen'.

This weakness is not restricted to the M&A field. It is a general weakness in Western strategic thinking and it has been recognised for some time. When Strategic Human Resource Management (SHRM) emerged in the mid-1980s (Beer et al., 1984; Fombrun et al., 1984), one of the central messages was the need for tight integration between commercial strategy and organisation and people. That message has barely penetrated the strategy field and now needs to be restated, this time in a different form.

N.R

People make organisations 'happen'. People make structures 'happen'. People make systems 'happen'. People make cultures 'happen'. People make almost every abstraction in management textbooks 'happen'. But so conditioned have we become by years of depersonalised academic analysis of management and organisations that we regularly forget the human fundamentals.

Likewise for strategy. *People make strategy and people make it 'happen'.* Strategy in every firm is the result of human processes and human interaction – one set of people formulating strategy and another (usually larger) set of people making strategy 'happen'.

> The *substance* of strategy is all about markets and competition, but the *processes* that conceive and deliver strategy are essentially psychological and social. *Strategy is about markets but it is formulated in hierarchies and implemented in hierarchies by people whose thinking and actions have been shaped by hierarchies.*

The twist in acquisitions is that strategy formulated in one hierarchy has to be effected in another. The organisational logic and guiding mindsets on each side are different. Bridging this gap is what strategic integration at a practical level is all about: creating the most appropriate organisational conditions to ensure that strategy conceived at the top of the acquiring firm is made to 'happen' by layers of managers in the target firm – usually by working through layers of managers on the acquiring side.

A common belief is that social engineering of the target organisation is sufficient to bridge the gap. The more the target can be reshaped to 'look like' the acquiring organisation, the better the chances of success. It is a highly questionable assumption and it will be scrutinised later. At this stage we will just note the following.

Changing the outer logic of the acquired organisation – the technical side of integration – is relatively straightforward. Changes to structure and reporting relationships, changing financial controls and IT systems, harmonising rewards and benefits, meshing supply and distribution channels – these tasks can be time-consuming and costly but they are relatively easy to grasp. They have a visible logic. Start and finish parameters are easy to identify. Technical solutions can be provided. Far harder to change are their social and psychological foundations – the invisible ways of thinking that justify each aspect of an organisation 'happening' the way it does.

Structures and systems and procedures have *meaning* for the staff who use them. They have 'taken for granted' justifications which often can be perplexing to an outsider. The beliefs, the values, the justifications for doing things 'our' way and not 'their' way, the political order, the hidden way the organisation works – these are the hardest to get to grips with and the hardest to change in a target.

But note that this is a two-way problem. For management and staff on the target side, trying to understand these aspects of the acquiring organisation can be equally perplexing. 'Getting into the minds' of the other side and bridging the mental gap is by far the hardest part of integration.

The Human Factor and Mindsets

These hidden or taken-for-granted ways of thinking in a company are best captured by the concept of mindsets. This is a shorthand term to convey the idea of mental programming in a company; that groups of people have 'welded-in' or taken-for-granted ways of thinking and acting which mostly go unquestioned. Mindsets are at the heart of organisations. Understanding how managers and staff are programmed to think and behave is central to understanding the way that organisations work and to handling change or interfacing effectively.

We now rephrase an earlier statement. *People* **with** **mindsets** *make organisations 'happen'*. For any organisation to function, all the different abstract components (structures, controls, systems, technology, values, and so on) have to combine and *come alive* to make the organisation perform as it does. The components have to be energised with human emotion, intention and commitment. All this connecting occurs *in the minds* of organisational members.

In ways that we only dimly understand, all the different organisational components combine, first and foremost, *within the minds* of organisational members, and one outcome of this combining is the formation of mindsets.

Individual intention and emotion drive an organisation but shared mindsets hold it all together and provide the logic and the orientation. Mindsets are the essential glue that binds all the different aspects of an organisation together into a functioning whole.

Mindsets are what give each firm its distinctive behavioural profile, its unique 'way of doing things'. When mindsets are shared, they operate a bit like mental 'lenses'. They govern:

1. how people *see* or perceive events

2. how they *think* about or interpret events

3. then how they *act* upon events.

Crucially for managing, mindsets shape how people *think about how to get other people to act* upon events.

Understanding these fundamental processes of how people see, think and act on each side is crucial if two firms are to dovetail effectively into each other. Yet most organisation theorists and integration specialists seem unaware of them – or choose to ignore them. They focus almost exclusively upon the outer aspects of an organisation and the technical aspects of integration. People – if recognised – are but adjuncts to an essentially technical rationality. If 'people problems' occur, they are to be resolved using personnel/HRM solutions (incentives, training, replacement, appraisal, counselling, and so on).

However, technical or personnel solutions do not create a meeting of minds. Merger history provides countless examples of companies spending small fortunes on the social engineering of target firms – changing structures, systems, procedures, controls, and so on – and then finding that that was exactly what they got: an engineered environment with precious little change in managerial thinking. Ways of perceiving and reacting to competition, attitudes to risk, selecting priorities and ways of doing business – these either changed little or the extent of change was patchy.

Obviously, some organisational changes will influence thinking, but the problem lies in knowing which ones will do so. Often in acquisitions it is a hit-and-miss endeavour, but much depends on how ingrained or 'welded-in' the thinking is. Any manager who has integrated a cross-border acquisition, especially across different continents, will be only too familiar with the problem of ingrained mindsets. The sometimes very different ways of thinking and behaving on the other side and the justifications given for courses of action (or non-action) can often confound comprehension and bedevil integration. Even in national mergers, buying into a different industry can expose similar issues – trying to 'see' problems or events through the same 'lenses' as the other side.

What we learn is that mindsets are partly function-specific, partly firm-specific, partly industry-specific and partly country-specific – the latter being the deepest and the most taken for granted and hardest to access. This, of course, is one of the biggest difficulties for global managers bridging national cultures. Integration requires them not only to access and try to understand the ingrained assumptions behind mindsets in another country, but also to start questioning those they carry with them from home.

Wrestling with such matters can be mind-bending, literally, but can also lead to rich discoveries, to the roots of integration wisdom. Like discovering how few of the certainties that managers work with, and business schools teach and advisers prescribe, have any solid scientific basis – most are products of time, place, custom and practice. Then realising how few solid grounds there are for imposing *any* management practice upon a target company – only a belief or a conviction that one practice may be better than another. However, not all managers get the opportunity to make such discoveries. Indeed, many might find the process highly uncomfortable. For the imperial manager, foreign mindsets are a nuisance to be 'normalised' into those of the acquiring company as soon as possible.

In Summary

Strategic integration is viewed here as a human or social endeavour with important technical dimensions. Fundamentally, at a practical level, it is about bringing together two sets of people with different mindsets and different conditioning environments – sometimes just top management teams; sometimes entire organisations – in the most appropriate way to deliver acquisition strategy.

- *Thought governs action*, so understanding the business and organisational thinking on each side is one vital component of integration.

- *Hierarchy shapes thought*, so a second vital component (assuming a change of thinking is judged necessary) is the social engineering of the acquired organisation – making the most judicious changes to vendor structure, controls, systems, responsibilities, and so on – to influence vendor behaviour in the most appropriate way to deliver results.

- *Culture shapes hierarchy*, so a third component (essential for international and global mergers) is understanding how both the 'home' national culture and the 'away' national culture(s) shape organisations and employee behaviour in each country. The proposition here is that organisations are microcosms of the national culture in which they are embedded and from which they draw their personnel.

- *Change destabilises*, so a fourth component is managing the reactions to the acquisition on both sides – especially fears and uncertainties – in order to minimise negative impact upon people and performance.

These abstract notions – the conceptual bones of the book – are outlined in Figure 2.2, and will all take flesh and become clearer as we progress. The mindset concept is absolutely central and runs through all the chapters. Mindsets of those who act (in this case, acquiring and integrating) and mindsets of those who are acted upon (i.e., acquired and integrated) are crucial for understanding what happens across the entire acquisition cycle.

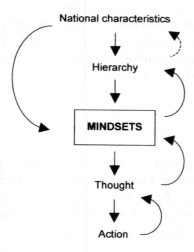

Figure 2.2   Mindset dynamics in strategy and implementation

There are, of course, other mindsets we could single out, such as those of academics from various disciplines, consultants, competition regulators, policy advisers, and others whose thinking is or has been influential in the M&A field. However, here we will concentrate on the main parties who make acquisitions 'happen'. We will examine them one by one, looking at (a) mindsets *as they are* (i.e., general, Western, taken-for-granted ways of thinking at each stage of the acquisition process), and then (b) mindsets *as they could be*. Along the way, we should be able to incorporate the thinking of many influential others.

In Part 2, we start by plugging the mindset concept into a strategic planning perspective. This allows us to begin exploring the strategic mindsets of top managers and especially the thinking that drives M&A strategies. Some of the really heavyweight assumptions that have driven M&A activity across the twentieth century will be put under scrutiny. For example:

- Few companies would sanction a massive investment where the statistical risk of failure was greater than 50%. Given the risks, what types of strategic thinking justify takeover activity?

- What is the source of top management pre-deal optimism? Does it derive from selective collection of data or from selective interpretation of data?

- Given the abrupt changes in strategic thinking across the decades, how susceptible are top management mindsets to changes in strategic fashion?

- When planning acquisitions, are top managers able to step out of their own strategic mindsets and recognise the 'taken for granted' assumptions under which they operate?

These are important questions for any strategy agenda. They are especially important for integration. Weaknesses in strategic thinking become amplified in the post-deal period. If value isn't there to start with, no amount of integration effort can deliver it. But if potential value really does exist, care must be taken not to destroy it. So Parts 3 to 5 examine integration in detail. Each chapter looks at a different aspect of bringing two companies together – moving from the national domain through to the international and global domains. Common to all is the question: what types of thinking can help or impede the value creation possibilities of integration?

Every chapter is about mindsets that drive action – acquiring top management mindsets, acquired top management mindsets, mindsets at different levels on each side – and the performance consequences that follow. Along the way, some of the least explored areas in mergers and acquisitions will be highlighted. For managers involved in acquisitions, the journey should open up whole new ways of conceptualising what they do.

Academic Note

For academics, the strategic mindset concept opens up a twenty-first century research agenda that is literally bursting with possibilities – both with reference to itself and with reference to the unimaginative and wooden nature of so much managerial M&A research to date. And it is timely to open up that agenda.

The proposition that acquisition outcomes were more a product of managerial processes than strategic choice was first suggested by Jemison and Sitkin in 1986, yet very little work of any substance – either conceptual or empirical – has been done to date to take the proposition forward. Here we lay some important foundations, the most important of which is to cement into place a fourth, new, cornerstone into the M&A mindset.

The typical twentieth-century merger mindset drew almost exclusively upon three academic disciplines: finance, economics and strategy. These were the cornerstones upon which most thinking and practice and research rested. Now in the twenty-first century, a fourth human or managerial cornerstone is

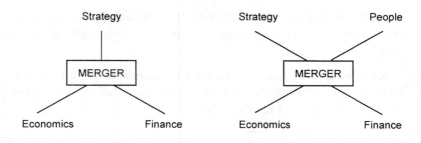

Figure 2.3   Cornerstones of merger thinking

added (Figure 2.3). It encompasses several related fields of knowledge – chiefly organisation behaviour, social psychology, cultural anthropology and managerial decision-making.

Note that this is more than just belatedly putting people in the picture. The emphasis on mindsets shaping action points to organisations as psychologically driven entities; that knowledge and nostrums from strategy, finance and economics are *psychologically interpreted* in each firm before being turned into action. This in turn puts human agency and enactment (Weick, 1979, 1995) right at the centre of strategy and at the centre of acquisition dynamics – the idea that people make the social world 'happen'.

All this should provide a strong focus for pulling together writers in the strategy field who have been moving in this direction – emphasising the social and psychological *processes* of strategy rather than the economic and market *substance*. However, mindsets and enactment raise some fiendishly tricky questions. Figure 2.2 can be a conceptual minefield for the unwary. For example:

- Thought shapes action, but action retrospectively shapes thought. How is this twin dynamic to be explained in the context of M&A?

- Which actions, in which circumstances, retrospectively inform mindsets, and which do not?

These are important questions for understanding and explaining and learning from acquisition activity – and for strategy in general – and they are by no means straightforward.

- People think, but they also remember and they anticipate. How do these three psychic states (present, past, future) all interact and shape mindsets and actions?

- How do these three states inform (and also misinform) one another? And under which circumstances?

- Across all of the questions, how much thought and action is rational (intellectually driven) and how much is emotionally driven?

These are not the easiest of questions to get to grips with. They require considerable mental agility to unscramble and pursue. Caution is therefore advisable. There is no suggestion of any Catch-22 research agenda here. Just a gentle reminder that investigating mindsets needs researchers with mindsets that understand mindsets!

To conclude: the purpose of this chapter was to outline some of the thinking behind the book and to explain the human factor and strategic integration as simply and succinctly as possible. It has been a conceptual exercise – inevitably – but has tried to be as jargon-free as possible. It probably is of more interest to academic readers, although managers who enjoy conceptualising about what they do and who are familiar with the literature should gain a lot out of it. There is plenty to 'get the mind round' and plenty of related issues still to explore.

For other readers, it may have left them feeling a bit lost and bewildered. If all this talk about mindsets and enactment and psychological agency is confusing or sounds too academic, *don't worry*. Just remember the Game of Golden Lemon (Box 2.1).

Box 2.1   The Game of Golden Lemon

If you look at a lemon through rose-tinted glasses, the colour will *look* like gold. If your critical faculties are not in good shape, you might believe it really *is* gold. If you then convince others to see it the way you do, you all might cheerfully part with gold.
Recognise the game? Of course you do!

Part 2

Value Destruction

CHAPTER 3

How Unsuccessful are Acquisitions?

'Nobody really explained the risks or the sorts of problems we could run into. Our advisers had a first-class reputation. To be fair, their procedures were faultless – absolutely smooth. But any mention of future difficulties was dismissed as untypical of the deals the bank handled. We were led to believe that failure statistics came from obscure academics with sampling problems.'

(Managing Director, engineering)

What do we mean when we say an acquisition underperforms? Most managers have come across the statistic on acquisition performance – *half to three-quarters fail*. But what does it really tell us? Apart from acting as a warning to would-be acquirers, by itself it says very little. If the statistic is to have any practical value, we need to know more about how it has been arrived at. In particular we need to know the following:

- What is meant by an acquisition failing?
- By how much do acquisitions fail?
- How is performance measured?
- What specific causes of failure have been identified?

These are highly complex questions. Teams of researchers throughout the world have been investigating them for decades and have not come up with a consistent set of answers. But they have given us the next best thing – clusters of answers which reflect the researchers' academic disciplines. Each of the disciplines (mainly finance, economics and strategy) acts like a lens illuminating different aspects of the acquisition process. When these different perspectives and findings are put together, a composite picture emerges about acquisition performance which makes for uneasy reading.

Every manager involved in merger and acquisition activity, whether as acquirer or as target, should be familiar with what this work has to say. However, with much of it tucked away on library shelves and in academic

journals, access can be difficult and time-consuming. This chapter and the
next are devoted to summarising what is known about acquisition underperformance in a readable and accessible way. Digesting what they have to
say should more than repay any effort involved.

How is Acquisition Performance Measured?

There is no single, universally agreed measure of acquisition performance,
and for good reason. An acquisition usually sets out to achieve several goals,
not just one. The various parties who have an interest in the acquisition
usually have different expectations and have a preference for different
outcomes. Some of these outcomes are easy to quantify; others are more a
matter of judgement.

Thus, in practice, we find acquisitions and mergers being judged across a
wide spectrum of measures ranging from hard (numerical) measures through
to soft (judgemental or impressionistic) measures, depending on which perspectives and interests are being taken into account, and also – most
importantly – the time period over which performance is being assessed.
There are five different types of measure in common use:

1. *Financial measures*. Has the acquisition improved earnings per share
   (EPS) or return on investment (ROI)? Has the acquirer's share price
   risen relative to the industry or sector average, or compared to estimates
   of the share price had the acquisition not been pursued? Are cumulative
   abnormal returns/residuals (CARs) positive?

   These measures are solidly numerical and usually allow direct
   comparison between firms in the same country. However, different
   accounting and regulatory regimes in different countries can distort
   straight cross-border comparisons.

2. *Economic measures*. Has the acquisition delivered higher efficiency and
   profitability? Have synergies and economies of scope or scale been
   realised? Does the acquirer have more market power? Has the
   acquisition allowed the company to grow faster than by internal effort
   alone?

   Some of these outcomes can be difficult to quantify accurately on a
   before-and-after basis. Major restructuring, for example, can result in
   operating units no longer being recognisable for comparative purposes.
   However, if efficiency or synergy outcomes are realised, they should
   translate into improved *profitability*, which can be quantified.

3. *Strategic measures*. Has the acquisition achieved the goals that top management set out to achieve?

Some goals are easily quantified (improvements in EPS/ROI, sales, market share, cashflow stability, and so on). Other goals can be shown to have occurred (acquiring a capability, repositioning the company, building foundations for future growth, defending markets, and so on), but how effectively and efficiently they have been pursued – the cost-benefits – are often hard to quantify, let alone gauge independently.

Sometimes managers are the best placed to form a judgement, given their inside knowledge of the companies and their awareness of what they intended the acquisition to achieve. But then they become judge and jury in their own defence.

4. *Executive measures*. Have the owners or CEOs and the top management teams from each side gained out of the acquisition? Have their salaries, bonuses, stock options and other financial benefits risen? Has there been an increase in their 'psychic income' – their power, prestige and industry standing?

Top managers commonly expect rewards to be related to the size of the firms they run. Merged firms are instantly bigger, so increases in financial rewards usually happen quickly. These are easy to quantify. Increases in psychic income require more indirect measurement, but these too usually rise with size.

But note: a 'feel-good' factor may be important for morale at the top but is little more than an indulgence if it does not translate into 'perform-good' as assessed by at least one of (1), (2) or (3) above.

5. *Regulatory measures*. Is the acquisition in the public interest? Does it comply with monopoly (anti-trust) legislation? Will it be anti-competitive? What are the likely economic and employment consequences?

Questions of this nature are directed mainly at large mergers and acquisitions. Generally speaking, the public interest is a notion that is notoriously difficult to pin down. In part because criteria vary from one country to another. In part because criteria are often political in that they usually reflect the economic and industrial and social policies being pursued by governments in the countries concerned. Such matters are not the province of this book.

Clearly, these measures are assessing very different things. They reflect different perspectives and interests, which is why discussions on takeovers often become heated and bogged down with people talking at cross-purposes.

For a meaningful analysis of acquisition performance we need a solid and numerical base from which to proceed.

> An acquisition is an investment. It is a strategic choice by a company to invest shareholders' capital in the purchase of another company rather than invest it in other ways. Therefore, it has to be considered like any other investment. Does the acquisition bring value to shareholders? Does it deliver as good or better returns compared to other investments that could have been made with the capital involved?

This is the base from which we start.

Do Shareholders Benefit from Takeover Activity?

The short answer is that generally they don't. There is now a substantial body of research that has attempted to measure the impact of takeovers upon shareholder wealth. The question these studies usually ask is: 'On average, do shareholders in acquiring and target firms gain from takeovers?' There are two different ways of approaching the question: one is to use stock market indicators and the other is to measure actual returns to shareholders. Both conclude negatively.

Studies using stock market indicators attempt to isolate that part of a company's share price movement which is attributable solely to the act of takeover. It is a highly complex procedure but, stated simply, a mathematical model is used to predict how the shares would have behaved if the takeover had not happened. Then a comparison of the prediction with the actual movements in share price is made. Any difference (the abnormal gain or loss, or the residual) is attributed to takeover.

When the procedure is applied to a large number of firms and averaged, then repeated across different time periods, the results should give a fairly accurate indication of whether bidding and target shareholders gain or lose from takeover activity and also the trend across time. CAR (Cumulative Average Residual or Cumulative Abnormal Return) is one commonly used index. Positive CARs indicate that shareholders have gained out of acquisitions, and the converse for negative CARs.

There is now more than 20 years of such research available. It involves dozens of studies covering thousands of takeovers on both sides of the Atlantic, and it shows a consistent pattern of poor long-run acquisition performance. The size of the underperformance varies with the mathematical models the researchers use and the time period under investigation, so care must be taken when interpreting their findings. However, there appears to be agreement on the following:

1. Any acquirer share price gains around the time of a takeover (fairly common during the 1970s and early 1980s) very quickly disappear, followed by a pattern of longer-term losses (see, for example, Firth, 1980; Franks and Harris, 1989).

2. Shareholders in target companies often do well out of the deal. Abnormal gains of up to 20% were reported in some studies in the 1970s and early 1980s, with smaller gains in later periods (Jensen and Ruback, 1983; Malatesta, 1983). Some analysts explain this as value transferring from bidder to target in the short term (Mandelker, 1974; Firth, 1980). In the longer term, both sides generally show losses.

3. There is strong evidence across the decades that cash bids do not perform quite as badly as equity bids. Negative returns to cash acquirers are less than half those to equity acquirers. But leveraged buy-outs usually perform well and deliver positive returns (Hansen, 1987; Agrawal et al., 1992).

4. Takeovers during the 1980s and early 1990s appear to have some of the poorest levels of post-acquisition performance. CARs of around –18% after three years are reported in some studies (Gregory, 1997).

The last finding is especially significant. Since the late 1980s, firms have had unprecedented amounts of computing power to improve and refine their financial and commercial projections. For this reason, one would expect a much closer match between projections at the time of takeover and performance in the years ahead. Yet the gap appears to be widening. We need to remember that when research reveals abnormal negative returns of 18% over three years (i.e., around 6% per year), these figures are benchmarked against a control, not against the returns management promised they could deliver. If we make the modest assumption that most takeovers promise to overperform by around 10% in the first few years, then in many instances the gap between promise (+10%) and performance (–6%) may be closer to 16% per year or nearly 50% after three years.

However, some people are uncomfortable with this approach because it is heavily grounded in complex finance theory. They also distrust the findings because they believe that financial markets are too fickle for solid bench-marking. They prefer the second approach, which is more direct and easier to grasp. This examines the actual returns to shareholders over an extended

time period, and then compares this performance either to an industry average
or to a control group of non-acquiring companies over the same period. The
method may be different but the conclusions are depressingly similar. Returns
to shareholders in acquiring companies are consistently lower than in non-
acquiring companies. A representative flavour of two decades of research is
given below.

- In 1982, *Fortune* examined the ten-year performance of the ten largest
  US acquisitions of 1971. All were massive; all promised golden
  returns; all performed dismally. Not one reached 13.8% (the *Fortune
  500* median return across the period). Three returned less than 5%
  (Louis, 1982).

- In two separate studies, McKinsey & Co. investigated the actual return
  on capital invested in takeovers. In their 1985 sample of 58 takeovers,
  only 6 (i.e., 10%) produced returns in excess of the cost of the funds
  involved. In their larger 1988 sample of 116 takeovers (60 in the UK
  and 56 in the US), the improvement was little better – 23% recovered
  the cost of capital compared to 77% that did not (McKinsey & Co.,
  1985, 1988).

- In 1996, Mercer Management Consulting analysed more than 300 large
  mergers and acquisitions from the mid-1980s onwards. In the three
  years post-deal, 57% of the merged firms lagged behind their industries
  in terms of total returns to shareholders. Longer-term underperformance
  appeared even higher (Smith and Hershman, 1996).

- In 1999, KPMG examined 107 cross-border takeovers and found that
  only one in six (17%) added to shareholder value. More than half (53%)
  destroyed value and the remainder showed no discernible difference.

The overall conclusion that these (and other) studies point to – albeit using
different methods – is both consistent and compelling. On average, there may
be modest initial returns to shareholders of acquiring firms, but these then
tail off rapidly. Between two-thirds and three-quarters of acquiring firms do
not recover the costs of their acquisitions during the first five years.
Shareholders in target firms often benefit around the time of the deal, perhaps
by value crossing over from acquirer to target, but then there is a pattern of
longer-term losses.

   However, these studies tell us very little about *why* mergers and acquisitions fail to deliver value. They simply paint a before-and-after picture. We
now need to turn to the field of economics, and then later to strategy, to shed
some light on the processes that can create but can also destroy value.

Do Takeovers Increase Efficiency and Profitability?

Economics theory tells us that size matters. Greater size should deliver a multitude of synergy and efficiency benefits – greater market power, financial synergies, risk reduction, higher productive efficiency with lower unit costs, lots of scope for restructuring and rationalisation – all of which should translate into higher profitability. So central are these propositions to managerial mindsets that there is scarcely a takeover or merger which has not been justified by invoking some or all of them.

However, economics research tells a different story. There is very little solid empirical evidence that the efficiency and synergy possibilities of greater size are actually translated into higher profitability. Throughout the twentieth century, economists have been investigating large samples of merging firms and comparing their before-and-after profitability. These are the most comprehensive and rigorous and reputable studies available.

One finding, which occurs consistently throughout, stands in stark contrast to most managerial claims. *Not a single large-scale empirical investigation has concluded that takeovers and mergers are profitable, in the sense of being 'more profitable' than alternative forms of investment.* Economically speaking, big is not always beautiful.

- In 1970, Hogarty reviewed the evidence from most of the major empirical investigations into pre-1960 merger activity (i.e., rock-solid economics research covering a period from the first two merger waves early in the twentieth century through to the late 1950s). He concluded his 'survey of the surveys' thus:

  What can fifty years of research tell us about the profitability of mergers? ... A host of researchers, working at different points of time and utilising different analytic techniques and data, have but one major difference: whether mergers have a neutral or negative impact upon profitability. (Hogarty, 1970, p. 389)

- In 1980, Mueller summarised the findings of a large-scale, seven-country study of the determinants and effects of mergers that occurred mostly in the late 1960s and 1970s.

  Mergers have but modest effects, up or down, on the profitability of merging firms in the three to five years following merger. Any economic efficiency gains from mergers would appear to be small ... as would any market power increases. (Mueller, 1980, p. 306)

- In 1987, Ravenscraft and Scherer published the results of a massive investigation into 6,000 US mergers and takeovers, examining performance up to nine years after the deal. They found compelling evidence that takeover damaged the profitability of acquired firms. Even the profitability of individual lines of business declined following takeover.

  In 450 of the targets studied (i.e., where data were available), acquired lines of business were on average 3% less profitable than comparable non-acquired lines in competitor firms in the nine years following takeover. One third of all acquisitions in the study were subsequently divested (Ravenscraft and Scherer, 1987a, 1987b).

- In 1999, in a much smaller-scale study but relevant here, Booz, Allen & Hamilton reported on the European insurance industry. Industry consolidation and market concentration across the 1990s should have delivered higher efficiency and increased cost savings, but they did not. For many insurers, as market share grew so also did costs.

  Overall, the ten largest European insurance firms saw their market share rising by around 25% between 1990–97 but their cost-efficiency remained static (see Figure 3.1).

Why Does Size Not Always Deliver?

Why do the predictions of economics theory not always hold? Why does size not always deliver? Seven reasons go a long way towards answering these questions (see Box 3.1). All concern the usually unrecognised problems of (a) creating greater size and (b) managing the complexity of increased size.

Human Costs of Scale

For every theoretical economy of scale predicted on paper, there is a corresponding human 'dis-economy' of scale in attempting to realise and sustain it. The costs of the latter usually go unrecognised in merger calculations, even though they often exceed the value of any predicted paper benefits.

Horizontal (related) mergers are where economies of scale are potentially greatest with duplication of similar functions. However, every function evolves surrounded by its own web of organisational components (structure, political order, managing systems, culture, and so on). Merging functions or sub-functions requires one or the other function to be 'disconnected' from its

> **Box 3.1   Seven obstacles to efficient size**
>
> 1. Human costs of scale
> 2. Displaced competition
> 3. Exponential complexity
> 4. Efficiency trade-offs
> 5. Weak innovation
> 6. Information overload
> 7. Invincible mindsets

own web and 'reconnected' to another. The human difficulties and resource consequences are often immense.

Synergy calculations can easily estimate the costs of physical relocation, systems redesign and downsizing. The costs associated with resistance to change – assuming that they are recognised – can rarely be predicted with any degree of accuracy.

Displaced Competition

If the two companies are direct competitors, each may have entrenched negative attitudes towards the other. When the companies are big, they often

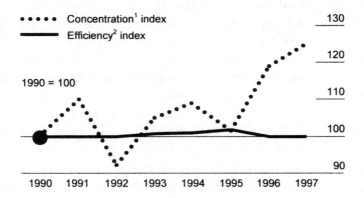

Figure 3.1   The European insurance industry: market share and cost efficiency, 1990–97
1 Market share of top ten insurers.
2 Inverse expense ratio.

Sources: Booz, Allen & Hamilton; *The Economist* (5 June 1999, p. 103)

define themselves from the top downwards in terms of what the other is *not*. Bring them together and the interfirm competition previously located in the marketplace becomes displaced inside the bigger merged organisation.

However, the competition is not about customers. It is about survival and power and control – who is to remain and who is to run different parts of the business; which systems are to be adopted and which culture is to be dominant. When the primary task shifts to winning internal wars, the main casualties are suppliers and distributors and customers, and ultimately the bottom line. It is a lesson acquirers regularly forget. Taking a competitor out of the market only takes a day, but stopping the two sides from fighting each other can take years.

Exponential Complexity

Even if all strategic fits happen as intended and culture integration is smooth and market power increases, all are offset by having a bigger organisation to manage. One bigger (merged) organisation is significantly more complex to manage than either organisation was prior to takeover. In the long run, size and complexity can constrain efficiency and market responsiveness.

We know from organisation theory that as firms get bigger their complexity increases not in proportion to size but *exponentially* with size. Ever-increasing amounts of effort need to be channelled inwards to coordinate and control the larger unit created. The *number* of organisational relationships to be managed increases exponentially with size, as does the *scope* of these relationships. In a large or diversified corporation, the complexity of the management task is potentially overwhelming (Caplow, 1964; Chandler, 1977).

How do managers handle this complexity? Usually they fall back upon that soldered-in component in almost every manager's mindset – the bureaucratic template. Managers at the centre (and at further decentralised centres) structure relationships by limiting the duties and responsibilities of others, then they establish formal rules and procedures for interaction, and then decide who will interact with whom, and so on.

These actions help to avoid fuzzy relationships and make control easier. On the plus side, they contribute to the smooth running of the organisation and give the bureaucratic structure its undeniable strengths. But the downside – almost always, as size increases – is reduced flexibility, lost market opportunities and wasted talent – well-recognised problems for more than thirty years (Lawrence and Lorsch, 1967; Jaques, 1976).

When large corporations combine, they usually *say* that they will build upon each other's organisational strengths. But it is often their pre-deal weaknesses that are amplified. When the newly merged unit is many times more complex than the sum of its already complex parts, managers tackle the new complexity using the approach they are familiar with, which is often the only one they know. They view the newly merged complexity through the bureaucratic template. The result is that large merged corporations almost invariably become even more structured, more rigid and less adaptable than either single entity was prior to takeover.

Box 3.2   Complexity in piggy banking

In the fast-moving world of finance, could anything be simpler than over-the-counter banking? Citibank thought not, until 1997 when it looked at how complex its operations had become. Even something as ordinary as a demand-deposit account turned out to be mind-boggling. Around the world, for reasons of local regulations and history, Citibank was offering not one such account but almost 150,000 versions of it.

Some accounts calculated interest daily, others monthly; some charged fees, others did not; daily withdrawal limits varied, as did interest rates, and so on. To handle such complexity, Citibank's back offices were using 28 different computer systems. The bank's response was a massive cost-cutting project to reduce complexity by up to 75% across all its operations and to cut computer systems in use to one or two.

However, not all firms are willing to get on top of their own complexity, or even to recognise it. What Citibank discovered is not uncommon in any sprawling global corporation where earlier acquisitions have not been fully rationalised. Merge any two of them and the integration complexity becomes horrendous.

If two organisations have difficulty grasping and simplifying their own complexity before they merge, what are their chances of rationalising the complexity of a much bigger merged entity when half of it is completely unfamiliar? (*The Economist*, 5 June 1999, p. 103)

Efficiency Trade-Offs

In the long run, size and complexity also constrain efficiency. Big organisations traditionally have been good at achieving one type of efficiency, *static* efficiency (i.e., highly efficient low-cost production with the firm operating at full capacity). But their inherent complexity and rigidity have made it harder to achieve *dynamic* efficiency (i.e., adapting quickly to changing competitive conditions and developing new technologies and knowledge bases) (Burns and Stalker, 1961; Leibenstein, 1976; Klein, 1977).

In the days when size and scale created an almost impregnable competitive advantage, static efficiency was a sufficient barrier for dominating markets. (But note that this worked more by keeping rivals out than by leading from up-front.) However, especially during the last decade or so, scale increasingly has been defeated by the pace of technological change. Competitive advantage no longer can be secured by doing efficiently what was done in the past.

Increasing numbers of smaller companies are competing profitably with global giants on the basis of their superior *dynamic* efficiency: through more flexible internal structures, a lower cost base, or by networking and strategic alliances. As a result, they have been able to offset the established concentrations of economic power enjoyed by many large firms. Dell provides a perfect illustration (see Box 3.3).

Box 3.3   Swell Dell

In the space of a few years, Dell's share of the worldwide PC market grew until it was neck-and-neck with IBM and second only to Compaq in 1998. By building customised computers only to order, the company achieved sales growth of around 56% and did what less dynamic rivals would have baulked at – it recast its production line every working day.

Weak Innovation

Innovation especially is affected by organisational size. In general, giant firms are not as innovative as smaller firms. Instead, they rely heavily upon a continuous supply of purchased innovation which they adapt or improve – and the bigger the organisation, the greater the dependence on external sources of knowledge and ideas to avoid decline. Ground-breaking research is much more likely to happen in small dedicated environments than in large corporations. But deep corporate pockets allow the large firms to acquire almost any innovation and knowledge they seek.

However, that rigid and bureaucratic character which comes with size, can work against acquired innovation in various ways. It can constrain the innovative spirit in smaller targets after they have been acquired. It can put a brake on application – large firms in general do not adopt acquired innovations as rapidly as smaller, fast-growing rivals. Sometimes it can stifle innovation completely if, for example, a new idea or process puts existing technology to shame and threatens to overturn large chunks of committed investment. Patents are purchased – then get locked away.

Information Overload

Another obstacle to efficiency is the capacity of managers to process and act upon the sheer volume of information generated by size and diversity. In any large organisation, managers are surrounded by a complex architecture of information and reporting systems, the content of which far exceeds the capacity of any one individual – or even a group of individuals such as a board of directors – to fully comprehend. The bigger the organisation, the more overwhelming is the volume of information generated.

To make such complexity manageable, managers commonly engage in simplifying behaviours, all of which can constrain performance. One is to limit the types of information they are prepared to consider. The human mind, after all, is psychologically unable to consider more than a handful of factors at any one time (March and Simon, 1958). Another is to limit the information they allow other managers to consider. The result is top-down information rationing (Cyert and March, 1963). Managers at lower levels develop mindsets sensitised to consider only those aspects of performance which higher authorities have deemed appropriate – or which they believe are important for their own appraisal and career purposes.

A vicious cycle can then develop. When managers at middle and lower levels are information-rationed, their capacity to interpret the market and generate new options, new choices, is heavily constrained. Equally, when managers at the top are insulated from the market by thick layers of hierarchy, what they often receive is a politically filtered interpretation of the market rather than being told what the market is actually saying. Selective attention, information rationing and market myopia all can be mutually reinforcing.

It is worth noting here that corporate raiders have long recognised these inefficiencies and regularly turn them to their own advantage. Raiders often make the decision to pounce on the basis of scant published accounts and other public data. They can detect hidden value from outside a company using only a fraction of the data that target managers have prepared – but failed to act upon.

Invincible Mindsets

Finally, there is the internalisation of size. Often there is a sense of invincibility within large corporations; that the market is so large it will always be there (give or take a bit); that most if not all of the corporation will have a long and secure life, even if ownership and name should change.

When this sort of scenario is widely shared, managerial thinking can become introspective and retrospective, shaped more by what happens *inside* the corporation than what is going on outside. If there is a conviction that 'our way of doing things' is best – and which large company does not believe this? – change will be expected to come mostly from within. Tomorrow will be much the same as yesterday – unless a higher authority deems otherwise. Long before it has happened, the future gets defined in terms of a logical and incremental continuation of the past (Weick, 1995).

This type of thinking contributes substantially to the conservative quality to be found in many large organisations. For example, new problems facing the organisation are often interpreted as variations on existing problems already in hand, rather than problems requiring radically different solutions. If the market does demand a really new answer to a problem, something may be selected from a menu of solutions the organisation feels comfortable to offer. Even then, what is offered may be a political compromise; a satisficer rather than a maximiser; something acceptable to different political groupings in the organisation and not necessarily what is best for maximising, for example, profit or customer satisfaction or market share (Cyert and March, 1963).

Dynamic efficiency requires a constant search for new options, new choices, new ways to create value. These depend crucially on mindsets which value high levels of *non-hierarchical* behaviour – a climate of continuous questioning, spontaneous information-sharing across boundaries, the closest

---

Box 3.4   Drugs and celibacy

Of the dozen or so large pharmaceutical mergers in the last quarter of the twentieth century, not a single one achieved a genuine increase in productivity or boosted the number of successful new drugs brought to market. With one exception, every drug mega-merger across the period was followed by a subsequent loss of combined market share. Drug companies that remained celibate usually did better. (*The Economist*, 7 February 1998, pp. 85–6; 22 January 2000, pp. 77–8)

of customer awareness and, above all, incentives which reward deference to markets more than deference to hierarchy.

All this can go against the grain of authority and tradition in a corporation. It can also be unsettling. Often there is a fear that too many problem searches or too many radical solutions might create new unknowns and even more difficult problems for managers struggling to control an already complex organisation. Mental overload and a sense of being out of control are uncomfortable and few managers like it.

The Real Message of Size

Essentially, all this is telling us that the obstacle to higher levels of efficiency and profitability in large merged companies is not size *per se*. Size and complexity are not the real villains. *The villain is the psychological capacity of managers to grasp and manage the complexity of creating and sustaining greater size.* To restate what was said in Chapter 2, organisation is the medium through which strategy is translated into results. People make organisations 'happen', and it is to people and human processes that we must look for explanations if strategic predictions about greater size fail to materialise.

At the heart of an economics puzzle about the inefficiencies of size lies a problem which is fundamentally psychological: managerial capabilities and mindsets. All the various responses to big-firm complexity we have looked at – information rationing and filtering, centralisation and standardisation, retrospective thinking, satisficing behaviours, over-reliance on procedures and numbers and formulae – all offer predictability and psychological comfort and a sense of being in control, but in fact can result in *loss of control*. They can lead to a major gulf between how the organisation and the market each 'see' critical aspects of competition and performance. The bigger the organisation, the greater the gulf can be.

Usually it takes something traumatic (such as falling profits and dwindling markets) to bring about change, and over the years various remedies have been tried. Delayering, creating Strategic Business Units (SBUs), contracting out, alliances and joint ventures, business process re-engineering and performance-related incentives are all steps in the right direction. They can help to make size less unmanageable and more market responsive. Ultimately, however, the limiting factor in the pursuit of dynamic efficiency is appropriate mindsets.

If that capacity is not there before a merger, it is most unlikely to emerge in the post-merger hubris. Merge any two large organisations with inflexible characteristics and the result is usually one larger, even more unresponsive unit. But even if combining firms are dynamic, bringing them together diverts enormous amounts of time and energy into trying to understand how the other side thinks and acts. Integration forces all managers to look inwards; to be concerned more with routines and procedures and less with the real business of competition.

> A newly merged mega-corporation can be a bit like a dinosaur with a left brain and a right brain struggling to understand and communicate with each other. Coordination and control get out of step and eyes go off the ball, off the market. There is increased market power but less coordinated capacity to sustain it. The longer the incapacity lasts, the more the potential value of the deal can seep away. Competitors love it.

- Quaker Oats' acquisition of US soft drinks manufacturer Snapple (bought in 1994 for $1.7 billion; sold in 1997 for $300 million) was reportedly plagued by indecisive integration and culture clashes. While the two companies sparred and dithered, rivals Coca-Cola and Pepsi stepped in and captured the value. They launched new soft drinks that took the market share that was the justification for the deal, and effectively sank it. (*Fortune*, 11 January 1999, p. 44)

- Researchers at Wharton examined the cost-cutting performance of banks in America, and found that merged banks cut costs more slowly than non-merging peers. Their explanation is that merging and integration distracts managers' attention from the real business of cost cutting. (*The Economist*, 9 January 1999, p. 23)

Who Really Benefits From Greater Size?

So, who really gains out of greater size? In the short term, of course, there are many beneficiaries. Shareholders – especially on the target side – usually show a modest short-term profit. Target firms can gain access to new markets and new capabilities, and so can acquiring firms. They can also capture meaty chunks of short-term value (financial and tax synergies, supply and distribution and marketing efficiencies, disposal of marginal businesses, and so on). The bigger the deal, the bigger the potential savings.

However, set against these are the transaction costs of the deal, the actual and opportunity costs of integration and restructuring, and the costs of managing the complexity of the larger unit created. In large mergers, reorganisation costs can be massive, as can external fees. Third parties always seem to gain when firms chase size. It is often the case for deal-makers and advisers that the bigger the deal, the bigger the fee. In hostile bids, third-party costs can cancel out any immediate gains, and can even wipe out years of future value (see Box 4.5, page 58). Put all these different costs together and most if not all of the short-term value can get gobbled up.

So everything depends on the long-term ability of the acquirer to create new and sustainable value. But the evidence on acquisition performance tells us that, on average, fewer than one in three really manage to achieve this. Mergers and acquisitions rarely benefit shareholder interests in the longer term. So who really gains from what looks like – contrary to all the confident theoretical assertions about the efficiencies of size – a long-term *inefficient* spiral?

One group appears always to gain out of increased size – top management teams. Acquiring managers gain power over a larger slice of the market. They gain control of more assets with minimum interference from shareholders. They get a larger organisation to exercise authority over. They can protect themselves from hostile takeovers when their companies are really big. And they gain financially.

For nearly forty years we have known that financial and non-financial benefits to directors and senior executives are tied much more closely to the size and the growth rate of a company than to its profitability (Marris, 1964). Even with the current emphasis on performance-related benefits in the boardroom, size is still the critical factor for thresholds. Salaries, bonuses,

---

Box 3.5   Daimler–Chrysler driver warranty

Prior to the Daimler–Chrysler merger in 1998, documents filed by Chrysler with the US Securities and Exchange Commission showed that the corporation's top executives were estimated to gain as much as $1 billion (£600 million) just from the deal. They would make the money by converting their existing share options into shares of the newly merged entity – and they would be free to sell the shares at any time.

Robert Eaton, Chrysler's CEO and reported architect and driver of the merger, was estimated on his own to collect shares worth $100 million. Other top managers would get proportionately less. In addition, any Detroit executives who lost their jobs as a result of the deal were to be offered multi-million-dollar golden parachutes.

When asked to comment on the status of his own options, press reports tell us that Mr Eaton was understandably reticent. 'My personal situation never came to mind', he is said to have retorted. 'We are trying to create the leading auto company in the world for the future of all stakeholders.' (*Independent*, 14 May 1998)

stock options and other perquisites usually ratchet up with company size, as does psychic income – the power, prestige and industry standing enjoyed by company chiefs. And there is usually a trickle-down effect to lower levels. Most managers can benefit in terms of wider promotion opportunities and extended salary scales and greater job security as companies get bigger.

So what's the bottom line on size? *Efficiency theorists* say that takeovers and mergers occur to improve the efficiency of the combined firms' operations and to create synergistic long-term economic value. Evidence to support the position is pretty thin on the ground. *Empire-building theorists* say that top managers seek to increase both their material and their psychic income. Size supplants shareholder value as the corporate goal. This seems closer to reality. Thick hierarchy can damage performance and shareholders' pockets – but it's usually great for executive careers! (See Box 3.5.)

CHAPTER 4

Strategy and Acquisition Performance

'Mergers must never become a strategy in their own right. That's an important lesson I've learned from watching the other side.'

(Chairman, foods)

The last chapter brought together a lot of finance and economics research in just a few pages. The evidence is compelling that, on average, mergers and acquisitions do not deliver the profitability and efficiency outcomes that theory predicts they should deliver. But it should not be read as a despondent conclusion – it is an **on-average** conclusion.

Every average has a spread, and across the spread can be found the disastrous failures as well as deals that delivered all that was expected of them, and sometimes more. So there is everything to play for in acquisitions, provided managers know how to play the game ... and that's the central problem. We don't know why some deals deliver and many don't. Theory that champions the benefits of merging goes curiously silent when deals go wrong. That is of little help to managers planning company growth or struggling to put two firms together and deliver results.

Good theory should do two things: predict accurately and explain convincingly. Managers probably have more interest in prediction, academics in explanation, but both are essential criteria for judging theory. Economics and finance are two bodies of theory that are immensely influential in merger and acquisition thinking. They are two of the cornerstones in the typical M&A mindset, but when it comes to predicting and explaining merger and acquisition behaviour, finance theory and economics theory both have serious limitations:

- They are weak at *predicting* – in the sense of specifying accurately the prior conditions necessary for an acquisition to be successful **at the level of the individual firm**. The best they can do is to predict on an aggregate basis – i.e. that if we take a large sample of acquisitions, some predicted benefits are likely to occur somewhere in the sample. They cannot predict which **particular** set of benefits will come through in a **particular** deal and which will not.

- They are also weak at *explaining* how outcomes and results come about. They shed little light on the chain of events between deal and results – especially how organisational processes and managerial actions contribute positively and negatively to acquisition outcomes. Any explanations offered are usually in terms of what theory says and not in terms of what managers do.

In fact, the fields of organisation theory and managerial behaviour do a better job of explaining inefficiencies of size and underperformance than do finance or economics (as we saw in the previous chapter). And – as the sharp-eyed reader must have noticed from the reference dates – much of the knowledge has been around for decades. But somehow it has remained very much on the margins of merger thinking.

Can Strategy Theory Explain Acquisition Performance?

We now turn to the field of strategy to see what light it can shed on acquisition performance. It is, after all, the third major stream in takeover research; the third cornerstone in the M&A mindset. A key aspect of strategy is managerial choice – that managers *choose* to grow their firms in particular directions then *choose* to acquire then *choose* the targets they want to pursue. This puts top managers in the driving seat at the centre of things and that, potentially, could be more illuminating.

So we ask the question: Is strategy theory *good* theory – good in the sense of being able to predict and explain acquisition performance? At first sight, this seems a perfectly straightforward question. However, before we can start to answer it, we need to go back a step and establish: *what exactly is strategy theory?* And that opens up a veritable can of worms.

Finance and economics may lack explanatory power in the acquisition field, but when we look at both disciplines we see solid bodies of tested theory and we see basic assumptions remaining consistent across time. This is as true for the disciplines as a whole as for the different branches, the different schools of thought, within each.

When we look at strategy, we see very little established theory to start with. In fact, there is very little consensus among writers about what strategy actually is – beyond the obvious recognition that it concerns those major policy decisions that shape the future directions of an enterprise.

Strategy lacks the coherence of an academic discipline. It is a field highly prone to fads and fashions. Prescriptions about how best to pursue strategy vary from one writer to another. The assumptions behind strategic thinking change abruptly at different periods in time. They also change as we move to different parts of the world. The cumulative result is that it is hard to find any consistent stream of strategic reasoning across the decades or any consistent set of assumptions from which to proceed.

In fact, it is hard to find anything really solid to latch onto in the strategy field. There is very little that is conclusively proven to be correct or incorrect. Different and often contradictory lines of thinking from different periods in time all persist and sit uneasily with one another.

Strategy is often hallowed ground for management scholars because it is the domain of industrial chiefs. But when the substance of strategy is analysed closely, especially Western textbook strategy, it often seems little more than a porridge of elementary economics, guru entrails and opportunism.

We will explore this only as far as identifying (a) how shifts in strategic thinking have influenced acquisition behaviour across the decades and (b) the changing beliefs about where sources of potential gain could lie in mergers.

Twentieth-Century Acquisition Strategies

Pre-1960: Horizontal and Vertical

Prior to the 1960s, most mergers and acquisitions pursued either horizontal or vertical integration. The patterns were set in America and gradually copied around the world. In the first great merger wave (1894–1907), almost all the deals were horizontal. Firms stayed in the same industry and increased capacity by buying out direct competitors until some got so big they had near-monopoly power from coast to coast. This was the period when America's mighty industrial base was forged – unmatched anywhere else in the world.

The second great merger wave (1920–29) saw vertical integration on a massive scale. Major US corporations formed during the first wave consolidated upstream and downstream by buying over suppliers, distributors and product outlets and incorporating them into the framework of a single organisation. This pattern – horizontal and vertical expansion – was the dominant pattern across the world until the 1960s. Although from the 1950s onwards there was a shift from single-business to multibusiness firms, diversification was usually around a dominant or related business.

Strategic thinking right accross this period was heavily influenced by mainstream economics theory. Competitive advantage was seen as coming predominantly from greater size in a *particular* industry. Two convictions drove most of the deals up to the 1960s.

- One was that a combination of increased market power and efficiencies of greater size would deliver higher profitability and give a sustained competitive edge. This justified horizontal merging.

- The other was that significant sources of risk would be better incorporated *inside* the firm under a single authority (hierarchy) than left *outside* and managed on a contract (or market) basis (Williamson, 1975). This usually justified vertical integration.

However, as examined earlier, all the problems of creating and sustaining greater size created a countervailing set of inefficiencies.

The 1960s: 'Instant' Conglomeration

The first radical shift in acquisition behaviour came in the 1960s with conglomeration. It turned all previous strategic thinking on its head and dominated the strategy agenda for more than two decades.

The takeover wave of the 1960s was the largest in the US since the turn of the century. The takeover wave of the 1970s was even larger. Conglomeration was central to both – but with very important differences. Activity in the 1960s was more tentative and experimental. There were, for example, no high-profile strategic models guiding conglomeration – practice raced ahead of prescription. The techniques of financial engineering were fairly crude. And big firms were involved only to a limited extent. Many still had to be convinced that full-scale conglomeration (i.e. having no dominant business) was a viable strategy.[1]

Thus, there were two sides to acquisition activity in the 1960s, an evolutionary dimension and a revolutionary dimension. The **evolutionary** dimension was continued *defensive* diversification. Large firms continued to acquire in unrelated fields until some became conglomerate more by accident than by any central intent. They reached a point where they ceased to have any identifiable core or dominant business – and thus became classified as

---

Box 4.1   The *de facto* message of conglomeration

In a nutshell, what conglomeration said to managers was this. If you want to be big *and* profitable, why slog it out in a single industry? It can be slow and risky, and requires lots of hands-on time and effort to deliver results. So why not act smart? Decouple the mechanisms for size from the mechanisms for profitability, and pursue each separately.

For *size*, buy juicy chunks of different product markets and buy undervalued companies across lots of industries. In next to no time, you can have enormous amounts of market power without infringing monopoly (anti-trust) regulations. You can stabilise lots of risks. You can pull out of an industry quickly if necessary. And you can enjoy all the material and psychic goodies that come with being really big without the stress and unpredictability of trying to grow in a single industry.

For *profitability*, don't just rely on your acquisitions delivering. You've also got to actively influence financial markets. Financial markets work mostly through perception, so work hard at managing these perceptions. Company reports, forecasts, briefings and especially justifications for the conglomerate mix, all need to carry the right 'spin' to feed investor perceptions. Remember that illusion is as important as reality. Your market rating and your borrowing capacity to do further deals depend as much on image and rhetoric as on hard financial results.

In short, *smart* managers act like managers but think like *investors*.

This, in essence, was the conglomerate message although it was never stated quite as directly as this. Nothing so transparently self-serving and so riddled with internal contradictions could have appeared in a strategy textbook. But it was the *de facto* message. Tiny could become big and big could become giant very quickly if managers stopped thinking like managers and thought like investors.

Some got it at once; for others it took a little time. But any managers who found the message appealing could easily gloss over the contradictions. There was no need to shift **conceptual** ground to justify conglomeration – only to shift **investment** ground and invoke some persuasive rhetoric.

---

conglomerate. By 1969, for example, the proportion of single-business firms in the *Fortune 500* had shrunk to a mere 6% of the total (Rumelt, 1974).

Weston and Mansinghka examined the acquisition history of these large 1960s conglomerates and confirmed that unrelated diversification was driven mostly by *defensive* business reasons – five in particular:

... to avoid (1) sales and profit instability, (2) adverse growth developments, (3) adverse competitive shifts, (4) technological obsolescence, and

(5) increased uncertainties associated with their industries. (Weston and Mansinghka, 1971, p. 928)

In other words, corporate conglomeration in the 1960s was the predictable consequence of unrelated diversification, of the defensive trend towards the multibusiness firm that started many years earlier. And the style of acquiring also remained consistent with the past. Deals were mostly amicable and typically involved large firms acquiring smaller public or private targets. Mega-mergers (deals greater than $100 million) or takeovers by one conglomerate of another were *not* a feature of the 1960s.

The **revolutionary** aspect, the really novel and ground-breaking feature of the 1960s, was the arrival of the new or 'instant' conglomerates – small and relatively unknown companies snapping up businesses in every industry and pioneering the hostile takeover. These 'go-go' early conglomerates hit the US business scene with truly breathtaking speed – many of them rocketing in size on the back of the booming economy and soaring stock market of the time. Four of the most prominent were Gulf & Western, ITT, Litton and Teledyne – all little-known firms at the start of the decade; all firmly established top hundred US companies at the end.

To give a flavour of their phenomenal growth, Gulf & Western was a single-product business with 500 staff and $8 million turnover in 1958. Between 1960 and 1968, the company bought assets worth almost $3 billion in 67 transactions. Teledyne – which did not even exist before 1960 – also shot into the ranks of America's top hundred companies by purchasing assets worth $1.2 billion in 125 acquisitions (i.e. acquiring one new company, on average, every three weeks for eight years) (Davidson, 1985, p. 140).

Activity on this scale resulted in conglomerate empires that were far too diverse and complex to understand, let alone manage effectively. These new conglomerates had no strategy – in the sense that we currently understand the term – for managing the diversity of what they had acquired. Target companies were viewed as little more than streams of future income to be bought and sold on the basis of whether they would boost share price, carry greater debt, or generate sufficient cash to fund further acquisitions.

Of these, boosting share price was the most crucial, and here the conglomerates had a very clear – albeit crude – strategy. The central pillar of that strategy was P/E 'magic' – low-value stock swapping in a way that did not dilute the higher value of the conglomerate stock. Everything depended on this working. It relied on a combination of factors – weak disclosure requirements, the most adroit of legal and accounting practices (some might say trickery) and armies of gullible investors. But when P/E 'magic' worked, nuggets of gold popped out of empty hats (see Box 4.2).

Box 4.2   1960s conglomeration and P/E 'magic'

P/E *'magic'* was the key to the wave of US conglomerate mergers in the 1960s. It financed many of the deals and made hostile takeovers possible. Relatively obscure companies with high-profile executives were able to build empires on the basis of stock swapping without diluting the P/E value of their own shares.

Conglomerates would announce that 'for a limited period only' they would be willing to trade their high P/E stock for the lowly rated stock of small companies. Target shareholders would rush to get in on the bargain – they were getting an above-market price for their shares. Then P/E *'magic'* did the rest.

Everything depended on 'spin' and image and market seduction. If the conglomerate was perceived as dynamic, the market often evaluated the combined earnings of the two firms at the *higher* P/E of the conglomerate, rather than applying a weighted average of the two P/E ratios. When it happened, both sides could show an immediate gain.

To realise the gain, all the conglomerate needed was a printing press to print new stock certificates to pay off target shareholders. They gained by receiving new stock worth more than their old stock. And the conglomerate became richer by having more high-value shares in circulation. A double instantaneous profit – obviously, it was magic! (Blair, 1972; Davidson, 1985)

For these early conglomerates, it mattered little whether a gain in earnings was real or illusory as long as it was accepted by investors. It took a market slump and rising interest rates to expose just how fragile some of these empires were, and especially how much of their performance depended upon dubious financial engineering and wide gaps in accounting rules.[2] When the US stock market slumped by around 30% in 1970, shares in new conglomerates collapsed by as much as 70%. Those financed through debt and new stock issues experienced a sharp decline in earnings and many ran into severe liquidity problems. The bubble had all but burst.

Financial markets may have been seduced but the possibilities of financial engineering were there for all to see. 'Instant' conglomerates demonstrated what was possible and their practices were catching on fast throughout North America and around the world. As *Fortune* magazine remarked at the time:

Perhaps the most damaging result of the (recent) conglomerate merger era was the false legitimacy it seemed to confer on the pursuit of profits by financial manipulation rather than by producing something of genuine economic value. (Beman, 1973, p. 70)

The 1970s: Mega-Conglomeration

By the early 1970s, conglomeration needed legitimacy fast. It needed a convincing strategic rationale to make its procedures respectable and to recover face in investment markets. The Boston Consulting Group (BCG) supplied it all. In writings which were highly influential at the time, the then head of BCG argued:

> Conglomerates are the normal and natural business form for effectively channelling investment in the most productive use. If nature takes its course, then conglomerates will become the dominant form of business organisation ... (Henderson, 1979, cited in Davidson, 1985, p. 179)

The implicit message from BCG was that diversity and complexity and size should be no obstacles to performance – provided that the correct investment policies were followed. *Investment* rather than management was the key to a successful corporate strategy.

The logic was straightforward and outwardly seductive. The PIMS (Profit Impact of Marketing Strategy – see Buzzell and Gale, 1987) database of 37 key profit influences had already begun to single out market share as the most important influence upon the bottom line – the higher the market share, the higher the profits. But single-industry investment was risky.

The BCG investment matrix got round the risk by recommending a portfolio of different businesses, each with high market share, for sustained profitability. As most readers probably know, firms were advised to invest profits from *mature* businesses ('cash cows') into *growth* businesses, which either

(a)   were already market leaders ('stars') or
(b)   potentially could become market leaders ('question marks').

By shifting investment from stagnant to growing industries, it would produce genuine economic value and create the 'cash cows' of tomorrow. But economic inefficiency was not to be tolerated. Any business with a small or a declining market share – such as a sluggish 'question mark' or an ailing 'cash cow' – was to be labelled 'dog' and divested (see Figure 4.1).

It was a simple virtuous recipe: Milk the Cows, Worship the Stars, Watch the Question Marks and Shoot the Dogs. The matrix recognised only two strategic variables: market growth and market share.[3] It was intended initially as a guide to internal capital investment. But it quickly became an icon for business strategy and a blueprint for conglomeration.

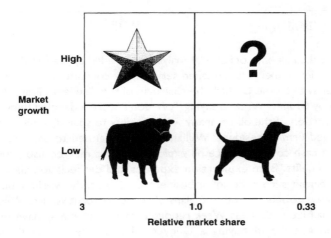

Figure 4.1 BCG Growth Share matrix

Source: © The Boston Consulting Group 1970. Reproduced with permission.

By overlaying the matrix upon *any* assortment of companies and classifying the mix into the four quadrants, it could transform them into an instantly recognisable strategic shape. No matter how large or diverse or eclectic the conglomeration, the matrix could provide a persuasive strategic rationale for why the companies were owned and where they were all going – and that in turn gave reassurance to financial markets.

And to top it all, there was just a hint of eternal growth and everlasting profits – provided, of course, that firms were quick to spot potential winners and equally quick to dispose of losers. *But there was one all-important catch. For the recipe to work, mature firms needed to start with an appropriate complement of 'stars' and 'question marks'.*

The result was a stampede of diversifications into unrelated or indirectly related industries and this time big corporations were driving the deals. By the mid-1970s when financial market conditions were again favourable, firms were stacking acquisitions in one industry upon acquisitions in another – often with little reference to production methods, technology, marketing channels or any other unifying basis for running a business.

Central planning departments in large corporations were scouring the lands for possible takeover targets. At General Electric, we are told that computers were spewing out daily reports twelve-feet high on individual businesses (Pascale, 1991, p. 199). Industry knowledge was often unimportant when selecting takeover targets. But that didn't matter. Businesses were just cash flows that could be mixed and managed by any competent executive with financial training.

Box 4.3   Seeing double

Testimony to the influence of financial analysis is provided by the fact that purely financial theories of mergers are taken seriously by corporations. At the time of its merger with Home Oil Ltd, the chairman of the distillery Hiram Walker was quoted by *Business Week* as saying, 'We don't know a damned thing about oil.' The attraction of the oil company was its ability to soak up liquor profits.

The merged firm's president, William Wilder, planned to use the liquor business as a cash cow to finance oil exploration. This merger also promised double tax benefits. Both exploration expenses and depreciation allowances could offset earnings from the liquor business. Of course, the world of business does not always cooperate with the plans of financial executives like Wilder. A year and a half later, *Business Week* reported that Wilder may have made a $295 million mistake in buying a Denver oil property for $630 million. (Davidson, 1985, p. 175)

It was a period when no firm felt safe from the unwelcome bid. If any firm could be targeted, then any firm could be a target. Second-guessing possible moves by rivals led to defensive diversification on a frenzied scale. Some firms made rush acquisitions solely to get rid of cash reserves; others to create anti-trust (monopoly) conflicts for prospective bidders. Some even bought 'dogs' as poison-pills to thwart potential approaches. The press labelled it merger mania, perhaps correctly.

And big firms got bigger. An unprecedented number of US industrial giants got locked in takeover contests to create even larger, more unmanageable corporations. Mega-mergers (i.e. deals greater than $100 million) increased annually from 15 in 1974 to 200 in 1984. Oil companies were especially prominent – first as targets, then as acquirers, and then both at the same time. The three biggest deals of the period certainly involved oil – Du Pont acquired Conoco for $7.5 billion in 1981, Texaco acquired Getty Oil for $10 billion in 1984, followed swiftly by the then largest takeover in US corporate history – the $13.3 billion acquisition of Gulf by Chevron.

Many of these mega-mergers, particularly between conglomerates, had no discernible business logic. Acquirers sometimes sold off valuable assets just to get the cash mountain to do the deals. Unease was felt in many quarters including Congress, where calls repeatedly were made for restrictions. Oil mega-mergers were put under particular scrutiny, even by Congressional friends of the oil industry. 'Absolutely no redeeming social or economic value', was a typical judgement, especially when future oil exploration funds got dissipated into windfall profits (Davidson, 1985, pp. 263–4).

Common to all the mega-mergers was the pursuit of size apparently for the sheer sake of it – and because companies had the resources to do so. But remember: size presented no problem. The key to a successful strategy was investment and mixing cash flows and engineering financial ratios, not managing the nightmarish complexity that had been created.

Box 4.4   Managing by numbers

The single most important message carried to executives by the BCG matrix was implicit: you can manage a diversified corporation by numbers. If believed, that message freed managers from any restraints surrounding acquisition policy. Any firm could be a target. No firm resulting from mergers would be too large, too diverse or too complex if the numbers – product market growth and market share – provided all the information necessary for good management.

For executives who needed acquisitions to place earnings that could not be invested in current businesses, this was welcome news. Mergers could be undertaken without raising fears that the firm would become unmanageable. Even if BCG was not exactly right in its prescription, the key to good management was in the numbers. And many executives were confident they could manage numbers. (Davidson, 1985, p. 173)

Excellence for the 1980s

In the 1980s, strategic fashion changed again. Evidence of conglomerate underperformance was difficult to refute. The more a company diversified into an unrelated business, the greater was the probability of failure.

- In 1982, *Fortune* magazine turned the spotlight on the ten largest US conglomerate mergers of 1971. All ten had chosen to diversify rather than grow existing businesses. It was not a successful strategy. They all delivered returns lower than 13.8% (the median for all companies in the *Fortune 500* across the decade) with three returning less than 5%. Half were judged to be in poorer strategic shape than a decade earlier (Louis, 1982).

- In 1987, Porter reported on the long-term acquisition performance of 33 of the largest diversified US corporations. The sample was huge – involving 2,021 acquisitions made by the corporations between 1950 and 1986. More than half were judged to have been failures and subsequently divested. In unrelated acquisitions, the divestment rate reached 74% (Porter, 1987).

- Across the decade, financial markets became more discerning. Companies that followed the portfolio management model were often awarded a 'conglomerate discount' – the market valued the whole at less than the sum of its parts. Similarly, bidders' share price movements across the decade showed an average 4% drop in non-related deals but a 3% premium when targets were related (Morck et al., 1990).

- Even BCG turned on its head. As early as 1981 the new head at BCG was quoted in *Business Week* as saying: 'The relationship between market share and profitability doesn't hold as much significance anymore. You can live as well as a small company or as a big company. And you can be as successful with a low-cost product or a high-value-added product' (1 June 1981).

A new strategic emphasis began to drive acquisitions and divestments – deconglomeration, demerging, unbundling (which encouraged the usually successful leveraged buy-outs (Kaplan, 1989)) and consolidation around core businesses. If this sounded dull, the strategic challenge now came from Peters and Waterman (1982) and the 'excellence' literature. Instead of buying and selling market share to engineer the bottom line, strategy was now all about mission and values and commitment to the customer.

> The new message said market share was precious. It was something to be earned and nurtured, not bought and sold at whim. A firm's mission was to understand and respond sensitively to each of its customer groups. A close-to-customer ethos should permeate every level of the business. Knowing the customer and being immersed in customer understanding was the key to a successful strategy and sustained profitability.

All of which made a lot of sense and required careful consideration especially at a time when power was beginning to shift from producer to consumer. *But along the way – perhaps because of the strong consumer emphasis – the message was hijacked by marketing specialists. The result was that much of strategy in the 1980s became almost indistinguishable from marketing – even though technology and the pace of technological development were the main drivers of market change.*

Two separate streams of *strategy as marketing* featured prominently in the 1980s – one inspired by Porter with the emphasis on markets; the other inspired by Peters and Waterman with the emphasis on the customer. Although different, they were really two sides of the same coin. Both were concerned with profitability through competitive advantage at the consumer interface.

The Porter approach emphasised market posture and positioning. In many respects it was a traditional marketing perspective – focusing on the 'hard', producer, supply side of the consumer interface. Strategy was a three-stage process of (a) analysing market forces using the Five Forces model. Then (b) choosing which of three (or is it two?) generic strategies to follow – lower cost or differentiation/focus. Then (c) examining each link in the value chain to see where value might be added more effectively compared to rivals (Porter, 1985).

These steps became touchstones in 1980s strategic thinking and were unquestionably a powerful antidote to the BCG matrix. For companies returning to consolidation after perhaps years of portfolio management, the approach was invaluable for restoring focus back to profitability through core product markets.

The value chain in particular encouraged firms to start looking at the internal organisational conditions necessary for external competitive success, for making strategy 'happen'. But the impact on how firms approached M&A implementation was marginal. Bungled integration and value destruction persisted across the decade.

The *'excellence' challenge* of binding strategy closer to the customer was the other – more populist – approach in the 1980s. Strategy from this perspective was all about mission and values and creating a consumer 'pull' towards the product – very much the 'soft', demand side of the consumer interface.

It was an approach that was evocative in spirit but weak on specifics. Lots of writers *urged* firms to move closer to the customer. Lots of firms *said* they were moving closer with customer-centred missions and values. But often it seemed as if little more than a new consumer 'front end' had been tacked onto existing ways of thinking and managing.

The result was the 1980s cult of 'spinning' the customer – image-makers heavily involved in engineering the customer interface and firms ritually proclaiming 'customer delight' regardless of the actual relationship that existed. It all conveyed a strong sense of strategic hype over strategic substance – as if financial engineering to a stockbroking formula (the BCG matrix) had given way to customer engineering to an advertising agency formula.

The impact upon acquisitions was negligible. The only noticeable effect was to provide an extra justification – 'in the consumer interest' – for doing deals. Other than that, it contributed little to acquisition or implementation thinking.

Merger Learning and Transaction Costs

Where M&A learning did occur in the 1980s was in two areas: hostile bids and transaction costs. Across the decade there was a sharp reduction in the number of hostile bids.[4] There was growing evidence that bidders in contested situations, and especially late entrants such as 'white knights', generally experienced negative returns in the years ahead (Bradley et al., 1988). There was also recognition that the negative attitudes developed during a hostile takeover usually exacerbated the already difficult task of integration. From the mid-1980s onwards, virtually all bids were agreed but often at a high premium – paying well above market value for the target.

The second learning feature of the decade was an increased awareness of M&A transaction costs. These are always high, with contested bids especially expensive (see Box 4.5).

Box 4.5   Brandy and cigars

Franks and Harris (1989) estimated that the transaction costs of an agreed merger may average 7% of acquisition value, excluding the costs of management time on each side. In hostile bids the figure can rise dramatically.

The now infamous contest in 1986 between Argyll Group (unsuccessful) and Guinness (successful) for control of Distillers is reckoned to have clocked up at least £150 million ($240 million) in third-party fees. The bid and its legal aftermath may have cost Guinness in excess of £100 million ($160 million). Argyll's fees *just for sustaining the bid* are estimated to have been nearly £50 million ($80 million).

In 1989 when the late James 'Marmite' Goldsmith teamed up with Australian Terry Packer to launch an abortive £13.4 billion ($21 billion) bid to unbundle BAT Industries, their shell company (Hoylake Investment, registered in Bermuda) announced it was prepared to spend up to £165 million ($270 million) in fees and commissions to brokers and advisers simply for doing, or attempting to do, the deals. (Pugh, 1987; *Independent*, 9 August 1989)

The Guinness scandal in the UK and the imprisonment of US arbitrageur Ivan Boesky were two high-profile events that more than any others put the spotlight on the costs of takeover – and on four aspects in particular:

1. Third-party and 'lubrication' costs are paid solely for making the deal happen and are not performance related. They are 'up front' costs the

size of which is related only to the value of the bid and the duration of any contest.

2. The expenditure produces nothing of any direct economic value.

3. In hostile bids the cost often has a magnitude so obviously out of proportion.

4. The sums involved frequently are much larger than any market-exploiting or inefficiency-reducing possibilities that a takeover might present.

The usual claim, of course, is that the costs are necessary to improve the efficiency of capital markets. The 1980s gave an insight into just how transparently self-serving that claim can be – especially when much of the potential value of a takeover can be lost before the ink is dry.

Capabilities for the 1990s

The leading edge in strategic thinking changed again in the 1990s, this time from product-based competition to capability-based competition. Hamel and Prahalad were among the earliest exponents. They argued that most models of strategy did not reflect the complexity of strategy-in-action. Nor did they help firms identify areas where they could develop a sustainable competitive edge. Most strategic models, in short, were just too simplistic.

> It is not very comforting to think that the essence of Western strategic thought can be reduced to eight rules for excellence, seven S's, five competitive strategies, and innumerable two-by-two matrices. (Hamel and Prahalad, 1989, p. 71)

Good strategy should catch rivals off-guard and keep them second-guessing. But following strategic models often does the opposite. When firms follow the same broad set of strategic nostrums, it frequently leads to cloned mindsets, copycat behaviour and predictable strategies that rivals can easily decode. Notions of 'strategic fit' and 'generic strategies' encourage firms to imitate one another instead of developing innovative and non-imitable approaches to competition.

What was required was a strategic recognition of the obvious. Products or services were the embodiment, the end result, of a whole spectrum of organisational capabilities, including:

- human capital (knowledge, competences, attitudes)
- technological processes
- organisational structures
- management systems
- organisation cultures
- external networks.

These and other capabilities were what brought products and services to market and gave each firm its distinctive edge. Hence the new strategic message of the 1990s:

> Firms are successful in markets not because of the *consumer form* of their products or services (price, differentiation, attractiveness or other marketing attributes) but because of the *capability substance* embodied in them. Successful products and services in the marketplace are a celebration of the organisational capabilities that delivered them. Hence, capability uniqueness is the real stuff of competition.

This new message said that *what* a firm competed with and *how* it competed were more important than *where* it competed. The sources of competitive advantage lay deep inside the organisation, deep in the value chain. Capabilities manifested themselves in the market but their origin lay much further back. Market leaders, for example, typically excelled on the back of one major capability – one that was difficult for rivals to imitate (see Box 4.6).

Box 4.6   The three value disciplines

In an interesting study, Treacy and Wiersema (1995) identified three core capabilities around which market leaders typically excelled. They labelled them **The Three Value Disciplines**. These were either Operational Excellence *or* Product Leadership *or* Customer Intimacy. The key finding was that market leaders did not seek to lead in all of them. They did not try to be all things to all people.

Instead, market leaders pursued competitive uniqueness by choosing *one* particular strength, *one* particular capability, and focused upon it relentlessly. They staked their reputation on it. The pay-off was a strategic capability that generated high value; that resonated with the company culture, and was difficult for rivals to imitate.

This was a direct challenge to the 'finishing line' emphasis that had dominated so much of strategic thinking across the decades. Too much emphasis had been placed on the final outcomes of strategy – profitability, ROI, market share, and similar – and insufficient attention to the processes and capabilities that delivered them. The bottom line was that strategists required deep, industry-wide and firm-specific understanding of products *and the organisational processes that delivered them*; not just financial and market and customer understanding.

This left many people uncomfortable.

- Strategy-as-marketing theorists found it difficult to accommodate product and process variables in models with (mostly) market variables. Some generic prescriptions began to look distinctly hollow without firm-specific knowledge – especially two-by-two matrices.

- It all ran counter to much of the business school training – that managers should be able to formulate strategy on the basis of finance and market information but without knowing much about the product or the processes which delivered it.

- It made life difficult for industry and investment analysts because capabilities, unlike market variables, are hard to quantify and systematically compare.

Capability Thinking and Acquisitions

However, capability thinking – more than any other strategic concept – captured the acquisition realities of the 1990s and into the twenty-first century.

Capability Focus

Across all industries, firms were much more selective and focused in their acquisition targets – seeking to plug clearly identified capability gaps in their competitive armoury or acquiring specific capabilities which they were unable or unwilling to develop in-house.

And – perhaps deterred by transaction costs and the complexity of merger integration – competitors collaborated to an unprecedented extent forming networks, joint ventures and other forms of strategic alliances. Some used collaboration specifically to challenge industry giants. Canon, for example, linked up with Kodak to refine the capabilities necessary to successfully challenge Xerox.

However, as always, the success of any collaboration hinged crucially on a further capability which not all companies possessed. The ability to bring the two sides together in the most appropriate way; to turn rivals into allies, and not to destroy value.

Smaller Companies

Capability thinking captured how most small and medium-sized firms approached acquisitions – not just in the 1990s but right across the decades. Remember that much of the high-profile acquisition behaviour in the previous pages has come from the largest of firms. They dominate attention and swell the statistics by virtue of their size – and overshadow the thousands of smaller acquisitions happening every year, perhaps once-in-a-lifetime events for the companies involved, which barely get a mention in the press.

What most smaller acquisitions have in common is *acquiring or being acquired around a specific capability*. Whether it is small firms seeking a specialist partner. Or R&D firms seeking a production capacity. Or expanding firms seeking the managerial and marketing expertise of a larger unit. Or owner-managers facing retirement and wanting the business to continue under a particular management style. The common thread is growing the business on the back of a clearly specified capability.

The End of Old Certainties

Another feature of the 1990s was that old certainties were dying faster than ever before. Firms could no longer lead by doing more efficiently what they had done in the past. They had to regroup and use their total company skills more effectively. New sources of competitive advantage were being discovered by breaking down functional barriers, improving flexibility, speeding up product development, integrating more tightly with suppliers and distributors, developing innovative relationships with customers, and so on – not just in one country, but spread around the world.

These were exciting developments but *there was no formula for understanding how they worked*. Firms were evolving with their own unique approaches to value-added and capability management. That meant acquirers had to have a sound *process* perspective. They had to understand thoroughly how value creation happened in any successful target they went after – otherwise inappropriate styles of post-acquisition management could destroy much of the value purchased.

Knowledge Industries

Knowledge-based industries were fast becoming the new engines of economic growth. By the mid-1990s, information technology alone was producing more than a quarter of all US economic growth. Other fields (such as genetics, biotechnology, pharmaceuticals, financial trading and similar) were also becoming high value on the basis of knowledge or capabilities that firms possessed or potentially could possess.

When knowledge, ideas and know-how are the key source of competitive advantage, everything hinges on a continuous creative output from the core people. Manage them the wrong way and much of the value of the business can walk out the door. Once again the spotlight turns on *having the ability to understand and manage capabilities* as a central issue in M&A and collaboration management.

As the century ended, mega-mergers were once again in the headlines. The ten biggest deals of the twentieth century occurred between 1997–99 (see Box 4.7). But they do not invalidate the capability argument; they reinforce

---

Box 4.7   The ten largest mega-mergers

The ten largest mergers of the twentieth century all occurred between 1997 and 1999.

1	Exxon and Mobil ($86 billion)
2	Travellers Group and Citicorp ($73 billion)
3	SBC Communications and Ameritech ($72 billion)
4	Bell Atlantic and GTE ($71 billion)
5	AT&T and Tele-Communications ($70 billion)
6=	Nationsbank and BankAmerica ($62 billion)
6=	Vodafone and AirTouch Communications ($62 billion)
8	British Petroleum and Amoco ($55 billion)
9	Olivetti and Telecom Italia ($34 billion)
10	Rhone-Poulenc and Hoechst ($28 billion)

(*Fortune* and *Acquisitions Monthly*, various dates)

it. These mergers occurred between global giants seeking to dominate global markets. The sheer size of these combined corporations is obviously a strength in that it protects against predators. But it is also a weakness in at least two respects:

1. Most of the deals were justified on the basis of scope and scale and cost cutting, and to be sure there are huge economies to be gained in production and marketing and distribution when operating on a truly global scale with truly global products. But set against these are the costs of trying to realise the synergies and also the integration complexity which can be truly horrendous when operating on such a scale.

2. The second weakness is that massive size can be an obstacle to innovation and growth. Mega-corporations may be the gatekeepers of growth in their industries, but the real engines of growth are the smaller companies pioneering new technologies and capabilities. Big corporations depend crucially upon a continuous supply of smaller innovative companies to retain a competitive edge. They usually have the resources to acquire whatever they need, but not always the ability to manage it successfully. Once again we get back to the central importance of having *the capability to understand and manage acquired capabilities, to turn competitors into allies and not to destroy acquired value.*

What Does All This Tell Us?

This chapter has given no more than a brief overview of M&A activity across the twentieth century – really no more than a series of snapshots. But it's sufficient to say something important about the relationship between strategy and performance.

We began by asking the question: can an examination of the strategy field help explain acquisition underperformance? Going further: could strategy be the *critical* variable affecting acquisition performance?

At first sight the answers might appear to be 'yes'.

• We saw how the dominant logic and assumptions behind strategy shifted abruptly across the decades – strategy as applied economics up to the 1950s; then strategy as financial engineering in the 1960s and 1970s; then strategy as sophisticated marketing in the 1980s; then strategy as capability competition in the 1990s.

- We saw the formula-based simplicity of many of the strategic models driving acquisitions – telling managers, in effect, that competitive strategy can be built upon a small handful of variables.
- And we saw claims that firms can copy a standard formula yet still retain a distinctive edge.

So it is tempting to blame simplistic or inconsistent strategy for decades of acquisition underperformance, and to blame managers for being so easily seduced into following strategic fashion. But that would be the *wrong* conclusion to arrive at – even though there are many examples of these weaknesses across the pages.

From the evidence put forward, the conclusion we must come to is that **the relationship between acquisition strategy and acquisition performance is loose and indeterminate**. The key point to note is that although strategic thinking changed across the decades, acquisition performance did not. Research at different periods right across the century has concluded, very consistently, that acquisitions *on average* are more likely to underperform, more likely to destroy than create value.

This seems to be telling us two things.

1. A small minority of acquisitions are likely to be successful – no matter what strategic logic and directions they follow.

2. And the majority of acquisitions are likely to be disappointing, again irrespective of the strategic logic that is driving them and the directions they follow.

So, maybe it doesn't matter too much which strategic approach a firm follows. Assuming that an acquisition's potential really exists and is not an accounting fiction, then what really matters is **the capacity to make a chosen strategy 'happen' and deliver value**. This is what has separated the successful acquirers from the rest across the decades – and will continue to do so in the future.

CHAPTER 5

Twelve Ways to Destroy Value

'When you ask why we made the acquisition, do you mean "business school" reasons or "real" reasons?'

(Managing Director, electronics)

The three fields of scholarship we have looked at – finance, economics and strategy – have provided some highly persuasive justifications for takeover activity. But they have shed little light on why some deals turn out successful and the majority do not.

We can get some on-average causes. Sometimes in a particular merger we can pinpoint a few likely causes. But usually it is not possible to attribute the performance of an acquisition to a single cause or set of definitive causes. Making and managing acquisitions is a long, complex set of *processes* that can take years to deliver results. There are too many variables acting together and too many decision points along the way to know for certain which have contributed most to performance.

There is, however, one thing we do know for certain. *Managers make acquisitions 'happen'*. Small groups of managers each choose to enact the acquisition process. They select the targets, interpret the environment, do the deals, choose the integration style and then manage the combined units. So it is to *managerial actions* we now turn to start getting at least some tentative explanations for acquisition outcomes.

Way back in 1983, Jensen and Ruback concluded that 'knowledge of the sources of takeover gains still eludes us' (Jensen and Ruback, 1983, p. 47). Research since then has not altered this conclusion. We can never really know the precise sources of gain in profitable mergers. But from the evidence we have amassed we can pinpoint some very likely sources of *loss* in mergers. We can identify managerial actions which, on the balance of probability and with our current organisational knowledge, are more likely to destroy value than enhance it.

Twelve of the most common contributors to value destruction are examined in this chapter. All have to do with managerial mindsets – how managers perceive; how they interpret; how they think and how they act – in an acquisition context (see Box 5.1).

Box 5.1   Twelve ways to destroy value

1. Tracker thinking
2. Political and personal motives
3. Over-reliance on numbers
4. Trusting forecasting models
5. Paying a market premium
6. Managing by wire
7. Lack of industry knowledge
8. Poor organisational auditing
9. Bungled integration
10. Mushy business planning
11. Deals separated from implementation
12. Not learning from experience

Tracker Thinking

'Big firms have superior performance. Copy their acquisition practices.' Wrong! Tracking and copying the acquisition patterns of large firms can be a sure way of destroying shareholder value. Size on its own cannot be relied upon to signify either effective strategy or good acquisition management. Large corporations may be pioneers in state-of-the-art management practices but only a few can claim to have made really successful acquisitions. Remember that the biggest failures in merger history lie at the feet of the largest corporations.

Tracker thinking is the raw fuel of strategic fashion. It can lead to knee-jerk strategy – moving in a particular direction even if there is no pressure or compelling rationale for doing so. And it can encourage acquisitions as a generic activity – if one does it, others feel they should do the same. Of course, the pressure to copy large firms is strong. Consolidation moves by industry giants can shape the industry and markets for years ahead. But reactive acquisition is seldom an efficient or an effective response. Every merger wave has had its large corporate trailblazers – and every merger wave has had its armies of disappointed followers.

Political and Personal Motives

Political and personal motives lie behind every acquisition. The problem is keeping them in alignment with financial and business motives. In the sample of companies in *Acquisitions – The Human Factor* (Hunt et al., 1987, the study that was an early stimulus for this book) only about a third of the deals were driven solely by financial or business concerns – or so overwhelmingly that other reasons were insignificant. The remainder (nearly two-thirds) was driven by a complex set of motives, with personal and political drivers often dominating (see Figure 5.1).

	Percentage of acquisitions where motive was significant
Financial and business motives	
Improve EPS	3
Improve ROI	33
Assets	15
Market share*	100
Technical capability	35
Management capability	33
Synergy/Economies of scale	25
Defending markets	18
Political and personal motives	
Sending signals to City	40
Chairman insistence	35
Retrieve 'face'	18
Rise in technology league	15
Impress competitor	8
Buying tradition or heritage	8
'Cash cow' for other bids	5
Sort out another problem acquisition	3

Figure 5.1   Diversity of acquisition motives

* All acquirers gave market share as a motive (new markets, increased share, or both).

Source: © Reproduced with permission from Hunt, J.W., Lees, S., Grumbar, J. and Vivian, P. (1987) *Acquisitions – The Human Factor*, London: London Business School and Egon Zehnder International, p. 13.

The business reasons in Figure 5.1 are entirely straightforward. All the acquirers wanted to capture markets, and the other motives were mainstream strategic reasons for wanting to purchase another company. So that aspect is unremarkable. Far more revealing – because they never appear in strategy textbooks – is the spread of political and personal motives. Some are worth highlighting.

- Top of the list was a preoccupation with investor perception, with sending the 'right signals' to financial markets. It figured in 40% of the sample and in half of these it appeared to be a dominant factor. *'We needed to be seen as a big player in the City.'* Or: *'A deal of this size would increase our financial muscle in the City.'* Or again: *'We **had** to improve our rating – it was essential. The acquisition did it.'*

- Chairman insistence figured strongly – like the division forced to acquire a target that it didn't want. *'The chairman told us to buy them. We didn't want them and they didn't want us.'*

- There were high-profile chairmen buying on the rebound after losing an earlier deal. *'It was a personally motivated project. I **had** to have them … there was no question about it. Most of the board were uneasy.'*

- Or taking a loss-making subsidiary from a rival and being seen to have turned it round in a short time: *'The chairman wanted to put one over on the other side, and our production people wanted to prove they could do it. It was a high-risk strategy, but worth it if we could pull it off.'*

- There was acquiring for image and prestige reasons. *'We wanted a traditional British company in our group. It didn't matter too much – as long as we could have "By Appointment to Her Majesty" on the front of the annual report.'*

- And perhaps the most oblique motive of all – making a second acquisition to sort out problems with a first. One company found it didn't have the necessary skills to manage a loss-making US acquisition. Instead of divesting, it bought a second US company in the hope that its managers (being local and closer) would sort out the problems with the first company. Two years later came the comment: *'We've now got two loss-making subsidiaries on our hands. We weren't expecting that.'*

This is a snapshot from just one study in the mid-1980s. Choose another decade and the examples would be different but the conclusion remains the same. When political and personal motives eclipse sound business judgement, getting the return on the deal is usually much harder.

Over-Reliance on Numbers

'**If the numbers look right, the acquisition will be right.**' This is the most common assumption in acquisition thinking and it is mistaken, so very mistaken. If the numbers look right, the acquisition in all probability will go wrong. Absolutely true! History tells us so.

Nearly two-thirds of all mergers and acquisitions have failed to deliver as expected, many in a spectacular way. But every single one started out with a set of numbers that conveyed bullish optimism. Managers believed them when they went ahead. Investors must have believed them to have parted with their money. Financial markets used to believe them when they marked shares up. But no more than about a third have actually delivered as expected.

Numbers are wonderful for crystallising the past and giving shape to dreams but they tell nothing about how the past happened or how the future is to be delivered. Numbers on their own tell nothing about the structures and systems and cultures and capabilities in a firm. Nor do they reveal how these variables interact to shape how a firm thinks and acts and does business. It is precisely this sort of *process* data that managers need to have at their fingertips to combine two firms effectively and get them to perform.

Hence the guiding rule for mergers: **Investors think numbers; managers think processes**. When acquisition managers think numbers, they think more like investors. They surround themselves with financial and commercial analyses, forecasts, projections, simulations, and ratios of every conceivable kind. These are the tools of the investment analyst and the financial adviser, not the tools needed to understand how two firms can be brought together and managed to deliver results.

And financial markets have now twigged it. This is the interesting twist to the guiding rule. Investors are now starting to think how managers *should* think. More and more they are looking to acquirers for a track record of process competence – proven competence at making merger numbers 'happen' – before favouring a deal.

Trusting Forecasting Models

Forecasting models are used at all stages of acquisition planning, from filtering out unsuitable targets to shortlisting potential partners. 'Running the numbers' on a potential target is such standard routine that there is scarcely a management team in the world that is not heavily influenced by what the models and the numbers have to say. However, it is when putting a deal together that accuracy in valuing a target is essential.

Putting a value on a target company is the most crucial calculation in any deal. It determines the maximum bid price, and that in turn sets the performance hurdles for years ahead.

We know that forecasting has never been an exact science. Forecasting models, to be of any practical use, have to simplify the real world and concentrate on just a few key variables and relationships. This, of course, is what makes the models seductive – their apparent capacity to reduce the complex, unknown future into a handful of simple dimensions. However, that simplicity disguises four major weaknesses when the models are used for valuation.

Consistency

One big worry is that forecasting models do not always agree on which variables and relationships are central to predicting the future and which are not. Nor do they always agree on how the different variables interact. This can lead to a wide discrepancy between forecasts and to a scattergun array of projections.

Historical

Commercial forecasting models are time-specific in the sense that they are developed at a point in time and then tested and validated against a *particular* set of economic and commercial conditions. Most models can handle incremental changes in boundary conditions but not major shifts. In times of unprecedented change when boundaries of markets and industries are becoming unrecognisable and when the ground rules of business are being rewritten almost every year, historical models have obvious limitations.

Strategic Fashion

There is also the effect of fads and fashions in strategic thinking. We noted in Chapter 4 how, in only a few decades, the dominant logic behind strategy shifted from being economics-based to finance-based to marketing-based to capability-based. Each of these approaches to strategy suggests very different possibilities for value creation. Feed the assumptions of each into a forecasting model and radically different projections will appear.

Realisation

Even if a forecasting model was demonstrated to be accurate within its limits, it tells nothing about how to realise the future. Synergy forecasts, for example, tell nothing about the nightmarish complexity and horrendous costs that may have to be confronted when trying to realise the gains.

Forecasting models, at best, can only try to predict the predictable, not the *un*predictable. The models cannot foretell, for example, how rivals might respond and regroup following a deal. Nor can they predict the thinking behind future competitor strategies.

Box 5.2   Forecasting wonderland

Consider a not entirely hypothetical example. Suppose a cash-rich firm was keen to acquire and set aside an entire week for evaluating possible targets. If on Monday the firm planned to consolidate; on Tuesday to integrate; on Wednesday to loosely relate; on Thursday to conglomerate; then on Friday said: 'Nothing's suitable. Let's dis-integrate'; do you know something?

It is possible to find a forecasting model for each day that will say: Yes, that is a good choice of strategic direction and here are some up-beat projections for the next ten years. Backroom analysts doing boardroom presentations might find this comforting but it is not very reassuring for the rest of us.

Paying a Market Premium

Paying an above-market price for a target company makes future value that much harder to deliver. The performance improvements needed to make the deal pay off are so much greater. Paying a high premium when markets are high seems doubly dangerous. Performance hurdles for managers get raised from the difficult to the near-impossible. In such circumstances, much of the potential value of an acquisition can be lost when the deal is signed.

But how much is too much? There is no such thing as a 'correct' price for a company. Everything depends on mindsets – on perception and judgement and how circumstances are interpreted. Hindsight might tell if a target was accurately valued or not, but at the time of the deal, market valuation (with all its imperfections) is the best indicator we have got.

When a firm pays an above-market premium for a target, it is saying that its single judgement is superior to the multiple judgements of the market. But acquisition history says the opposite. The odds against success are loaded even at market price. Start paying premiums and it becomes even harder to break even, let alone get a deal to pay.

This used to be the problem in hostile takeovers. Competitive bidding jacked up premiums to the point where the chances of the acquisition breaking even became remote. Then around the late 1980s, it seemed that firms had finally got the message – but not quite. Hostile bids virtually disappeared but the problem of overpaying persisted. Acquirers in agreed takeovers are still willing to pay well above market value to get targets to give up control.

1998 was a record year for merger activity – both in volume and size of deals. *Fortune* magazine took a closer look at some of this activity (see Table 5.1). In six of the most celebrated US mega-mergers of the year, the magazine revealed that acquirers had paid astonishingly high premiums for their targets – ranging from 34% to 86% above market valuation at the time the deals were announced. In some instances, astronomical improvements in target performance would be necessary to make the deals pay.

Table 5.1   1998 mega-deals: impossible hurdles?

Companies (acquirer/target)	Value of deal ($ billions)[1]	Premium over market price[2]	Expected growth of target before deal	Required growth of target to make deal pay
AT&T/TCI	$26.7	48%	18.1%	20.7%
Conseco/				
Green Tree	$7.1	86%	0.4%	9.3%
Deutsche Bank/				
Bankers Trust	$8.9	42%	2.6%	7.1%
Exxon/Mobil	$77.2	34%	9.9%	12.9%
Nationsbank/				
Barnett Banks	$14.3	44%	10.3%	14.8%
Newell/Rubbermaid	$5.8	65%	13.9%	19.2%

[1] Price on announcement.
[2] For more details on how these and other figures are calculated see *Fortune* (11 January 1999, p. 44).

Source: Fortune (11 January 1999, p. 44)

Some of these hurdles seem close to impossible. Conseco paid nearly double the market price for Green Tree. According to *Fortune*'s calculations, synergy potential was weak – one selling insurance to the middle classes; the other sub-prime mortgages to lower-income groups. A 23-times improvement in target performance would be needed just to make the deal pay.

But even apparently modest increases in target performance can be daunting. The Exxon/Mobil deal at a final price of $86 billion was the largest merger of the twentieth century. *Fortune* reckoned Exxon paid through the nose. At the time of the deal, Mobil stock was high. The company was judged to be performing well – nimble management, little slack, and certainly not undervalued. The market had high expectations of Mobil and this was reflected in the share price.

By offering a 34% premium, Exxon chose to value Mobil's total assets at one-third more than the already high valuation of the market. That puts a different slant on increasing Mobil's annual growth from 9.9% to 12.9% per annum. It may look modest, but according to *Fortune* the Mobil investment required a return on capital of 17.6% to make the deal pay. But in the six years prior to the deal, high-performing Mobil's best annual return had been 12.2%. So it's not such an easy hurdle to jump.

Managing by Wire

What encourages firms to pay such premiums and believe they can be recovered? In particular, large corporations with world-class managers, with armies of expert analysts and with usually a conservative approach to risk? We know every acquisition is unique so the reasons will be different in every deal. Nevertheless, there is one characteristic of large corporations – not often examined – that can encourage over-bullish mindsets at the top. Senior and top managers have increasingly become accustomed to managing by wire.

We noted in Chapter 3 that as firms got bigger and more complex, information overload became a major problem. The limitations of the human mind and the need for simplification resulted in practices such as selective attention, data rationing, political filtering, introspective thinking, and so on. To this we now need to add IT. Data reaching the top of corporations is no longer just selected and filtered. Increasingly, it is also IT-interpreted.

The realities that top executives now manage are more and more computer-reflected and software-interpreted images of the real world. The 'lenses' they look through to plan and control are computer-assisted. The sheer size of mega-corporations is such that little else is possible. They are now so large and complex that those at the top cannot possibly grasp more than a tiny proportion of what is happening below and around them without IT assistance.

Increasingly, top managers are managing virtual worlds. Their mindsets – how they perceive and think and act – are more and more shaped by the technological infrastructure that surrounds them and feeds them with data. The result is that computer realities and business/managerial realities become harder to distinguish.

There are advantages, of course. Managers might feel relieved when massive number-crunching tasks are delegated to the machine – leaving them more time to deal with what they believe to be the substantive issues. Erratic strategic choices can be filtered out very quickly by the dogged rationality of software.

But there are also downsides. That same rationality can reject innovative strategies that deviate too far from the mainstream. And when top executives manage by wire they collectively can become dependent on wire. A culture of dependence on software can deskill critical judgement – and that in turn can make wire-dreams easier to believe and accept.

Box 5.3   Delegating up the wire

There is an old IT joke that computer boffins in large corporations still enjoy telling.

> *Question*: Why did the central computer issue redundancy notices to the main board?
> *Answer*: Because the board kept referring all important decisions to the computer.

A juvenile joke – or a sharp mirror of truth? Suppose a potential acquisition is evaluated by two different lots of software. If one jangles gold and the other spits out lemons, are receiving mindsets able to identify which might be the more accurate? More importantly, can they explain *why*?

Lack of Industry Knowledge

Lack of industry knowledge can cripple an acquisition. It was the curse of conglomeration in the 1970s and some residues still persist. Two common mistakes are to believe that industry and technical knowledge is really only necessary for implementers and others further down the line. Or if knowledge of a particular industry is not in the acquiring firm, it is sufficient simply to buy it in. Nothing could be further from the truth.

Knowledge of the target industry – and sometimes the sector – has to permeate at least a significant proportion of top and senior management in the acquiring firm. It is essential at every stage along the way:

- for judging the feasibility of forecasts

- for anticipating competitor reactions

- for accurately valuing a target

- for real understanding of market and customer behaviour

- for credibility in day-to-day management following the deal.

In all sectors it is crucial. In the high-tech knowledge sector, it is simply not possible to evaluate choices and manage competently without an intimate knowledge of the industry and its technology. Few acts are more certain to dissipate value than acquisitions driven by managers who do not understand the industry or the technology they have bought into.

Poor Organisational Auditing

It is hard to imagine a firm embarking on a multi-million-dollar capital investment programme without conducting the most detailed appraisal and risk analysis. Data of every relevant type would be gathered in detail. Not to do so would be considered highly *irresponsible*. But when it comes to mergers and acquisitions, exercising *due diligence* traditionally has been little more than conducting financial and legal and commercial audits of the target firm.

During the last decade we have seen more firms moving towards some form of pre-deal organisational audit – such as investigating IT systems or core production or senior management calibre. But few firms extend their investigations into the human capability and the social and psychological underpinnings in a target – how the company collectively thinks and acts and does business. It is rare to find an acquiring firm that regards a fully comprehensive audit of the structures, cultures, controls and people in the vendor on the same level of importance as the financial and legal and commercial investigations.

- Thorough organisational audits are essential for understanding the processes that deliver the financial and commercial figures that make a target attractive in the first place.

- They are absolutely vital for knowing if two firms can work together and where culture clashes might occur.

- They are essential for understanding and costing the often complex task of integration.

- Most important of all, organisational audits are usually the *only* source of data for indicating when to abort a deal that otherwise on paper looks promising.

Insufficient knowledge of how a target company actually works remains the single most common reason for implementation difficulties. Too many firms wait until after the deal to discover what they really have bought – and that's when lemon harvesting begins!

Bungled Integration

How two firms are brought together shapes attitudes and performance for years into the future. Like a genetic process, apparently simple decisions and actions in the early weeks can be amplified throughout both companies – often with unintended and costly consequences. Later chapters will examine integration in detail. At this stage, we will just note the four most common mistakes acquirers can make.

1. Not having an agreed integration plan during negotiations. If a plan is not agreed before the deal is signed, different parties on each side will proceed on how they *imagine* integration is to happen. Fudged responsibilities and vague reorganisation plans are a sure recipe for political intrigue, distrust, and people working at cross-purposes.

2. Not having a full-time integration manager. The majority of managers assigned to the task do it on top of their main job and often have little experience of what is involved.

3. Not fine-tuning integration. A common error – especially among novice acquirers – is to go for total integration rather than carefully tailoring the extent of integration around the business goals of the acquisition or merger.

4. And the most frequent error of all – to be found even among experienced acquirers – is to regard integration as predominantly a technical matter and to overlook the complex human underpinnings of the process.

Generally speaking, firms that conduct thorough pre-deal organisational audits are usually sensitised to the psychological and cultural and mindset components of integration. And they are usually better prepared to handle them.

Mushy Business Planning

Top-down strategy has got to be matched with a detailed bottom-up business plan of how the acquisition is to generate value. That is the only way managers down the line can know what they are expected to deliver. Yet it is surprising how many acquirers – large and small – rely on projections to indicate future value and delay detailed business planning until after negotiations are completed.

Newly acquired managers don't like it. The delay can signal indecision and lack of focus, especially when they are left unclear on what their new targets and directions are to be.

Financial markets don't like it either. Fund managers and analysts are now far more discerning and scrutinise deals on the fine print of where value is to be created. If markets don't see it and don't believe value can be delivered, shares are likely to be marked down. Gone are the days when an acquisition by itself could be relied upon to boost share value.

Deals Separated from Implementation

A theme running through many of the factors here is the separation of deal-making from implementation planning. The practice is endemic. Boardroom teams and financial advisers negotiate deals often with only the haziest grasp of how results are to be delivered and with even less appreciation of the complexity of implementation. Integration managers then learn about the deals often at the last minute and are then charged with making the acquisition work. Sometimes they may know very little about what was agreed during negotiations and maybe even less about the real strategic logic behind the deal.

It is a practice that reflects the narrowest textbook interpretation of strategy. It perpetuates inefficiency. And it signals a worrying lack of trust in key senior executives. They are trusted to do the really difficult bit – implement the deals and deliver the return on capital (otherwise they would not be chosen for the job). Yet they are not trusted to be included in planning the very process they are supposed to implement. From an efficiency perspective, it is hard to defend.

Most of the factors that cripple acquisitions can be identified in advance. But there has to be a willingness to seek them out and evaluate them long before negotiations are completed. So why is that willingness not always there? We know it is not in the interests of efficiency – but it can be in the interests of psychology. For example:

- There is the **gambling** hypothesis. This argues that managers who make acquisitions are like gamblers who want to believe in their luck. They know the odds are stacked against them but they want to believe that their deals are different and really will deliver. If they hear themselves saying often enough that they can win *and hear it without contradiction*, then they start to believe that their luck will hold and that stiffens the will to proceed.

- There is the **mental overload** hypothesis. Top managers know only too well how complex and mind-bending integration can be – especially in large mergers. They may also be aware of how little they know about the realities of managing change further down the line. So they defer the implementation agenda to avoid mental overload. They simply cannot take the task on board during the hubris of negotiations.

- And there is the **empire-building** hypothesis. When large chunks of material and psychic income are at stake, some managers might not want a bubble-pricker at the negotiating table saying that, really, two plus two only equals three and a bit. Neither might financial advisers.

Three very different scenarios; three very different justifications for avoiding or postponing the integration issue. But all utilise the same comfort solution – retreat into a virtual world of ratios and projections and computer-calculated certainty.

> Psychologically, being cocooned in a virtual world of numbers can be more reassuring and protective than embracing the political and emotional unpredictability of making acquisition numbers 'happen'.
>
> Selective attention and listening to mirrors are two of the oldest psychological defences known to mankind.

Not Learning from Experience

Finally, that oft-quoted phrase: **'If only we knew what we know.'** It is especially relevant here. Knowledge, not capital, is the scarce resource in the M&A world.

A culture of secrecy surrounds so much of M&A practice. Firms seldom reveal how they make their acquisition decisions or how they value their targets or how they decide upon a particular implementation approach. Any firm with a successful set of procedures is sure to keep it under wraps. On the other hand, when things go wrong (as they often do), curtains tend to get drawn around the entire episode. The result is that learning in the M&A field is not made easy. Case material is hard to come by. Quality knowledge is very thin on the ground.

So the main – and sometimes only – way managers learn is by trial and error and building upon experience. Those managers who develop expertise in the field – especially hands-on experience of integrating or being integrated – are valuable assets to a firm. But if they leave, so does the capability.

> That is why from a strategic perspective it is important that individual know-how and experience is brought together into a collective knowledge base. Only that way can it grow into a unique, in-house, competitive capability.
>
> It is something any shrewd Human Resources (HR) Director/Vice President should be able to initiate. And to do it in a way that protects the knowledge base, keeping it in-house without attracting third-party interests.

Given that most firms acquire infrequently, there is usually plenty of time between deals for significant learning to take place.

It is now more important than ever. Firms of all shapes and sizes are becoming involved not just in mergers and acquisitions but in joint ventures and strategic alliances and other collaborative ventures. Globalisation is pulling firms into unknown territories – many for the first time into cross-border deals, into emerging markets, and navigating the complexities of cross-cultural management. Knowledge of what to do and what *not* to do is now harder to obtain than ever.

Hence the importance of firms **knowing what they know**. Firms with successful M&A practices probably have made every mistake in the book – and many others as well! But step by step they have revisited what they did and learned what not to do next time around. By systematically examining and refining their practices, they have developed a capability that many of their rivals lack. And that can make all the difference.

Part 3

Integration Strategy

CHAPTER 6

The Integration Agenda

'Vision is often sufficient to carry a deal. To deliver results you need detail, detail, detail ...'

(Finance Director, oil)

Now there is a change of emphasis – less on analysis and more on action. The remaining chapters are written mostly from the perspective of an integration manager who – as best practice dictates – is incorporated early into the acquisition planning team. The chapters explore some of the major issues an integration manager is likely to confront and how to think about them, and they also suggest some models and frameworks to guide action.

Before proceeding, three points should be emphasised.

1. Although integration is a post-deal event, *all* the aspects covered are essential pre-deal considerations and require careful preparatory planning and synchronising before negotiations are completed.

2. Remember that there are many other aspects of integration – financial, legal, accounting, etc. – which are either mandatory or regulated by sets of rules or established procedures. These are not addressed here. We are concerned solely with those discretionary strategic aspects for which there are no rules or conventions, only judgements.

3. Remember the general caveat that applies to all chapters. Every acquisition is unique, so models and frameworks need to be tailored to the specifics of each situation.

The Integration Manager

There are two main sources of potential gain when companies combine: markets and hierarchies. Some gains can come directly from increased market power – especially in product markets and financial markets. Other gains can come directly from reorganising and managing hierarchies more efficiently. But the majority of potential gains depend upon a long-term interactive relationship between markets and hierarchies. Bigger organisations with greater market power create new opportunities which allow the organisation to grow larger, and so on.

Likewise for sources of loss. Some losses can be attributed to unexpected market changes. Others to a failure to realise internal efficiencies. But more commonly they can be traced to the inability of newly combined hierarchies to integrate effectively and respond appropriately to changes in external markets (see Figure 6.1).

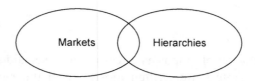

Figure 6.1   Sources of gain and loss in mergers

That is why every acquisition needs a *commercial manager* and an *integration manager* – one manager focusing predominantly on market processes and the other on organisational processes. *Both* sources of gain and loss need to be addressed with equal measure during acquisition planning.

The commercial manager (usually the CEO or equivalent) is concerned primarily with driving the business aspects of the deal – the market and technical and financial aspects. He or she starts off with a strategy or maybe just a vision, and has to deliver the vision and results in the years ahead.

Vision and strategy are effected through people and organisations. The integration manager has to design how best to combine two hierarchies and two lots of people to turn vision into reality.

Both managers need to work hand in hand from the earliest stages. They bring together different capabilities and ways of thinking: one focused externally on markets, the other internally on hierarchies. But the integration manager has to deliver first. He or she has to design the conditions for the commercial manager to work through to turn strategy into reality in the years ahead. The integration manager is the commercial manager's right hand.

The Integration Agenda in Acquisition Planning

There is, however, much more to the integration manager's job than just bringing two companies together. There is also the question of whether the companies *ought* to be brought together in the first place. If we go back to the definition of strategic integration in Chapter 2, it reminded us that integration had to be for a purpose – to realise strategy *and* to create value (which most acquisitions don't). But perceptions of value are very much organisationally conditioned. Strategic mindsets and notions of potential value are often firm-specific: what is gold to one firm can be a lemon to another.

An integration manager with good insight into organisational and psychological processes can help an acquisition team to 'step outside' their mindsets and recognise some of the taken-for-granted processes by which they operate. That can make an invaluable contribution to acquisition planning and to minimising value destruction.

When this aspect is added to the integration agenda, it opens up at least ten major dimensions to the integration manager's job. They are put in the form of questions that a shrewd integration manager will start asking long before negotiations begin.

1. **Value checking**
   Does the acquisition value really exist or is it an accounting creation?
   If real value is not there or gets destroyed by overpaying, no amount of integration effort can deliver it. Here the integration manager will be probing the strategic assumptions behind the deal – and also wondering if struggling to join two firms together will be worth the effort. High-pain-low-gain acquisitions were a feature of the twentieth century and the shrewd integration manager will want to steer the firm well clear of them.
   Issue: Strategy checking (Chapter 4)
   Issue: Forecasting assumptions (Chapter 7)

2. **Sustaining value**
   If potential value is really there, can it be sustained?
   Market value is sustained by effective and responsive organisations and quality management teams. But history tells us that bigger merged organisations are often less efficient and less responsive than either was prior to takeover.
   Issue: Inefficiencies of size (Chapter 3)

3. Information

What types of information on the target company are needed to verify value and assess the costs and the complexity of integration?

Due diligence has to extend far beyond financial and legal and commercial audits. Carefully refined human and organisational and capability and cultural audits are also essential.

Issue: Auditing/due diligence (Chapter 8)

4. Controls

What controls need to be in place in an acquired company?

Having the right people in the right place with the right controls is a priority in any acquisition.

Issue: Essential Controls (Chapter 9)

5. Interfacing

What is the best way to combine the two companies to deliver value?

The business goals of an acquisition should determine how far the two organisations should actually be combined. Under what circumstances should the acquired organisation stand alone, be partly merged or fully assimilated?

Issue: Structural interfacing (Chapter 10)

6. Human reactions

What are the essential elements of an acquisition-specific Human Resource strategy?

Change, career shifts, relocations and new responsibilities often lead to high levels of uncertainty and stress after a takeover. Performance often drops as a result. Planning an acquisition-specific Human Resource strategy is the first step in securing commitment.

Issue: Acquisition Human Resource strategies (Chapter 11)

7. Handling the implementation

How best to start bringing the two firms together?

Gaining commitment on both sides from the time of the announcement is essential to avoid post-merger problems.

Issue: Three-stage commitment building (Chapters 12 and 13)

8. Mindsets

What ways of thinking on either side have the potential to destroy value, both pre-deal and post-deal?

There is a whole basket of mindset issues here – from differences in values and priorities and attitudes to risk through to justifications for all the different ways each firm is organised and managed. These lie at the root of culture clashes in mergers. Can they be predicted?

Issue: Organisation culture (Chapters 14 and 15)

9. **Acquiring across national cultures**
   What do we know about the impact of national culture upon management styles in national organisations?
   Cross-border deals have to take into account differences in national culture and their impact upon how a business is organised and managed.
   Issue: National culture (Chapter 16)

10. **Global integration managers**
    How best to develop and prepare managers for managing across one or more national cultures?
    Global mergers need highly skilled managers who are able to operate effectively across many continents. How best should they be developed?
    Issue: Global integration managers (Chapter 17)

These ten questions go straight to the heart of the integration agenda. All will be explored in the following pages, but note that they are repeating – now in more detail – what earlier chapters have been saying.

The integration agenda is much broader than joining two firms together. It is also about probing *behind the idea* that there is value to be had by bringing the two firms together in the first place. Value must always be the central consideration at every stage of acquisition planning.

A shrewd integration manager with sound organisational and psychological insight is perhaps best placed to identify *impediments to value* – not in markets, but in hierarchies and mindsets shaped by hierarchies – right across each stage. He or she will want to know first of all – is the value really there? If it is, what will it cost to deliver? Then is it worth the effort? These are three of the most fundamental concerns in any deal. Addressing them is one sure way of avoiding high-pain-low-gain acquisitions and building genuine shareholder value.

Who Should be Chosen to be an Integration Manager?

Who should be chosen to be an integration manager? Many of the detailed qualities will become apparent in the following pages, although there are some very obvious qualities that set that person apart from the typical acquisition team.

- The essential skills for making acquisitions are finance, market and product knowledge. For integrating acquisitions, change-management and people skills are vital. In cross-border deals, deep understanding of national culture and the problems of international management are also essential.

- The top management acquisition team are probably excellent at *driving* an organisation. The special expertise of an integration manager is in *designing* an organisation and *social engineering* the appropriate working environments.

- Modes of thinking are different. The acquisition team with an eye on markets are mostly thinking competition – themselves *against* others. Integration managers with an eye on blending two firms together are thinking cooperation – themselves *with* others.

Background and personality factors are crucial. Most experienced acquirers believe the role should not be used as a proving ground. It should not be a stepping stone for fast-trackers. Too much is at stake. Nor should it be a HRM appointment unless the person has an appropriate line background and a good track record of turning human resources into resourceful humans. Wisdom and sound judgement, and not just knowledge and technique, make an effective integration manager. And that generally points to:

- A person who is senior, not necessarily at board level but comfortable at that level, and who understands the industry and how the organisation actually works.

- The sort of person who speaks with authority and carries respect at many levels including board level, but doesn't always 'buy into' the firm's ethos. Instead, he or she will often rise above it and may often question the way business is done. If there have been earlier acquisitions, the person will have a good knowledge of how they were handled.

Psychological disposition is important when pulling two companies together and negotiating a new organisational order. It can make all the difference in situations where conflict may be endemic and where politics may cloud business priorities. Generally speaking, experienced acquirers have found that:

- Managers with a 'large ego' or a 'need to prove themselves' can sometimes exacerbate conflict, as can persons considered 'devious'. Hidden agendas can make integration many times more troublesome – like using integration to pursue private agendas or to promote sectional interests or the interests of external advisers.

- Being indifferent to status and salary differentials can be helpful – especially when there are significant differences on each side. Former owner-managers staying on to provide continuity can present a special problem – especially if they flaunt their newly realised wealth at the same time. A salaried executive integrating 'millionaire Californian beachboys', for example, may require a particular kind of personality – an ability to run with the pack, not get materially distracted, and still deliver results.

- A flexible social style is another essential quality especially in cross-border acquisitions – someone who is socially at ease in different contexts and good at reading social and cultural norms. Imperial managers and managers oversaturated with their company's values and culture may find this difficult. A 'them and us' attitude – with 'us' being superior – is usually bad news for integration. The cultural missionary type – 'I'm on a mission to spread the XYZ values around the world' – can spell disaster.

Every acquisition is unique so all these considerations need to be balanced against the specifics of context. However, these are the sorts of qualities that companies with a history of acquiring or being acquired would emphasise as being important in anyone in a bridging role – whether as integration manager or as a member of the integration team.

In Summary

Primary responsibility for an acquisition rests with the CEO or equivalent on the acquiring side. He or she is usually driving the deal and is heavily involved in negotiations. Post-deal, responsibility for making it all happen gets delegated. Sometimes to a few – like to the vendor CEO or to a director/vice-president on the acquiring side. More often to many – to specialist teams on both sides.

However, regardless of how it happens, the two sources of gain (and loss) – the market dimension and the hierarchy dimension – remain common to all deals and each is dependent on the other. Each has to be addressed with different mindsets and competences. CEOs with a typical strategic mindset focus on the market dimension and will ensure that this aspect is headed by persons with appropriate expertise. But the person who creates the conditions to make it all 'happen' – the organisational conditions for delivering market performance and acquisition value – and who can identify thinking that can lead to high-pain-low-gain outcomes, is rarely trusted to be included in the deal.

CHAPTER 7

Forecasting Models and Value Probing

'We believed it; we saw it; but the value just wasn't there.'

(Finance Director, engineering)

Many integration managers, given their background and expertise, may not be able to evaluate the specific *content* of acquisition strategy (especially if in a highly specialised or knowledge field). In fact, they may not be fully familiar with the strategic thinking behind a prospective acquisition or the real intentions behind it. But probing the mindsets that generate strategy and questioning the *processes and assumptions* that lead to perceptions of value is an expertise they can bring to acquisition planning.

In Chapter 5, twelve of the most common ways of destroying value were identified. If (as we are assuming here) the integration manager is included early into the planning team, then at least one of the factors has been dealt with. And that, in turn, opens the door to the others getting addressed. But every acquisition is unique, so all the factors need to be considered in context. A shrewd integration manager will want to establish very quickly the motives behind the deal and how consistent or diverse they are. Who are driving it and who are not fully committed? Is there a detailed bottom-up business plan? And how much knowledge do they have of the target business?

But the really big questions concern strategy and value. *For practical and comparative purposes, all strategy ultimately boils down to numbers.* In every acquisition, a figure gets quoted about its potential value. 'The merger is worth $X billion.' Or 'They are paying £Y million for the target.' Few people know exactly where the figure has come from or how the price has been calculated. But the figure sticks. It gets widely quoted and people believe it although very few know the assumptions it is based upon. And that is where the integration manager starts to dig.

Typically, before an integration manager gets involved, the target has already been selected and preliminary discussions have taken place. Positions will have already been taken up regarding the merger. However, they need not be set in stone.

Box 7.1   A boardroom scenario

One afternoon, a senior corporate executive was invited by the CEO to attend a boardroom presentation about a prospective acquisition. He was told that if the deal went ahead, he was the board's preferred choice to handle the implementation. Was he interested?

The presentation was slick and professional. Two Harvard-trained partners from a prestige global consultancy gave a penetrating analysis of the target and the synergies that could come from merging. Every strategic aspect was considered in detail. And every question seemed to have been anticipated.

What if markets should change in this way or that way? What if competitors did X or Y or Z? What about technology yet to hit the market? What about economic changes? Integration costs? Even down to possible taxation and labour market changes in every country in which both companies had an interest, there were buttons to press and out popped tables, charts, simulations and forecasts about the likely effects upon acquisition value.

Everything pointed to one conclusion. The two companies, it seemed, were meant for each other. Whichever way they looked at it, the deal was a winner.

The boardroom scenario set out in Box 7.1 is commonplace. What is the best way to take it apart? In this instance, the executive began with the integration costs and demonstrated that they would be several times greater than forecast. And that many of the synergies would cost more to realise than their worth. Interfacing structures, replacing systems, culture clashes and political factors would all make their contribution.

And that in turn started a process of further probing and questioning that not only threw the acquisition into sharper focus but also uncovered some of the hidden motives that lay behind considering the target in the first place. In the end, it was not pursued.

That is the way most managers will probe a prospective acquisition – they take one particular figure (an output) in the value projection and probe around it. The difficulty here is benchmarking. For every manager who says 'That forecast doesn't square with my experience', there may be another who is quite prepared to accept the figure on other grounds.

Probing Deeper

So we need a more incisive way of probing value assumptions. Every forecast of acquisition value is an *output* of one or more forecasting models. These models, as noted in Chapter 5, can vary considerably in terms of the assumptions they make and the gains they predict.

Therefore a more systematic and penetrating approach to value probing is to examine the fundamentals (the inputs) of the models that are used to predict acquisition value and synergy.

Any competent manager can do it – no special expertise is needed. Some starter questions that can be asked are these:

- *Presenter Knowledge*
  At a presentation like the one described above, ask the speaker directly: which forecasting models are being used to predict synergy and value? If the models cannot be named and their essential features cannot be described, be wary.

- *Test Specifics*
  If you know something about forecasting models, ask why a particular model has been chosen in preference to another. Otherwise, take an area you feel knowledgeable about – economics or finance or markets or technology or whatever – and probe around it. Get the presenter to state up-front the basic assumptions the model makes about the area in question, then see if you believe those assumptions. In the now globalised world, industry and market boundaries are becoming increasingly fuzzy. Any confident assertions about industry size and market size are always worth examining – especially at the national level.

- *Strategic Fashion*
  How much predicted value hinges on strategic fashion? Look for evidence of transient assumptions being built into the models. If you are unsure what they are, there is plenty of material in earlier chapters about merger waves that soared upon golden beliefs – then came crashing to earth a decade later.

- *Validation*
  Find out when the forecasting model or models being used were last validated, and against what sort of economic circumstances. *This may appear to be an esoteric point but it is absolutely crucial.* Validation means that a model has been *independently* verified as being an accurate predictor of whatever it claims to predict. There are lots of forecasting models in existence whose predictive accuracy has never been put to

independent test. When shareholder value is at stake, it seems sensible to choose a model with a solid pedigree.

Also remember that a model that was an accurate predictor in one set of economic circumstances may not be accurate in another. What predicted accurately in the 1980s and 1990s might not be appropriate today. What predicts accurately in Western economic contexts may fare badly in other economic environments.

- *Recognise Bluff*
  Some advisers might make reference to other areas where they have a forecasting expertise – like economic forecasting. They might say: we are one of the leading economic forecasting units in the world, so (by implication) why not trust our market forecasts? It is a plausible but deceptive stance.

  Economies and product markets have very different characteristics. Capitalist or free market economies, despite the name, are among the most tightly managed economies in the world – which is one reason why economic forecasting in these countries can be fairly accurate across long time periods.

  Product markets on the other hand cannot be managed to anything like the same extent. Global corporations shape them as best they can, but many industries are evolving so fast that it is simply not possible to predict accurately what will be happening in five years' time. That is especially the case in the knowledge sector.

- *Networking*
  Get second opinions on any assumption about the future you are unsure about – and from as many sources as possible. Large firms have in-house teams of experts and lots of external contacts. It is relatively easy for them to find out how different advisers' forecasting models have fared with hindsight.

  Smaller firms and novice acquirers may have to shop around. Talk to a local business school, to think tanks, to any group of experts that don't have a vested interest. There is no need to reveal strategic intentions – just get as broad a range of readings as possible about what the future *might* look like.

- *Timescale*
  Finally, over what sort of time horizon are gains predicted? Sometimes advisers will project glowing synergies 10, 15, even 20 years into the future – into a time period that is wholly unknown. Be suspicious of long-term predictions – apply the Six-Year One-Third rule instead (see Box 7.2).

Box 7.2   The Six-Year One-Third rule

Most managers who have handled acquisitions will say that five to six years is about the maximum a forecast can hold. Beyond that it is impossible to predict what competitors will do or where threats will come from or what sorts of opportunities will present themselves.

   Hence the *Six-Year One-Third* rule. It is a crude but useful rule of thumb. Take the projected six-year return, divide by three (because only about one-third of deals deliver as intended), and that in all probability is the likely return on the deal – *unless* it can be convincingly demonstrated through the most detailed competitor analysis, organisational auditing, business planning and implementation planning that a better return is possible.

These are just some indicative questions for starters. Others will suggest themselves in the context of each acquisition. Every deal is different, so not much more can be said. But all interested managers – with the aid of a shrewd integration manager – can do some deep probing.

The message of the chapter is clear. Managers have got to get behind the calculations, get behind the value assumptions in their strategy, and rigorously examine them.

CHAPTER 8

Due Diligence or Shrewd Diligence?

'Numbers don't tell you much. You must walk the business – get out and see what's going on.'

(Corporate planning director, retail)

Financial, legal and commercial audits have always been at the very heart of the diligence process. In part because they are a legal necessity (although it is worth noting that what is mandatory varies with the legislation in each country). In part because managers believe they are the most important investigations prior to any deal. However, these are not our concern here. The procedures are well documented and there are armies of experts in every country who can offer whatever advice and assistance is required when going global.

Far more important is the question: *When auditing a target, what does being duly diligent really involve doing?* We know from research that most acquirers do not have sufficient intelligence on the inner workings of vendor organisations at the time of negotiations. So the answer we suggest is this.

> Due diligence is not just about compliance with legislation, custom and practice. Much more importantly, it is about judgements concerning the sorts of information an acquirer *ought* to gather on a target company before finalising a deal. That in turn is shaped by the strategic mindsets through which acquisitions are viewed.

Up to the early 1980s, strategy had a strong financial bias and it is reflected in how firms investigated prospective targets. It is neatly captured in the study: *Acquisitions – The Human Factor* (Hunt et al., 1987). All acquirers in the sample conducted detailed financial and commercial and legal audits of the vendor prior to signing, but only about one-third extended the audit process into the inner organisational workings. Even then it was mostly superficial (see Figure 8.1).

To illustrate: audits of management calibre typically covered only the most senior ranks in the target company and barely penetrated middle management

Type of audit	Frequency of conducting (%)
Financial/legal	100
Business/commercial	98
Engineering/production	40
Management/personnel	37
Systems	20
Other	5

Figure 8.1   The typical pre-deal audit profile

Source: © Reproduced with permission from Hunt, J.W., Lees, S., Gumbar, J. and Vivian, P. (1987), *Acquisitions – The Human Factor*, London: London Business School and Egon Zehnder International, page 27

levels. Personnel audits covered little more than pensions, salary levels, special contracts and general personnel policies. Production audits and management control/system audits were often cursory and conducted in much secrecy – 'quick tours round' or 'visits disguised as bankers' – even though most negotiations were amicable and open access was available.

There were exceptions, of course. A tiny minority of acquirers investigated the vendor in almost forensic detail before finalising a price, but these were rare. The vast majority relied almost totally upon financial and commercial data, and waited until after the deal to fully investigate what they had purchased. And they paid the price – even when some provision had been made for the unexpected. One-third of the sample found 'skeletons' that, if known, should have reduced the purchase price considerably. In deals that proved to be unsuccessful, the surprises contributed directly to years of underperformance (see Figure 8.2).

Note that skeletons were found across all areas – not just in the (mostly unaudited) human and organisational domains. Some of the biggest headaches came in mainstream finance and legal areas. For example: claims of 'dishonest' presentation featured strongly – in areas as diverse as profit forecasts, systems capability, new product development, licensing arrangements and especially in the detail of joint-venture contracts with foreign partners. What was significant here was that acquirers believed auditing had been thorough, *and in many instances top-notch firms of consultants had been used to conduct the investigations.*

By the late 1980s and into the 1990s, strategic thinking had changed again. Strategy-as-marketing and strategy-as-excellence were firmly in fashion and both influenced the diligence process. Most consulting houses reported a significant increase in commissioned market research and organisational

Areas of post-acquisition surprises		Frequency of occurrence (%)
'Dishonest' presentation		31
Lack of management control		23
Management calibre		19
'Problem' vendor subsidiaries		15
Personnel policies		8
Production capability		4

Figure 8.2   Common skeletons

Source: © Reproduced with permission from Hunt, J.W., Lees, S.,
Gumbar, J. and Vivian, P. (1987), *Acquisitions – The Human Factor*,
London: London Business School and Egon Zehnder International, page 29

audits – especially in the human areas of management calibre, attitude surveys, personnel systems and organisational culture. These were important steps in the right direction – except that the organisational audits were often more like fishing expeditions than systematic exercises.

The big problem was *performance benchmarking*. Lots of information was collected on vendor organisations but often nobody was quite sure which aspects were significant for vendor performance and which were marginal. Culture audits were a case in point. Differences on each side could easily be identified but knowing which were critical for performance and which were not, was often hard to pin down. So the audits – although well intended – were not always helpful. They shed little light on how best to bring the two organisations together. And they seldom pinpointed what to change on each side and what to leave alone to ensure acquisition performance.

A more general observation about due diligence in the twentieth century is this. Right across the century, two of the most common justifications for avoiding organisational auditing were insufficient time and the need for secrecy. However, the extent to which these are genuine barriers is highly questionable. There are clearly some instances where speed and discretion are of the essence – like when companies come up for sale at short notice or when it is vital that rivals are kept in the dark until the last minute. But mostly time and confidentiality are not the problems – an attitude of mind is. Narrow mindsets mean narrow diligence.

Some managers will argue, of course, that post-deal surprises are inevitable in any takeover and hence the most practical option is to make a reasonable *financial* provision for the unexpected. This might make sense if auditing was only to establish the value of a target business. But auditing is also to provide essential data for integration planning. A financial provision, no matter how generous, sheds absolutely no light on how best to bring two firms together to make strategy 'happen'.

However, as we will see below, building *capability profiles* of prospective targets long before any deal is considered, can provide invaluable intelligence both for value checking and integration planning.

Capability-Based Auditing

Capability-based auditing derives out of capability-based competition – and addresses a gigantic puzzle at the heart of strategy. Environmental scans have always been an essential aspect of business. Firms routinely collect vast amounts of intelligence on what competitors are doing. Consultancies specialising in providing such information are an almost institutional feature of the corporate landscape. Yet in most instances the data collected is product and market intelligence. Seldom do environmental scans probe deeper to identify the human and organisational capabilities that actually bring particular products or services to the market in the first place. Capability intelligence, if sought at all, is gathered mostly in an unsystematic and piecemeal fashion.

Here lies the puzzle. Managers know that capability intelligence is essential for planning post-acquisition fit and realising calculated synergies. And despite claims to the contrary, managers also know that they usually have plenty of time to gather whatever information they need. Studies show that firms can shadow targets for years before making an approach – an average time is about three years – which is plenty of time to gather whatever intelligence is needed for merger planning. But mostly they choose not to (see Box 8.1).

One reason is that the dominant logic (Prahalad and Bettis, 1986) that guides their strategic thinking is the logic of product-based competition and not the logic of capability-based competition.

Box 8.1   Long Shadowing

Firms often claim that there is insufficient time to conduct detailed organisational audits before finalising negotiations. Research tells otherwise. Acquirers will often shadow a target for years before making an approach. In *Acquisitions – The Human Factor* (Hunt et al., 1987), the average shadowing time was almost three years, with some acquirers watching and waiting up to five years for the opportunity to pounce. Which is more than sufficient time to build up a solid database on the inner workings of target firms.

We noted in Chapter 4 that when the logic of product-based competition drives strategy, there is a marked tendency to define products or services according to price, attractiveness, differentiation, or some other market-referenced attribute. In-house capabilities are important only in so far as they support a predominantly marketing mission. The effect – as we see in many firms and in numerous textbooks – is that strategy has become virtually indistinguishable from a sophisticated form of marketing.

The logic of capability-based competition turns much of this on its head. Products and services are viewed as embodiments – celebrations even – of organisational capabilities. Markets are media through which bundles of such capabilities are displayed and linked to customer needs. Firms dominate markets not because of their products *per se* but because of capabilities embodied in their products.

When managers think this way, a direct strategic linkage is perceived between capabilities and customers.

- When managers *think* competition, they think capabilities first, markets second.

- When managers *see* competition, they see capabilities first, products second.

However, to think this way is not always easy. It requires a different mindset – one that goes beyond conventional strategic thinking and against the grain of a lot of business school training. It can take time to get the thinking in place – but it pays dividends in the long run and contributes enormously to integration planning.

Building Capability Profiles

There are three essential steps to building capability profiles.

1. Identifying in each firm the full range of capabilities – 'hard' and 'soft' – that are critical for competition and performance.

2. Developing a system of performance benchmarking for each capability (i.e. identifying the contribution each capability makes to value and understanding how it makes the contribution).

3. Systematic gathering of 'hard' and especially 'soft' intelligence on the inner workings of competitor and potential target organisations.

Each of these steps will be examined in turn but note that building capability profiles is not the sort of management technique that is easily bought in. It is not another 'add-on' technique. The procedures have to be developed in-house because much of it hinges upon attitudes of mind and ways of thinking – and these have to be in place first. Firms have got to know themselves before they can know another firm. Any acquirers developing their own embryonic systems most certainly will keep them under wraps. They are valuable competition tools.

Box 8.2   The tale of the deadwood ship

Once upon a time, a European company bought a subsidiary from an American corporation. The corporation was consolidating and pulling out of markets – one of which was the main line of business for the European company. So the deal made obvious strategic sense.

Negotiations were smooth and amicable. Every request for information was answered in full. All figures on past performance seemed to add up. All projections appeared sound. And every assurance that each side asked for was given. So both sides agreed a price, shook hands, and the subsidiary crossed the Atlantic to her new owners.

But the first year wasn't quite as expected. The acquisition was performing well below what it should have, and there were no obvious reasons why. External conditions were much as predicted and internally there had been very few changes. The same top management team, the same budgets, the same structure had all been kept in place. Heads were scratched and computers whirred ... then the answer came. Most of the middle managers had been with the subsidiary for less than two years prior to the deal.

About three years before the sale, the corporation had started moving underperforming managers into what were called 'new project' positions. They were told they would be playing an essential part in revitalising the company and that the challenge would enhance them. Good managers were given the same message – but their career shifts were within the core divisions that were not being sold off. When all the deadwood was gathered together, it was neatly parcelled up and floated off – without incurring a penny in severance costs.

What's the moral of the story? *Lift the hatches and inspect the crew.* Check the management development records as an integral part of the diligence process.

Identifying Capabilities

The key question here is:

What gives us our competitive edge?

The answer, of course, lies not in products or markets but in human and organisational capabilities that deliver products or services to markets. A good starting point could be Porter's value chain (Porter, 1985) (see Figure 8.3).

This is a comprehensive map of the organisation processes that all combine to create value. Most managers should be familiar with it and may well have used it to improve internal efficiency. However, *maps are not territories on the ground*. Every firm has its own social and cultural foundations. Each of the processes in the value chain is embedded in a human context that can vary enormously between firms. That is why Porter's classic model has been amended. Identical *technical* processes can deliver very different outcomes depending on the mix of people and industry and nationality that surround them.[1] This is evident in all acquisitions, but especially in cross-border deals.

Performance Benchmarking

What is the relative contribution each process in the chain makes to value, and can we explain exactly how the contribution is made?

Capability profiling requires a system of performance benchmarking for comparative purposes. There have to be yardsticks – both for comparing the relative contributions to value of in-house capabilities as well as for comparing competitor capabilities. Firms need to examine each element in the value chain in turn and ask the questions: what is the contribution this element makes to value, *and can we identify how it actually happens?*

One capability might seem to stand out and be regarded as the primary source of value. It could be a patented technology or a leading-edge knowledge base. It could be speed of design-to-manufacturing time. It could be a highly flexible structure or state-of-the-art logistics. Or it could be human (like an exceptional person at the top or a highly talented management team). But reality tells us that performance and value depend upon a whole range of capabilities and processes all interacting and reinforcing one another. Some may be less visible than others but that does not diminish their importance.

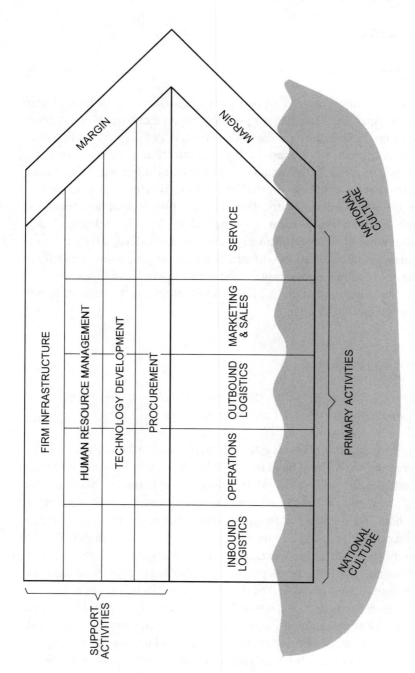

Figure 8.3 Porter's value chain in national context

Source: Reproduced with permission of The Free Press, an imprint of Simon and Schuster Adult Publishing Group, from *Competitive Advantage: Creating and Sustaining Superior Performance* by Michael E. Porter, © 1985, 1998 Michael E. Porter

Whether we think of them as chains or systems or bundles, links and inter-dependencies are at the heart of the value creation process.

Out of this initial exploration should come some tentative judgements about dominant and contributory capabilities, and maybe even an embryonic system of performance benchmarking. But note the difficulties along the way. Deciding which dimensions of each capability are to be used for bench-marking and then establishing the relative value contributions of each, are two tasks that are by no means easy. There are at least four reasons why.

- First is the influence of corporate mythology and its make-believe *becauses*. Every company is stuffed full of beliefs like: We are successful – *because* we are lean and thin. Or *because* we have the leading edge on something. Or *because* we recruit the best people. Or *because* we pay higher salaries. Or *because* we are faster than our competitors.

  Lots of these *becauses* may be true to an extent. After all, every myth contains a grain of truth. The problem is when the grain gets amplified out of all proportion. The *becauses* get elevated into almost sacred beliefs that few dare question – regularly asserted but seldom challenged. They can distort perceptions of capability strength.

- Then there is the accounting influence. Budgeting procedures and cost allocation and transfer pricing conventions can influence judgements. There is always the danger that managers might assume that proportions or allocations in common use actually reflect the value contributions of different parts of the business. But as any finance manager will admit, accounting conventions are often arbitrary or at best the loosest of approximations.

- 'Soft' capabilities present a further difficulty – like tacit knowledge and attitudes and beliefs and all the human components that make up an organisation's culture. These can contribute enormously to performance and value but in ways that can be fiendishly difficult to pin down and measure. Many of the strategic HRM goals – like commitment and flexibility and mission identification – fall into this category (Beer et al., 1984; Guest, 1987, 1997).

  These sorts of qualities are ambiguous and 'woolly' in that they can mean different things to different people – even in the same organisa-tion. For example, two managers could *say* that their staff are committed and flexible, yet they could be thinking about quite different behaviours when they use the terms. Benchmarking is not easy in these circum-stances yet the attempt must be made.

Some firms use attitude survey data as a proxy. The data can be useful – but with the limitation that it usually captures perception and intention (i.e. what people *say* they would do) but not always what they actually do. Nor does it capture the determinants of action (i.e. the organisational conditions that encourage staff to act as they do).

For example, attitude surveys of two combining firms might reveal that staff on each side feel highly committed and integrated and motivated. That might look encouraging at first sight but (a) the reported feelings may not always get translated into action, and (b) if they do, it could be because of very different management styles and organisational cultures in each firm.

- Even with 'hard' capabilities, even although it may seem intuitively obvious, it is not always easy to measure precisely the direct connection between a process or a capability and its value outcome. When there is a weak link in the value chain, the effects (inefficiencies and losses) are more easily isolated and quantified. But not so when all the links are more or less equally strong.

These difficulties are mentioned not to discourage but to help managers anticipate. They all can be worked through and in the end should deliver a workable system of capability benchmarking. But no matter how primitive the first attempt may be, it is still the beginning of a system of codified *organisational* knowledge – of firms beginning to know in a systematic manner what they already know and using this knowledge for strategic purposes. And that provides the basis for building competitor profiles.

Competitor Profiles

The third step is to build up similar profiles on competitors and potential targets using the in-house benchmarks as reference points and following a similar procedure. The key question here is:

On each capability, 'hard' and 'soft', where does the competitor or target have the advantage and where not?

This requires *organisational* intelligence-gathering about competitors and prospective targets in an innovative and systematic manner. Most firms of any size have employees who have worked for rivals. Most employees know something about the inner workings of competitor organisations. They get it from all sorts of sources – from contacts and colleagues, from consultants and advisers, from journals and the business press, from outsourcing and alliances and other collaborations.

The puzzle in strategy (as mentioned earlier) is that firms avidly collect commercial and technical data as a strategic priority – but not organisational data. Knowledge of the inner workings of rivals usually gets left 'in the air' – dissipated into gossip, stories, stereotypes and folklore. Seldom does it get collected systematically and rigorously into a competitive weapon.

But it can be done – by all firms large and small – provided there is a will to do it and at least the basics of a capability benchmarking system in place. For example, HRM chiefs (if they have a strategic perspective) could make competitor intelligence-gathering a routine follow-up to selection. For every new manager, there could be a diagnostic debriefing at some point after the person is immersed in the company and is fully sensitised to the differences. Likewise for the appraisal process. A systematic debriefing of existing employees with relevant backgrounds or contacts could be linked to appraisals – extending right down to the shopfloor where appropriate.

The agenda questions (one factual; the other judgemental) would be:

On each capability or process, how in detail do we differ from the other company you are familiar with? Where and precisely how do we have the edge and where do they have the edge?

Note that these are not informal chats. They would have to be focused, diagnostic, intelligence-gathering exercises conducted by persons with specialist knowledge in each area. Intimate familiarity with each capability or process is essential for pinpointing (and then trying to quantify) differences between any two firms.

Using Capability Profiles for Target Auditing

The strategic benefits of capability benchmarking and competitor profiling are many and extend across all functions and levels. At top levels they stimulate greater process awareness in strategic thinking. At middle levels they encourage more value-added thinking. And more generally they can contribute to a process of cultural change – especially mindset change – right across a firm. Managers and staff become more competitor-aware – not just in terms of what competitors are doing but *how* they are doing it.

But it is when investigating target companies and planning integration that capability profiles come into their own. Figure 8.4 illustrates how. If the acquiring firm has profiled its own major processes and capabilities and

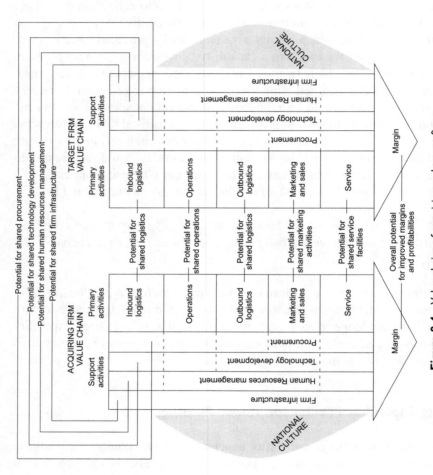

Figure 8.4 Value chains of acquiring and target firms

Source: adapted from Payne (1987)

knows exactly which dimensions are value-critical and which are not, and if there is already the beginnings of such profiles on the target firm, then acquisition planning gets a headstart.

1. Target valuation becomes more accurate. Vendor profiles get behind the numbers and ratios and shed light on the processes that actually deliver the figures. That can be invaluable in situations where, for example, corporations invite bids for subsidiaries solely on the basis of prospectus information and refuse internal access.

2. Synergy prediction can be more realistic. Figure 8.4 shows the theoretical potential for synergy that acquirers typically see prior to a merger. But it also shows what acquirers usually *don't* see – the sources of entropy (i.e. the tendency of two firms to repel each another). When critical points of similarity *and* difference between two firms are visibly to hand, the difficulties and costs of synergy realisation become clearer.

3. The cost and complexity of organisational meshing also become more obvious. Detailed profiles can indicate quickly where incompatibilities exist – in structures, systems, processes and cultures (both organisational and national).

4. Organisational audits then become more refined and focused. If intelligence on the inner workings of target firms is readily to hand, audits can be directed straight at those areas where information is really required rather than fishing about almost from scratch. And that is especially important when time is limited or confidentiality is an issue.

What are the Objections?

Building capability profiles takes time and effort. What sorts of objections might managers raise?

- *There usually isn't sufficient time*. Not true. Firms have more than ample time to build up comprehensive capability profiles on competitors and potential targets. Research (see Box 8.1) has shown that acquirers will shadow targets for an average of almost three years – in some instances, up to five years – before making an approach. And that is plenty of time to build up a detailed knowledge base on how target organisations *really* operate long before any approach is made.

- *Building capability profiles signals acquisition intent.* Not true. It is simply another prudent aspect of strategy and competitor awareness.

- *It is relevant only in high-tech or knowledge-based industries.* Again, not true. Firms in all industries are making acquisitions to plug specific capability gaps in their competitive armoury or to buy in new knowledge and skills that they are unable or unwilling to develop in-house. When capabilities purchased are the product of a unique combination of people, systems, structures and cultures, it is essential to understand how that special combination actually works – how it delivers value – before deciding on a style of post-deal integration and management. Otherwise, value-purchased may just seep away.

- *What about global deals that straddle every continent? How can we possibly know how different national cultures shape processes and capabilities?* This is a fair point – but only from smaller firms. Global corporations have international managers by the hundreds – managers who have years of 'hands-on' experience of managing across one or more cultural divides. But the knowledge often remains dispersed through the corporation and is not systematically collated for strategic purposes.

- *It's too resource intensive.* Not necessarily. Building capability profiles takes time and effort – and the bigger the organisation arguably the greater is the task. But it doesn't always require extra resources. What it does require is a particular kind of analytical perspective, and one suggestion (Lees, 1992) was that large firms use the internal audit function to do much of the legwork. Smaller firms without such a reserve may have to set up teams of selected managers to help.

  But no matter who does the legwork, setting up the system and establishing the criteria for benchmarking have to be done by leading experts in each functional or capability area. And if they are on the ball, it should come second nature to them.

CHAPTER 9

Essential Controls

'Day One must be planned like a military operation. You've got to have the right people in the right place with the right controls at their fingertips.'

(Chairman, retailing)

Getting the controls in place has various meanings in an acquisition context. It can mean *hard* controls like budgets and financial controls and IT systems and procedures. It can mean *human* controls like getting key people in charge on each side. Or it can have a *softer* connotation like management styles or the invisible control exercised by an organisation's culture.

This chapter is short and will deal only with the absolutely essential controls that have to be in place at the very beginning. It will be more relevant to novices to the acquisition game. Experienced companies *should* be familiar with what is required although it is surprising how many of these matters remain ambiguous during negotiations.

Essential Controls

Eight essential controls should be put in place as soon as the acquisition is announced (Box 9.1).

Key Responsibility Holders

First and foremost are the key managers – the right people in the right places. Who is responsible for what on each side must be agreed before negotiations are completed and be crystal clear. Deferring invariably leads to long-term problems – regardless of the size of the deal.

Usually target chiefs report to acquiring chiefs – but not always. Who occupies various driving seats can be a major stumbling block during negotiations especially when firms are large and of comparable size. A lot of

---

Box 9.1   Eight essential controls

1. Key Responsibility Holders
2. Financial Controls
3. Targets and Performance
4. Reporting Relationships
5. Business Philosophy
6. Bottom-Up Business Plan
7. Information Technology
8. Boundary Management

---

ego and rivalry can be involved. High-profile presidents or CEOs often resent reporting to an industry rival. Each will want the merger for business reasons – but each will want to stay top dog.

Fudging these sorts of issues is seldom satisfactory – like denying any differences and putting on a united front to get the deal through quickly. Or retaining two corporate headquarters and appointing co-chief executives – but not establishing the precise business relationship between each side.

Box 9.2   Move over, darling

The first attempt to merge Glaxo Wellcome and SmithKline Beecham is reported to have collapsed because neither boss was prepared to play second fiddle. It caused their share price to nose-dive. A year after the merger of Citicorp and Travellers (which created the world's biggest financial-services group), employees of the new Citigroup still couldn't work out which of their two former bosses was in the driving seat.

When Sweden's Pharmacia and America's Upjohn joined in 1995, rapid value was promised through cost cutting and matching drug portfolios. But Pharmacia had not integrated an earlier Italian acquisition. So the new company started out with power bases in Stockholm, Milan and Michigan. After a botched attempt to make everybody report to a new office near London, the firm moved to New Jersey and appointed a new boss at the top – and that's finally when things began to get pulled together. (*The Economist*, 9 January 1999, pp. 21–3)

Financial Controls

Tight financial controls are crucial and must be in place early. Due diligence usually reveals what is required, but not always. If the target firm is of any size, existing controls should be sufficient with perhaps some modifications.

If the firm is small and if it was run for income-generating ~~~~ some owner-manager firms), adequate controls may not even e~~~~ acquisitions need special attention. Procedures that satisfy accoun~~ regulatory regimes in each country (and hence pass the local diligence~ may not be sufficient for the level of control the new owners wish.

In general, even if nothing else changes in an acquired company, financial controls will (see also *information technology* below).

Targets and Performance

Expectations on each side have to be fully clarified and future targets agreed. Both sets of top managers need to be clear on precisely how business between the two firms is to be conducted. Normally it's business as usual for the first year or so, but not always. Two different management teams going into the future with diverging notions of what they are to do together and how performance is to be measured, can pull the acquisition apart.

Also important for target top managers is to learn the new criteria for capital investment and the procedures (and the politics) behind budget allocations. For smaller or owner-manager firms, all this can be a whole new learning experience.

Reporting Relationships

Further down the line, each senior manager must know exactly whom he or she reports to after the deal, and for what. There may be few changes, or may be many. Either way, clear unambiguous reporting lines are essential to minimise post-merger uncertainty and maintain a performance focus.

Sometimes a status issue arises when smaller companies are acquired by giants. High-profile CEOs or owner-managers have been known to resent reporting to an executive further down the line. They have been used to high status and want to report to someone of boardroom standing. Sensitivity here is important – especially if it's a knowledge company. Handle it crassly and the value-purchased can get up and walk away.

Business Philosophy

A business philosophy is a *soft* control – but it governs how *hard* controls are used. Acquired managers need to learn this. They need to learn about the values and beliefs and priorities and strategic assumptions they are being

v how the new owners do business on a day-
n verbal assurances.

tions acquiring firms will pick an earlier
a role model for targets to visit to show how
an be very useful – getting a recently absorbed
ke under the new owners. But it cannot be relied
in the pay of the acquirer are unlikely to shout
it should be.

Bottom-Up Business Plan

Also important is a *detailed* bottom-up business plan for the combined firm
showing where business is to come from and how value is to be generated.
Again, not a direct control as such but so essential for giving a ground-level
focus and a justification for performance targets and any changes. Too many
acquisitions begin life with a vague strategy and insufficient business detail
about how the strategy is to happen and where the value is to come from.

Information Technology

IT systems usually get standardised into acquirer format, especially
information and financial control systems. But that can take time depending
on the type of acquisition. If the target was formerly part of a large group,
the old systems would simply have been unplugged at sale and managers
would be expecting replacements. In smaller companies without adequate
controls, new technology will be introduced almost at once.

Most other acquisitions will get a total systems strip-out and that can take
years if the firms are big. In the short term, interfacing for critical data is the
critical management priority – being able to communicate and retrieve
essential information across both firms. *The key priority with IT is early and
effective interfacing* **to avoid loss of control**, *not necessarily standardising
the systems on each side* (see Box 9.3).

Boundary Management

Any changes to the target have to be in tune with acquisition strategy and be
the most appropriate to deliver that strategy. There may be few changes or
there may be many – like restructuring that can take months or even years

---

Box 9.3   Irritation technology

The merger between Union Pacific and Southern Pacific in 1996 was supposed to deliver a seamless rail service and $800 million in annual savings by using Union's top-notch computer systems to drag Southern up to scratch. But technical glitches (plus the sacking of too many of Southern's good IT people) derailed a good idea. At one point in 1997, 10,000 wagons were stalled in Texas and California. Operating profits fell, dividends were cut and the share price two years later was down by a third.

When Wells Fargo bought First Interstate in 1996, interfacing their respective computer systems proved to be a nightmare. Thousands of the banks' customers left because of missing records, long queues and administrative snarl-ups. (*The Economist*, 9 January 1999, pp. 21–3)

(see Chapter 10). Whatever the option, the key control is boundary management from Day One. That is a central task for the integration manager – to act as a gatekeeper between the two sides. *To help bring together what has to be brought together, to keep apart what has to be kept apart, and to minimise unnecessary interference or premature changes.*

These are eight essential controls to have in place as soon as the acquisition is announced. There will be others, of course, to do with security and technology and logistics and much more depending on the business of each firm. But these eight controls are essential to *any* acquisition. And the onus is on *both* sides to ensure that they are in place early.

CHAPTER 10

Integrating Structures

'We got their cashflow and their markets ... then bungled the integration and lost the lot.'

(Finance Director, leisure)

Deciding on the structural relationship between the acquiring and the target companies is the first critical consideration in integration planning. It is the organisation design question:

How best to design one new organisation out of two different organisations to achieve acquisition goals?

This is a complex social engineering question with enormous implications. How the question is answered impacts upon almost everything else – the changes that are to happen, the controls needed, the reactions to the merger, the commitment to the new owners, the degree of culture clash, and much more besides. Ultimately it determines the cost of integration.

Yet there is virtually no guidance to be found in any of the literature – academic or managerial – on how to start *thinking about* the question, let alone how to answer it. Nevertheless, right across the world, advisers are telling companies how best to merge and restructure their acquisitions with hardly any theoretical or empirical reference points to fall back on. This is worrying given the amount of value that hinges on the decision.

Note that the urge to impose changes on target companies is strong. Typical acquirer thinking goes something like this. *We own the vendor. It is now part of our group. We have to control it and we want to get value. So merge the different functions together and standardise as much as possible into our own format.* Novice acquirers are especially prone to thinking this way but they are not alone. In any acquisition, managers who have responsibility for something on the other side often share a sentiment that if only 'they' were more like 'us', control would be easier. It is an understandable but simplistic way of thinking. Familiarity brings comfort, not performance.

More sophisticated thinking asks a different question:

What *type* of organisational relationship between acquirer and target is most appropriate to achieve the strategy behind the deal?

This opens up a whole continuum of possible structures ranging from keeping the two firms separate and autonomous through to complete assimilation, with many other types of relationship in between. The crucial issue is to decide which is most appropriate for each acquisition (i.e. which is more likely to enable acquisition strategy to 'happen' and least likely to destroy value). Figure 10.1 illustrates the range of possibilities and some situations where each might be appropriate.

Model 1: Wholly Independent (Portfolio Model)

Here the acquisition is approached essentially as an investment, a self-generating income stream. The value of the deal lies in the capabilities and potential the target already possesses and not in any changes the acquirer might impose. Hence, there are no alterations to the structure or inner workings of the acquired business. Post-deal, it becomes a wholly independent subsidiary of the parent, with near-total autonomy. This structure involves the least disruption (maybe none) to the acquired business and culture clashes are unlikely.

Targets in these circumstances are likely to be:

- well-managed companies with little slack

- maybe with a highly specialised or even state-of-the-art technology

- and with good growth prospects.

The strategy behind the deal can vary a lot. It could be simply to get a lucrative slice of a growing market. It could be to build a platform for sector growth. There could even be ambitions for large-scale diversification in the years ahead. Whatever the reason, the approach in the early years is literally 'hands off'. Acquired managers continue doing what they are already pretty good at doing, sticking to their existing strategy and structures and ways of managing.

However, it can never be as simple or impersonal as an investment. Structures may not change but controls have to be put in place and boundary processes managed. Financial controls and information systems have to be ensured. Performance targets have to be agreed and reporting relationships

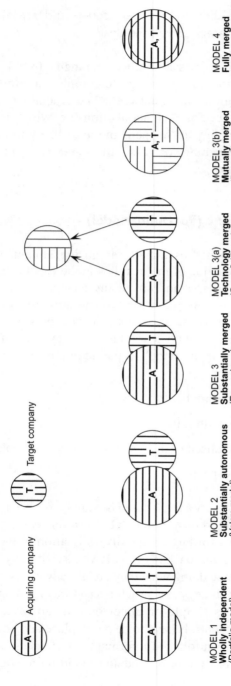

Figure 10.1 Categories of structural relationship between acquirer and target

Acquiring company

Target company

MODEL 1
Wholly independent
(Portfolio model)

No changes in target apart from financial controls and IT systems, and setting up new reporting relationships

MODEL 2
Substantially autonomous
(Velcro model)

Changes limited to target top management and their strategic thinking. Performance to be improved by know-how or capability transfer from acquirer to target

MODEL 3
Substantially merged
(Re-engineering model)

Major but not total restructuring of target organisation. Some functions merged into acquirer format. Others retain their separate identity and ethos

MODEL 3(a)
Technology merged
(Greenfield model)

Selective merging of R&D and some technical functions to build a dedicated environment for knowledge sharing and know-how transfer

MODEL 3(b)
Mutually merged
(Best-of-both-worlds model)

Building a combined organisation that incorporates the best practices from each side

MODEL 4
Fully merged
(Blitzkrieg model)

Target totally merged and transformed into acquirer format and style

have to be established (see Chapter 9). And – most important – is keeping the two sides apart.

Remember the task of the integration manager: *to bring together what has to be brought together, to keep apart what has to be kept apart and to act as a boundary manager or gatekeeper between the two sides.* If there is little to be brought together, then regulating the interfaces between the two sides becomes the priority.

It was mentioned earlier that there is always pressure to intervene on vendor territory. It is not just the urge to control and standardise. There is also a genuine curiosity about the other side, to meet opposite numbers, to find out what they do and how they do it. These interactions always have to be tightly regulated to avoid destabilising the target – especially so when it is intended to remain independent and autonomous. Take the example of a British company making a US acquisition without an integration manager in place to regulate the boundaries. In the words of the acquired president:

'It became a full-time job just receiving visitors. Although they promised no interference, in practice every function came over to have a look – endless strange faces asking: "What do you do?" and "Why don't you do it this way or that way?" We never knew exactly what they were after or what they would do with the information we gave them.'

Now make the contrast with a large UK financial institution acquiring a small knowledge-based firm. Here the integration manager exercised a tight boundary control function – a gatekeeper regulating what transferred between the two sides, ensuring that business transactions were speedily responded to while at the same time preventing the bureaucracy of the large firm swamping the entrepreneurial spirit of the smaller:

'I was determined to protect their innovative spirit. I stopped our people interfering unless they could justify it in terms of value creation. At the same time I tried to mirror their culture – like making sure all requests to us for information were answered within a day. I sat on our people until they learned not to intervene.'

Model 2: Substantially Autonomous (Velcro Model)

This structure is more typical of 'hands-off' acquisitions. The target retains a high degree of autonomy with changes confined mostly to the top management team – usually a reshaping of their strategic thinking with maybe some new faces at board level. Some managers from the acquiring side may also be placed in key positions further down the line. Otherwise, very little is changed apart from what was agreed during negotiations (like disposal of surplus businesses). No restructuring leaves the acquired business more or less intact and this in turn makes divestment easier should it become necessary. (Hence the Velcro model: stick-'em together and peel-'em apart).

Target companies that benefit from this type of structure are generally in reasonable shape but judged to be underperforming in some respect:

- some slack may be evident

- markets may be troublesome

- there may be a history of underinvestment by previous owners

- they may be small companies with good management but in need of large-firm expertise

- there may be hidden potential that only the acquirer sees.

Whatever the reason, the value of the deal lies in the approach – to encourage acquired management to do what is necessary to improve performance while maintaining business as usual. Various labels can be applied – 'suggestive' or 'gentle nudges' or 'mature parenting'. But common to all is the idea of *capability transfer*. Acquirers believe they possess some capability that will create value if transferred across to target management – 'using *their* management and *our* know-how and skills to improve performance'.

The strength of this structure is that it avoids many of the factors that routinely drive up the cost and complexity of integration. For example:

- *Change destabilises*, especially when imposed from outside. So change is kept to a minimum. Destructive culture clashes are also minimised.

- *Disregarding target knowledge*. Acquired managers often know better how to operate in a particular industry or a sector (especially in foreign markets) and that knowledge is respected.

- *Insensitivity to organisation*. Performance in any firm is a complex product of people, structures, systems, cultures and controls all interacting in ways that are often difficult to pin down. Change can have unanticipated consequences when the mix is not understood. In cruder terms, if the organisation ain't broke, why meddle and try to fix it?

- *Control vacuum* is avoided. Keeping the organisation intact keeps the controls intact, both formal and informal. That makes it easier for target managers to initiate change in ways they are familiar with.

- *Jackboot change* is also avoided. There is recognition of the many other ways of bringing about change without costly and messy restructuring – like redirecting strategy, replacing managers, creating SBUs, reformulating budgets, introducing new technology, refocusing incentives, and similar.

But again, it is not as simple as it may seem. There is still a complex agenda for the integration manager to get on top of.

- The essential boundary regulation processes described earlier have to be dealt with (financial controls, information systems, performance targets, new reporting relationships and regulating the interfaces between both sides).

- Not all capabilities transfer across easily. Those that are formula- or procedure-based probably do better (like a successful trading formula or a manufacturing expertise). They are relatively easy to transfer and copy with some training support.

  Other capabilities may be culture-specific (like excellence in innovation or customer intimacy). These may be so deeply embedded in the culture of the acquiring organisation that they require a similar context on the other side to manifest themselves. Trying to create that context can take time and draws the acquirer deeper into changing the target culture.

However, the advantages of this structure are many. A further strength is that it buys time – especially if a deal has been made in haste. It allows time for a detailed implementation strategy to be worked out and agreed on both sides before any changes are set in motion. Again, the role of the integration manager is critical both for keeping the two sides apart while the details are worked out and also for ensuring that the most appropriate mix of people from each side shape the agenda.

Model 3: Substantially Merged (Re-Engineering Model)

Here there is major (but not total) restructuring of the target into an acquirer format. Systems and procedures are usually standardised. Acquired top managers lose much of their autonomy and may be replaced. But only *some* functions from each side are merged – others retain their separate identity and ethos. When merging happens, there are human consequences right down the line. Duplication usually means job loss for some and relocation for others. When merging is also physical (like relocating manufacturing or centralising distribution), job loss can be considerable.

This structure is likely in four types of acquisition.

1. When the acquiring company already has centralised or group-level functions. These functions in the target usually get assimilated as a matter of policy.

2. When seeking economies in *loosely related* targets. Front-end, back-end and support functions are likely candidates for merging, but not the core primary activities.

3. In vertical acquisitions – upstream and downstream. Financial and administrative functions are usually standardised into an acquirer format, but not always the technical functions.

4. When buying to turnround. Deep but selective intervention may be necessary to turn the targets round. Functions in poor shape often get remodelled around acquirer practices.

The big consideration in any structural merging – partial or total – is the risk that costs might exceed benefits. That the time and costs and effort of bringing two sides together might outweigh any operating efficiencies achieved. These risks cannot be avoided if firms choose to go for these sorts of deals. But they can be minimised if the reality and complexity of integration are appreciated beforehand. Partial merging creates a battlefield where change can be tortuous and vigorously contested. There are at least five reasons why.

1. *Culture clash.* The more two firms are drawn together, the greater is the likelihood of culture clash and destructive conflict. The various elements that make up each organisation's culture (values, attitudes, management styles, controls, reward systems, etc. (see Chapter 15)) are placed side by side in a multitude of locations. What was previously taken for granted suddenly becomes explicit and writ large and open to challenge. The differences become a basis for differentiation rather than integration, for people on each side to say: 'We do it differently from you.' It can be a recipe for conflict rather than cooperation unless skilfully managed.

2. *Political agendas*. The more two firms are drawn together, the more integration becomes a political agenda fought around enhancing and protecting territories – the question of whose values and systems and cultures and *modus operandi* are to dominate and survive. When merging firms are big, we know from acquisition history that some power struggles can be long drawn-out and very public – and eat into the value of the deal.

3. *Loss of control*. The more two firms are drawn together, the greater is the number of people becoming involved in the integration agenda and trying to shape bits of it towards their own ends. The integration team often lose control of the agenda and become less certain about the timing and shape of the final outcome. That in turn creates further uncertainty for everyone else.

4. *Eyes off the market*. The more two firms are drawn together, the more managers look inwards, preoccupied with internal procedures and learning how the other side operates. Eyes then go off the ball, off the market, and that is when rivals can steal the value.

5. *Split organisation*. Merging bits of an acquired company can give it a split character, almost a split mind, and gives the combined organisation a messy, hybrid structure. In one part are the merged functions operating (usually) to an acquirer format and style. In the other part are the non-merged functions operating pretty much as before – on the acquiring side, to their format; and on the target side, to their old format. Yet somehow all of the pieces are expected to dovetail together to make one larger organisation that is just as effective – or even more effective – than either was previously. When stated like this, the contradictions become apparent – both conceptually and in practice.

So the idea that the structures of two firms can be 'partly merged' or 'half-merged' and still deliver performance seems inherently suspect. On paper with numbers it might look convincing but not always in practice. Sometimes it works and sometimes it doesn't. Large firms with group-level functions will usually absorb these functions in a smaller target as a matter of policy – and it will probably work. If functions on the acquiring side have a proven lead over opposite numbers in the target, then again it might work. Otherwise, much depends on how different (technically) the merging functions are, the mix of personalities involved and how different the cultures of the two firms are.

Some examples can illustrate the types of problem that can arise.

* *Merging distribution* should be straightforward. Efficiency and logistics are what they share in common. But these in turn are heavily dependent upon IT support and cooperation. Take the experience of one company:

  'We thought IT people would be able to work together because they are technical and rational. But they were locked into their own systems and wouldn't see any merits in any other. They blocked integration for over a year.'

* *Merging IT* in banking can run into similar problems.

  'Banking is IT-driven. Computer people want power, to order and regulate the corporation, and we let them have it. We are dependent on them and they on their systems. Take away their systems and you cut their legs off. So they fight for their own equipment first and rarely take the overall business need into account.'

* *Merging supply and procurement* should bring cost savings – but not always if ways of doing business are different on each side. Acquiring in other countries often runs into the problem of suppliers embedded in social or family networks. They want to do business on a personal basis with customers they know, and these feelings might not extend to a foreign company. There is no guarantee that they will continue supplying or on similar terms when the target becomes foreign-owned.

  This is a common problem when acquiring in emerging markets or where targets are state-owned – for example, in China or the former Soviet Union. It is also important in *any* small-company deal anywhere in the world. One UK company consolidated its experience into a policy.

  'We now visit all the suppliers to show our face and reassure them before signing. It reassures us as well. That was one lesson we learned from buying-out US entrepreneurs.'

* *Merging marketing* functions should bring efficiencies and a more powerful market presence – but not if the mix doesn't blend. Bringing former competitors together can be a recipe for conflict – as two different acquirers found.

  'We had two marketing teams under one roof rubbishing each other for two years, knocking every idea that came from the other side. The end result was a drop in sales.'

  'It took nearly three years for marketing just to agree on the shape of a new logo for the combined company.'

These examples tell us that the core problem in partial merging is the persistence of two organisational cultures and their respective subcultures *side by side* in the same company. When acquired firms remain mostly autonomous (Models 1 and 2), the two cultures persist but in different companies. When targets are fully merged (Model 4) one of the cultures is intended to go. But in Model 3 both cultures persist side by side – and legitimately so. If they are broadly similar then maybe only a few problems will arise. But if the cultures are different and antagonistic and rigidly value different ways of thinking and behaving, it can block integration and rot the value of the deal.

Model 3(a): Technology Merged (Greenfield Model)

This is a variation on partial merging that is suitable for acquisitions in the high-tech or knowledge sectors. It can work well given the right mix of inputs. The idea is to create a new organisation – a dedicated environment – by selectively bringing together the most appropriate elements from each side to develop know-how or technology.

Two typical situations where this structure is likely are:

1. When a large firm with a small specialist business acquires a similar specialist business – either a small independent company or a divestment from another corporation – with a view to bringing the two businesses together for technology development.

2. When the two R&D functions in a large acquisition are brought together in a dedicated environment to develop know-how or technology that will be the engine of growth for the combined firm.

The new environment may be in a new location – a genuine greenfield organisation. Or it may be no more than some specialist groupings (like the R&D functions) drawn from each side bonded together under a mission and managed in a special way – a 'virtual greenfield' organisation. Either way, the intention is to create a dedicated environment – maybe even a leading-edge environment – that should best encourage know-how sharing and capability transfer between the two sides.

Building a dedicated environment takes time and requires specialist skills. It takes time to select the various organisational practices from each side and blend them together into a functioning whole. It takes time to bring the most appropriate expertise into the planning team – especially the contribution of the key technical people (who, after all, probably know best what will motivate and drive their staff and what will not). And it takes time to resolve political issues of ownership and control and ensure that they take second place to the needs of strategy and technology.

If both sides know each other and are already collaborating – perhaps on a joint venture or an R&D project – then much of the preparatory work can be completed before a deal is signed. Creating the new unit can begin fairly quickly thereafter. Otherwise, time must be allowed for planning to take place – and that means falling back on Models 1 or 2 as the immediate post-deal structures until the groundwork is completed. Boeing provides the example here (Box 10.1).

Box 10.1   Boeing's Phantom Works

When Boeing acquired McDonnell Douglas in 1997, integrating the merger wasn't the only problem the company faced. There was fierce competition from Airbus – the Europeans had grabbed massive chunks of Boeing's civilian jet market. There were production problems. Boeing had cut the price of its civil jets, but the extra demand clogged factories, overstretched suppliers and brought costly delays (nearly $4 billion written off in 1998). And there was an earlier acquisition waiting to be integrated. Boeing had acquired Rockwell (a medium-sized defence contractor) in 1996 to reduce dependence on the civil aerospace market – just at a time when the US Defense budget was being slashed following the end of the Cold War.

For McDonnell Douglas, being taken over was a further dent to its prestige. In 1996 it had failed to be shortlisted to develop a prototype for the new Joint Strike Fighter (JSF) for the US military – potentially the biggest defence procurement contract ever. For a leading manufacturer of military aircraft, exclusion from the contract was a bitter blow.

So at the end of 1997, Boeing found itself fighting to retain its dominant position in the global civil jet market while at the same time having to integrate not one merger but two – Rockwell and a dispirited McDonnell Douglas – both of which were in a different sector (defence) and had one major customer (the US government) who had cut defence spending almost by half.

Pentagon advice (not to be ignored when contracts are dangling) was to split the new Boeing into two divisions – one for commercial aircraft (broadly the old Boeing) and the other for information, space and defence systems (broadly McDonnell Douglas and Rockwell). This was rough and ready, with little focus on products, technology or specific customer needs. But it was a holding position (roughly Model 2 in Figure 10.1) to allow time for an integration strategy to be thought out.

The new Boeing recognised that it had three major customer groups. Government for defence; government and private business in space; and increasingly privatised airlines for commercial jets. So a separate third division was created to tackle space and communication markets. That included everything from launching satellites to using satellites to provide high-powered data links to and from aircraft (like using satellite navigation for air traffic management in the future). This three-divisional structure now mirrored the company's major markets.

Then came the question of who should head up the various business units, given that each had different requirements and offered different possibilities for the future. The top dozen or so senior executives in the enlarged Boeing were chosen from – but did not specifically represent – the three merging companies. They began to reshape existing businesses around the new structure and gradually started to pull the new Boeing together. But it was top-down integration. There was still the bottom-up question to be tackled. How was the vast reservoir of knowledge and know-how scattered around different parts of the huge company to be hoovered up and developed and fed into the business plan?

Boeing's answer was 'Phantom Works', a specialist R&D unit not unlike the famous Lockheed Martin 'Skunk Works' (where secret defence systems are developed as 'black programmes' for the Pentagon). Phantom Works included the research and development heart of McDonnell Douglas, but enlarged to comprise some 4,500 scientists and engineers scattered right across the combined company. When selected, these experts would come into the unit on three- or four-year assignments before returning to operating businesses.

There would be short-term projects – like improving rockets or developing fighters including the JSF. There would be ongoing projects – like applying know-how from civil projects to military use and vice versa. And there would be more futuristic endeavours – like the Blended Wing Body which one day might replace conventional airliners.

Phantom Works was envisaged initially as the R&D organisation for the company as a whole. It became more than that. It became the bottom-up engine integrating the three companies together – pooling a vast range of technical and management talents to feed current business plans and potentially to be the engine of future strategy.

How successful has it been? Building a 'virtual greenfield' organisation (Model 3(a) in Figure 10.1) out of not two but three leading-edge firms is difficult. Moulding three sets of competing employees into one cohesive team is even harder. Boeing's estimate of 40% success in the first year or so is commendable given the inevitable rivalry and culture clashes that are bound to occur.

A better measure comes from other US Defense contractors who were forced to consolidate around the peace dividend. Many suffered post-merger confusion, falling profits and diving share prices. On that check, the new Boeing cleared take-off and started to climb way ahead of the pack. (*The Economist*, 12 August 2000, pp. 83–4)

Model 3(b): Mutually Merged (Best-of-Both-Worlds Model)

Another variation on partial merging is when the two sides in any deal (large or small) decide that they will create a combined organisation that incorporates the best practices from each side. It can be tricky to pull off.

If there are obvious strengths on each side and they stand out unambiguously, then it will be fairly obvious which functions and practices are to survive. Otherwise, defining 'best' can be problematic. There seems to be two ways of dealing with it:

- One is for the integration team to take the lead and make the decisions on what they judge to be the desirable qualities on each side then drive implementation forward (i.e. they back their best judgements). This is more likely to succeed.

- The other way is to delegate decisions about what is 'best' to a series of specialist groups or committees made up of representatives from each side. This usually is unwise. It is an open invitation for all to stake claims on their own practices and that can bring all the downsides listed above – political manoeuvring, jockeying for position, culture clashes and performance decline. It also sucks the acquirer and the integration team back into the target culture and opens up all sorts of past agendas and matters of contention that are usually best left buried. In effect, the target culture is reaffirmed and reinforced in the early post-deal period *before* any decisions are made about which aspects are to survive. The integration team then lose the ball, they lose control of implementation, and often it is difficult to get it back (see Box 10.2).

Whichever approach is taken, it takes time to work out the final shape of the combined organisation. Even if the integration team takes the lead and drives the merger from on top, it still takes time for each side to understand the other, to work through the political and cultural blocks, and to decide how the practices from each side are to be combined into a smoothly functioning new organisation. Again, the fallback position is Model 1 or Model 2 as the immediate post-deal structures until all the preparatory work is completed.

Model 4: Fully Merged (Blitzkrieg Model)

This is the model most classical economists have in mind when they talk about *economies of scale* by merging. The acquired business is fully merged – fully transformed into acquirer format and style. There may also be physical

---

Box 10.2   In debt to a curate's egg

What's the best structure for rationalising two credit agencies with competing branches in every town? Do you think your financial adviser would know best?

When a division of a major UK bank acquired a credit agency from a rival, it was delighted to get the extra volume (50%) as a boost to its sluggish credit business. So the bank gave substantial assurances. The target's name and head-quarters building would be retained. Staff would be merged on a scrupulously fair basis. And there would be no compulsory redundancies. But managers in both agencies (over 6,000 staff in total) saw things differently. They opposed the deal on the grounds that they each managed credit in completely different ways.

Implementing the merger was the responsibility of a three-man team – the managing directors of each agency and the systems director from the acquiring side. In their view, there were only two structures that would work and simul-taneously satisfy the assurances in the deal. Either (a) to have one totally integrated organisation lending under two different names. Or (b) to have two separate divisional offices, each controlling a different branch network.

One member of the team had reservations about both options, the other two had no preference – they were content with either. Unable to agree, they set up three working parties to advise them. These in turn sought further help, and within a month 14 working parties were planning the merger.

The working parties met in secret, pulling information in and giving little out. With no leadership or vision or policy directions coming from on top, fear and uncertainty ran rife on both sides. There were two rival branches in each town, and branch managers knew only one would survive. The best protection, they reasoned, was volume of business. High-risk lending soared almost at once. Any bad debt wouldn't show for at least two years – and that was long enough for everyone to look good on paper.

After three months came the first decision. The two treasuries were to amalgamate. One lot of staff promptly resigned. A further five months went by. Then came the announcement everyone was waiting for – the new organisation structure, which branches would close and how harmonisation was to happen. All was presented at a slick conference for the 200 or so area managers – and it fell flat. Nobody could figure out how the new structure was going to work.

What structure was chosen? Was it (a) or (b)? Was it one of the structures in Figure 10.1? It was none of these. The implementation team settled for a compromise that had failed in the past – *two* separate divisional offices controlling *one* set of branches. This had been tried in an earlier acquisition – and simply didn't work.

'The compromise organisation was the worst of all worlds. It was the curate's egg', remarked another director. Why did it happen? 'We didn't have one single person driving the integration. We had a triumvirate with two abstainers.'

merging – with plant closures, relocation, career disruption and job loss. The impact is usually greatest on the target side. For acquired managers and staff, full merging can have a post-Blitzkrieg quality. Little remains that is recognisable and a new regime is in control.

Note that full merging is appropriate only in selected deals – in particular, low-tech *horizontal* deals where there is nothing very special about the target company. Individual bits of the asset mix – markets, cash-flow, production capability, management calibre, etc. – will have strategic significance for the acquirer and may be highly valued. But there is nothing particularly special about how the mix combines to deliver performance. The target is the sort of company that probably would do just as well (and maybe a lot better) under different management.

There are four situations where full merging is likely.

1. In horizontal deals where the acquirer has a *proven* manufacturing or management or retailing capability in the industry or sector – and certainly superior to the target. For example, a leading retail chain acquiring a rival chain to expand its own brand name. Post-deal, one larger, seamless organisation is what is sought.

2. When small firms in the same industry come together to build one new, fully integrated company for growth.

3. When taking capacity out of an industry – like two steel companies merging in the hope of survival. Again, financial and administrative efficiency dictates one seamless organisation at the end.

4. When buying to in-fill – like buying a production facility to fill a gap in a product range. Targets by definition are comparatively smaller and usually are fully integrated except in special circumstances.

Full merging promises a glut of paper (theoretical) efficiencies – which could be why deal-makers seize upon them without always recognising the cost and complexity of trying to make the efficiencies 'happen'.

Merging two organisations is a massive programme of organisational change that is time- and effort-intensive and raises enormous opportunity cost questions. The bigger the deal, the more complex and time-consuming is the task. When the combining firms are sprawling global corporations, the integration task can be truly horrendous – and doubly so if there are earlier acquisitions on each side still not fully integrated. Full merging in global deals can take years to complete and diverts enormous resources inwards.

All the downsides of partial merging (see above) are amplified. Culture clash is at its maximum – invariably with more people from each side interacting and all levels of the target being incorporated into an acquirer format. Political manoeuvring and resistance to change are also at a maximum, especially when functional duplication means job loss and competition for survival. More people involved in reorganisation means more eyes off the ball, off the market. Add to these the psychological processes of disorientation and relearning; add the logistics and costs of any closures and relocation, and the picture is well-nigh complete.

And when it is all over, acquisition history tells us two things in particular. One is that the costs of merging can be many times greater than any benefits realised. The second is that two different organisations can still exist. Structures and systems and procedures can all be standardised but mindsets on each side may not change. 'Our way' and 'their way' can still persist and compete destructively.

So, are there any situations where full merging can proceed more easily? Much depends on the industry in question and what the deal is intended to achieve, and also the level of acquirer experience. How the integration team relates to target managers and the level of professionalism they bring to the process can make a significant difference. However, two general situations stand out. One is where the acquiring company has a significant advantage over the target – either in terms of size or in terms of capability. The other is when integration can follow standard procedures rather than being a one-off or craft endeavour.

(a) *Brawn or brains.* When acquirers have a significant **size** advantage over the target, they can bring more resources (and usually more experience) to the integration process. These can drive the process faster and perhaps handle resistance more effectively. Alternatively, when acquirers have a **capability or performance advantage**, it can act as a 'pull' towards the new owners. Target managers are more likely to recognise they will be better off under the new regime and that in turn can weaken political inclinations and culture-clinging. In cruder terms, an excess of brawn or an excess of brains on the acquiring side can speed up integration.

But when merging firms are of comparable size and capability and performance, very little stands out on either side. Acquirers think there will be full merging around their own format (Model 4) and may well have agreed on this during negotiations, but target managers often think otherwise. They think Model 3. That is the model 'in the mind' – that integration is negotiable and that at least some aspects of their own culture and systems and practices can be preserved because there is no perceived 'better off' by copying the other side. This can prolong integration and is tricky to handle.

(b) *Routine or one-off*. The other situation where merging can be smoother is when it can follow **standard procedures** (as in retailing) rather than being a one-off, craft exercise (as in manufacturing). For example, rationalising two manufacturing enterprises requires one side to be carefully **crafted** onto the other. The final shape will be known only in outline form. That means that much of the practical detail has to be delegated, with lots of negotiation and judgement and head-scratching along the way until the job is completed. There is no master blueprint to guide action.

In contrast, merging two retailing chains or two high street banks can be far more straightforward. If the goal is one bigger chain of cloned outlets all looking much the same, integration can be centrally driven using **standard procedures**. The target can be transformed relatively quickly to a formula already in place long before the deal is completed. Dixons provides the example (Box 10.3).

Box 10.3   Dixons' fast Curry blender

When UK electrical retailer Dixons acquired the comparatively larger Curry's electrical chain in 1984, the *commercial* strategy was to keep both names competing in the high street with some product segmentation between the stores: Dixons to concentrate more on high-tech or specialist goods (PCs, cameras, etc.) and Curry's to concentrate more on lower-tech, household products (fridges, hoovers, toasters, etc.). Behind this consumer front, the *organisational* strategy was to have one seamless integrated organisation driving the two businesses.

Integration planning had the precision of a military operation. The day after gaining control, Dixons' chairman (Stanley Kalms) and the integration team visited the target headquarters. Eye witnesses tell that, after some brief formalities, the new strategy for the combined business was presented in detail to the Curry's board. Key office holders were then appointed, performance targets agreed, and the integration plan explained. Within an hour, a 30-page manual was distributed to Curry's senior managers detailing how it was all to happen.

Was this a successful acquisition? Nearly two decades later, the two chains are still competing and expanding across the UK. The stores have retained their distinctive ethos with most of the public perceiving them as separate companies.

Choosing a Structure

These four models of integration capture the spread of post-deal structures – from the stand-alone to the fully merged. They are, of course, just points on a continuum. In practice there are many variations in between. Nevertheless, as a starting point for integration planning, one of these models – in broad shape – will be selected as the most likely for the deal in hand, after which there will be fine-tuning.

How do managers choose the most appropriate for acquisition performance? The likely situations where each model might be suitable have been indicated – but these are very general. Fine-tuning has to take into account the *unique* context of every deal and how the various parties view integration. There is also the matter of *organisational politics*. Functional chiefs on the acquiring side often see their opposite numbers as extensions of their own territory. A common attitude is: 'We acquired you, so we call the shots.' Sometimes the 'we control you' attitude can extend right across the acquiring company and that can create strong pressures towards merging – doubly so when backed up with pages of rosy projections. On paper the justifications are usually efficiency or cost saving or synergy. But underneath, the real drivers are often control and empire expansion.

> Getting the balance right between performance and politics, between market demands and administrative comfort, is never easy. It is even harder when all sorts of material and psychological goodies accrue to the acquiring side as size increases.

That's what makes the job of the integration manager so difficult. There are no easy solutions or simple prescriptions. But there are six useful ways of thinking that can help to keep performance sharply in focus.

Depth of Cut

The first and most obvious point is that the deeper the cut, the higher the cost of integration. The more an acquirer cuts into the target (i.e. moving from Model 1 to Model 4):

- the greater is the destabilisation of the acquired business

- the more 'hands-on' management time and effort are required

- the greater is the likelihood of serious culture clashes

- the greater is the number of people getting involved in integration and trying to shape the integration agenda to their own ends

- the more attention is focused inwards, off the market and off the competition

- the greater is the complexity and cost of integration.

All this is obvious to an organisation specialist – but not always to the strategic mind. Novice (first-time) acquirers and especially smaller companies often try to standardise as much as possible after an acquisition irrespective of the strategic logic. Global corporations sometimes do the same when they are driven by an unswerving corporate philosophy. Then what both learn – in time and maybe at a huge cost – is the lesson that successful acquirers have discovered. **As little interference in the target as possible to achieve the strategy behind the deal**.

Let Markets Decide

When there is tension between acquisition performance and administrative comfort, let markets decide. The underlying principle here is to concentrate on the strategic goals of the acquisition and be guided by where the *major* sources of future value lie. There is more to this than just structuring the new organisation around markets or major customer groups.

Acquirers often start by scanning the target to see where potential cost savings or operational improvements might be made. That is to start at Model 3. It usually produces an eclectic set of integration directions that confuses short-term and long-term considerations. It also blurs the distinction between **strategic** and **operational** goals of the deal, and between **internal** (organisational) and **external** (market) sources of value.

A minimum intervention approach starts at Model 1 and asks two questions:

1. What minimum changes are absolutely essential for acquisition strategy to be realised?

2. How much acquisition value can be realised through efficiencies happening external to the organisation in various markets?

If the bulk of the value is dependent upon reorganising and managing hierarchies more efficiently (to improve competitiveness and not just to recover the cost of the deal), then obviously the knife of change is going to cut deep. But if the major sources of value lie external to the firms in market efficiencies (or synergies), these usually can be realised without any reorganisation at all. For example:

- Financial market synergies (like those deriving from capital restructuring) can be realised without any internal reorganisation.

- Product market synergies (like increasing market share through two sales forces carrying each other's products). The gains are immediate and of themselves require no structural merging. Some firms, however, might want sales and marketing to come closer together.

- Labour market synergies (like acquiring in countries with lower labour costs or more flexible labour markets). Provided the acquired business is sound, production can be placed overseas without any reorganisation at all – just mechanisms for control and communication.

- Knowledge market synergies (like acquiring to gain knowledge or pool know-how). Again, what is required are mechanisms for capability transfer and sharing, not structural merging.

These examples are simple to illustrate a point. Few deals are ever as straightforward. Acquired companies are often a portfolio of several businesses – major and minor – all rolled into one. Yet the principle is still the same. **Separate the businesses – then choose the most appropriate minimum intervention structure for each business to preserve the value of the deal**. It often results in different approaches to different parts of the same acquisition, and that may be resisted by the uniform mind with a one-size-fits-all approach. The skill of the integration manager in these circumstances is keeping a performance focus. And that's not always easy when powerful personalities are competing over who will run what and how it is all to happen.

Capability Profiles

At a very practical level, capability profiles (see Chapter 8) can provide a fairly accurate scenario of the cost and complexity of merging. They can help pinpoint areas of incompatibility and also similarity between the two firms. And they can give a comprehensive picture of what merger change would *really* involve – decoupling acquired staff from their old methods of working, then doing whatever changeovers are necessary, then recoupling staff to the new formats, and all the adjustment and learning processes that follow. If there is something special about either company, profiles can reveal what delivers that special value – and whether merging might destroy it.

If target capability profiles are not available, thorough pre-deal organisational audits are the next best thing.

Forget Synergy; Think Entropy

Synergy – as every merger strategist can recite even in deep sleep – means **the spontaneous creation of energy by two entities coming together, one enhancing the performance of the other**. As a concept, synergy is great for raising capital and wooing investors – but pretty hopeless for the nitty-gritty job of integrating two organisations to get returns on capital. *Entropy* as a concept is far more useful, particularly when the bulk of future value hinges upon reorganising hierarchies. But ask merger strategists what entropy means and the chances are that some will be stumped – even although both terms have been around for decades in systems thinking.

Entropy essentially is about disorder and decay – about the tendency of all higher levels of organisation to move towards simpler, less differentiated forms. **'The entropic process is a universal law of nature in which all forms of organisation move towards disorganisation or death'** (Katz and Khan, 1966). All higher levels of organisation – plant, animal, firm, corporation – have an inherent tendency to move towards a lower form; all complex forms have an inherent tendency to move towards simpler forms – *unless* energy is channelled inwards in a maintenance function to prevent the entropy or decay. The larger and more complex the organisation, the greater the amount of energy that needs to get channelled inwards to arrest entropy and maintain the higher or more complex state.[1]

However, managers don't 'think' entropy. They seldom remember that the structures, systems, controls and procedures that serve the economic and technical imperatives *simultaneously* act to contain the forces of disorder and decay. How the balance is struck depends on many factors and involves careful regulation of the many boundaries both inside the firm and with the wider environment.

The important point is that when the balance is right and the firm is successful, a steady state evolves with a minimum amount of energy getting directed at containing disorder and as much energy as possible to systems output – to survival and growth and productivity.

Merging two structures disturbs that balance. It disturbs the steady states that delivered performance on each side and the value components behind the deal. Substantial or full structural merging is an exercise in disorder management that accelerates rather than contains the entropic process.

- For the target, major merging dissolves the many boundaries that retain a state of equilibrium and the socio-technical balance. The organisation falls to a lower state – disorganised, unbundled and sometimes atomised – with an inevitable decline in performance.

- On the acquiring side, energy is diverted away from markets and competition into preventing the disorder of absorbing an alien culture and unfamiliar procedures. In global mega-deals the distraction can last for years if the firms are incompatible and again with enormous performance implications.

- Then one bigger organisation is a more complex, higher-order entity than either was beforehand. Greater amounts of energy get diverted inwards to sustain the larger unit and keep it efficient and competitive. (See Chapter 3 for the many implications of greater size.)

Most predicted synergies from organisational merging turn out to be illusory or trivial or cost more to realise than they are worth. So before embarking on a major process of organisational change, concentrating on the downsides, on the barriers to synergy, on *entropy*, seems a sensible way of proceeding.

Socio-Technical Balance

Another way of looking at the balance in organisations is through socio-technical theory (Miller and Rice, 1967; Cherns, 1976, 1987). From this perspective, every organisation is a compromise, a joint accommodation, between the 'hard' economic and technical demands of the enterprise and the 'soft' psychological and social and cultural requirements of the staff.

These two dimensions, the 'hard' and the 'soft', often work against each other so they have to be brought into equilibrium to achieve an efficient steady state. But that state is always a suboptimal state – each dimension satisficed but not maximised. Any attempts to maximise one are almost always at the expense of the other and can be counterproductive. The people affected divert energy into trying to restore the original balance and that often leads to a *less* efficient state.

Hence the socio-technical principle of *joint optimisation*. To maintain an efficient steady state, both sides of the enterprise (the 'hard' and the 'soft') have to be in balance. And – most important for integration – any changes on the technical side must be accompanied by appropriate changes on the social side, and vice versa. The big implication for merging is, of course, that acquirers need to understand how the socio-technical balance is achieved in both companies *before* any changes take place (see Box 10.4).

Box 10.4   Mergers and transplants

Consider what happens when two firms – two different socio-technical orders – are brought together in the name of efficiency. The technical part of integration (harmonising technology, systems, procedures, etc.) is an exercise in logistics that can be programmed step-by-step with help manuals if necessary. But bringing together the two different social orders is far more complex. It often arouses rejection mechanisms – not unlike what happens in transplant surgery.

A common problem is that the patient's immune system rejects the donor organ. So extra management efforts in the form of anti-rejection drugs have to be applied to suppress the immune system and encourage transplant acceptance. But that weakens the patient even further. The longer the immune system is suppressed, the more vulnerable the patient is to infection, and that requires further management effort in the form of more medication, and so on. Performing again at full capacity can take months, even years, to return – sometimes never.

The parallels with organisational meshing are many and compelling. When technical efficiency brings together two very different social orders – like two antagonistic organisational cultures or two national cultures that proceed on very different assumptions – resistance and rejection can persist for years. Trying to achieve a working blend of the two cultures draws more and more management time and effort into integration, with enormous performance implications.

Structure as Shorthand

Finally, remember that structure as depicted on charts is not something concrete or tangible – except perhaps at a ceremonial level of portraying office holders within a reward hierarchy. Structure *in action* is a shorthand term that captures a range of elements that include:

- A consensus on strategy and who determines it.
- A consensus on who exercises power and allocates resources.

- The controls and information flow and the regulatory and HR systems within the enterprise.

- The individuals who each energise the organisation and make it 'happen', both formally and informally.

- The mindsets – the collective ways of seeing and thinking and doing things – that are the social characteristic of the enterprise.

Merging structures involves merging all of these and trying to get them all to dovetail and work together in some kind of harmony. And that is much more than bringing together organisation charts on boardroom walls.

In Summary

These are six different ways of thinking; six different ways of looking at the implications – especially the downsides – of structural merging. All are about keeping acquisition performance firmly in focus but coming at it from very different angles. The concepts are fairly mainstream and should register with most managers and integration teams.

> But note again what was emphasised at the beginning of the chapter. *There is no solid body of tested theory on how best to merge companies.* There are only judgements – and judgements can be influenced by many factors including self-interest and political pressure.

Both can lead to more merging than is necessary. So also can pressure from outside. Large-scale organisational merging has always been a lucrative source of business for external advisers. Carefully probing the assumptions behind any recommendations for major restructuring seems sensible.

Remember also that the message of this chapter – and the whole principle behind Models 1 and 2 – is 'hands off' the acquired structure in the first couple of years or so – unless there is a compelling *business* reason for doing otherwise and only in carefully selected areas. Then across time as opportunities arise and market circumstances change, different parts of the business might grow closer together. But that will be slowly, driven mostly by a business logic (not an administrative or political logic), and usually with support for any changes coming from below.

Part 4

Human Resources

CHAPTER 11

People and Human Resource Strategies

'*Alienating the acquired people is disastrous. One must win the new people over. Bring them into the team.*'

(Chairman, engineering)

People are the vital core of our business. These words or something similar have appeared at some time in the annual reports of almost every company around the world. But words don't always match deeds. Often there is a gulf between noble statements of intention and how people are actually managed on a day-to-day basis. In mergers and acquisitions, that gulf can be enormous.

Box 11.1   People as a bulk buy

Suppose you apply to another company for a post. Before you can join its ranks, you will be assessed on your job competence, social skills, leadership potential, networking ability, and much more besides. You will be put through grilling interviews, job previews, all sorts of psychological tests, maybe even days at an assessment centre. Then if you're accepted, your entry will be smoothly managed until you feel comfortably adjusted to the new environment. All will be conducted with much seriousness because ... you're important.

But if that same company acquires the firm you work for, you will be bought as one of a job lot, a bulk buy, sight unseen. At best, only the most superficial audit of the human qualities of your firm will be conducted. And very likely you will be left to swim in a sea of stress and uncertainty for weeks, maybe months, after the event. But you'll still be told: you're important.

The employment market and the market for corporate control have different rules for bringing new people into an organisation. Unless, of course, you happen to be *really* important!

A similar point can be made about Human Resource strategies. Most firms will emphasise the importance of people to their mission and purpose, and usually they can point to how various HR practices (selection, appraisal, reward, training, development, etc.) are all shaped towards realising the mission or purpose. But ask the same firms what their HR strategy for mergers and acquisitions looks like and what its end goals might be, and in all probability you will get blank looks.

This chapter will explore what a M&A Human Resource strategy might look like and what it might be trying to achieve. First, however, it will highlight some of the more typical human reactions to an acquisition – especially to *being* acquired – and their dysfunctional consequences.

Typical Acquisition Behaviours

The behaviour and reactions of people on both sides of an acquisition are well documented (see, for example, Marks and Mirvis, 1986). We can start by listing some of the most typical.

On Being Acquired

Shock

For most managers and staff, the first they know of being taken over is when the public announcement is made. Typical reactions are a mixture of conflicting emotions – shock, disbelief, maybe anger if a small company has been sold out and people feel their efforts have not been rewarded. There can be relief when a cash-starved or struggling business is acquired by a more successful company. There can also be a feeling of betrayal if they have been sold to a competitor. And then there is fear – fear of the unknown, the future.

Fear of Job Loss

Fear of job loss is often rife. It is a fear that goes deep – deep into the unconscious. Mostly it is unspoken but the fear is there and can be numbing and paralysing. From senior executive to van driver, take away the trappings of role and there is the same psychology asking the same question: Do I still have a job? And it is not only on the acquired side. In horizontal mergers where only one lot of managers are likely to survive, the fear can extend across both companies.

Career Uncertainties

Even where jobs are secure, there are career uncertainties. Taken-for-granted understandings about likely job moves and the shape of future careers often come crashing to earth. A new authority is in control and people are expecting change – even if none is intended. For some managers it presents a challenge; for others it can be unsettling and have enormous family implications.

Sense-Making

Sense-making goes into overdrive. Divining the reasons for being taken over and the likely consequences can preoccupy managers for weeks. In the first two or three days, work can sometimes stop altogether as managers huddle in corners or have impromptu meetings in corridors, talking up each other's uncertainties and trying to agree some consensus on the implications of being taken over. A sense of personal vulnerability and loss of control can permeate all managerial levels. Putting 'horns' on the acquirer is commonplace.

Information Vacuum

'Hard' information is usually thin on the ground. There are usually a multitude of questions in the air and few people able to answer them in the detail expected. Rumour and speculation take over. A multitude of scenarios compete for attention – with most built upon *assumptions* about acquirer motives and intentions. In fact, most of the scenarios that do the rounds in the first few weeks after an acquisition are based upon third- and fourth-hand information.

Brain Drain

Some managers choose to bale out rather than go through the process of being merged and integrated – especially if they have been through it before. And it can be the most able managers who get out first, preferring to direct their energies to what they are best at. In fact, the experience of being taken over and merged can be so traumatic and unsettling that over 80% of acquired managers would not wish to go through the experience again – even when they are better off financially and their firms are in better shape as a result (Hunt et al., 1987). In the longer term, there can be an 'acquisition drift' factor

– talented staff drifting away because they are unhappy about life under a new regime.

There can also be loss of senior talent on the acquiring side if the acquisition is a drain on other businesses. It can also happen in failed bids. Managers who have spent months preparing to run and maybe turn round a prospective target, then finding out that it is not to happen, will still be 'psyched up' to do the job. If the challenge is really strong, some are easily induced to cross to the other side.

Wanting to Look Good

Uncertainty about the future encourages short-term, self-serving behaviours. CVs get polished up. Budget surpluses get used up. Options and benefits get taken to the hilt. And there are lots of public demonstrations of effectiveness – crisis meetings, new initiatives, bullish forecasts, maybe taking on new business without proper risk assessment – all with an eye to looking good in the short term.

Stress

Finally, there is stress. All these factors can combine to raise stress levels. The usual symptoms of stress – inner tension, withdrawal, heightened aggression, migraines, not sleeping properly, poor concentration, perhaps smoking or drinking more than usual – are commonly reported in the period following a takeover. And they impact directly upon both morale and performance.

However, it is worth noting two points about stress. The first is that it occurs in any major process of organisational change and cannot be avoided. The second is that stress levels vary enormously between people, depending on personality type (some people are more prone to anxiety; others have better defences); previous experience of mergers (knowing better what to do and not to do), and the organisational context (particularly how acquirers behave in relation to acquired staff).

There is nothing acquirers can do about the mix of personality types and experience in a target company. But there is a lot they can do to make the organisational context in an acquired company less uncertain. M&A stress can be minimised with a carefully prepared implementation strategy.

Collective Behaviours

The collective or company-wide ways of perceiving and relating to the other side constitute another set of post-acquisition behaviours. Two in particular are worth noting.

A 'Them and Us' Attitude

Sometimes managers in merging companies can behave a bit like two rival groups of football fans. We have all seen it. Supporters of the winning team somehow feel superior to the supporters of the other side – *'We* won; *you* lost.' And that sense of superiority is often real, as can be the sense of loss and inferiority on the other side.

Likewise in mergers. Managers on the acquiring side sometimes take the attitude: 'We own you so we control you. We are superior to you. We call the shots.' Or: 'If you were any good, why did you let yourselves get taken over?' It is a very primitive attitude – tribal even – and can be highly damaging. It can push morale even lower among target staff who may already be taking the acquisition very personally. Even when deals are amicable and for sound business reasons, acquired staff will still ask themselves: 'What did we do wrong to get taken over? Did we not work hard enough? Didn't we try our best?'

Some of this might be understandable following a rescue or a contested bid but not (as in most instances) when the deal is amicable and voluntary. What it reveals is the amount of identity that is at stake in a merger. For many managers, their notion of who they are, a large chunk of their public identity, is projected onto how one group of key players perform against another group of key players. In a football match, it is the two teams. In mergers, it is the two boards.

Stereotyping

Related to them-and-us is the tendency to stereotype the other side, particularly seeing only the strengths of the home side and the weaknesses of the other. For example, in a recent merger between two major UK banks, a senior executive on the acquiring side was heard to mutter: 'That lot couldn't even *spell* debt.' More common examples are 'They cheat' or 'They play by different rules' or 'They're less quality-conscious than us' or 'We have better managers or systems or conditions or whatever' – most of which are based on negative *assumptions* about the other side.

Again, it is partly understandable when direct competitors merge – often their mission was to emphasise how superior they were to the other side. Such a position makes it harder to acknowledge strengths on the other side and weaknesses on the home side. Otherwise, it has to be seen as another psychological way of coping with uncertainty and fear of the unknown – that the familiar is 'good' and the unfamiliar 'bad'. It is a polarised position that reinforces culture-clinging and is unhelpful for bringing two sides closer together. It is more typical of the middle and lower levels that have had little contact with the other side but it can be pervasive across all levels.

Hostile Bids

Hostile bids are particularly unsettling – for all levels including the board. The bids are by definition unfriendly – bypassing directors and appealing directly to shareholders – in effect, a vote of no confidence in the board. And they catch companies on the hop. Most do not have a set of procedures to hand for dealing with the unwelcome approach.

Fighting a hostile bid requires a coordinated and integrated effort on many fronts – not just top managers dealing with financial markets. If, for example, the bid poses a genuine threat to the company or its environment, getting support from many quarters is essential if the bid is to be judged on its broader impact, not just its economic consequences.

But what we often find is top management going into retreat. They withdraw into themselves to plan tactics. They closet themselves in crisis management meetings, demanding more and more information and giving little out. Middle management often do the same. And lower levels are left in a vacuum. Often they learn more from the media than from their own bosses about what is happening. Which is no way to unite a company to fight off a predator (see Box 11.2).

Goals of an Acquisition Human Resource Strategy

We return to the question: What would an acquisition Human Resource strategy be trying to achieve? What would the end goals be? Most people who have been through an acquisition would say that it should try to bring out the 'best' in people and avoid the stresses (as listed above) and the destructive conflicts and culture clashes that bedevil integration. At a deeper level, it should be about getting all sides committed to the new strategy,

---

Box 11.2   Smoke and glass

Hostile bids are less frequent now but a decade or so ago they were commonplace. How targets behaved in two such bids still can provide useful lessons.

In one firm, the bid sent the board into a defensive retreat. They had no strategy to deal with the approach. So they insulated themselves from the rest of the company, then became gripped by a collective paranoia. Directors came to believe their offices were bugged – by the bidder, the media, maybe even by their own managers. Security sweeps found nothing, but still they wouldn't decide tactics in their offices.

Instead, they would break off meetings and whisper decisions to one another in the corridor then return to their seats. Even when trusted executives phoned about something on the deal, they insisted on phoning back to a known number – just in case the caller was an impostor with a familiar voice!

Now make the contrast with a large glass manufacturer in the north of England, a company that was the mainstay of the local economy. A hostile bid by a perceived asset-stripper sent the board on an integrated offensive that galvanised the support of managers and workers, major customers, trade unions, civic dignitaries and even MPs.

It saw the bidder off – and brought an extra bonus. Managers and workers were brought closer together, and that created a culture shift that enabled the company to push through major changes to working practices that would have been unthinkable prior to the bid – and which delivered greater cost savings than either side thought possible at the time. (Hunt et al., 1987; Starkey and McKinley, 1990)

---

keeping a performance focus, minimising resistance to change, not losing key staff, and so on.

> All of which is fine as a general wish-list, but how are the building blocks to be put in place to make it all happen?

Here we need to draw upon some leading HR theorists. David Guest at Birkbeck College, London in a highly influential paper (Guest, 1987) has suggested that there are four goals which *any* HR strategy should be aiming to achieve – high levels of integration, commitment, flexibility and quality. If these qualities can exist in an organisation, higher levels of productivity and performance should follow. In another influential source, Michael Beer and his colleagues at Harvard Business School (Beer et al., 1984) have argued that strategic policy choices are the key to achieving effective Human

Resource outcomes. These two strands of thinking have been combined here and adapted to a merger context (see Figure 11.1).[1]

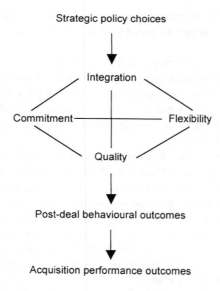

Figure 11.1 Human Resource policy choices and acquisition performance

Sources: adapted from Beer et al. (1984); Guest (1987)

The central idea in Figure 11.1 is that acquirers have a range of choices about which policies to adopt in respect of implementation. Whichever policies they adopt will affect people's behaviour on both sides (even if the policy is to have no policy at all!), and that in turn will affect implementation and eventually acquisition performance. This part is fairly obvious.

What is not so obvious is the question of *which policy choices* are more likely to get desirable levels of behaviours (i.e. behaviours that will support implementation and enhance acquisition performance) and which are more likely to achieve the opposite.

A strategic HR perspective doesn't answer the question directly, but indirectly gives some powerful pointers. People make organisations 'happen' and people make performance 'happen'. So try to bring out the 'best' in people by aiming for four specific Human Resource goals – aim for high levels of integration, commitment, flexibility and quality (as defined below). If these four goals or outcomes can be achieved, the *preconditions* will be in place for implementation to go more smoothly. Bringing two companies together is thus less likely to be troubled by 'problem' behaviours and desired levels of performance more likely to be realised.

Hence, from a Human Resources perspective, the four critical areas of strategic policy choice are:

- *Integration*
  This has three components because integration can have various meanings.
    1. The tight integration *at source* of Human Resource strategies into commercial and administrative strategies (a theme of this book, not just this chapter).
    2. The coordination *at source* of all aspects of implementation into a coherent programme of action.
    3. The most appropriate level of *structural* integration between the two firms (as examined in Chapter 10).

- *Commitment*
    1. Getting all levels of the acquired business committed to the new owners.
    2. Getting *commitment* on *both* sides principally around the business need of the combined company, rising above functional or divisional or career needs. The American notions of goal congruence, of building a large cohesive team, come to mind here.

- *Flexibility*
    1. Aiming for flexibility of thought and action on *both* sides. Getting mindsets on each side to understand and engage with one other.
    2. Creating a willingness to accept whatever changes are necessary in the business need – structural change, changes to policies and practices, job and career flexibility, and similar. And avoiding the rigidities of each side sticking to the familiar just because it is familiar.

- *Quality*
  This also has three components.
    1. Quality of *staff* in key positions – especially the integration manager and the implementation team, and having the most appropriate people in key positions on both sides. And handling implementation in a way that does not cause quality staff to leave.
    2. Quality of *performance* – implementing the acquisition in a way that has minimum impact upon performance on both sides.
    3. Quality of *image* – that the image and reputation of both sides are not damaged by implementation. How the two firms are brought

together should send a positive message about the acquirer to the target and to the wider industry and public. Known qualities on the target side should be preserved and not disparaged.

These HR goals are, of course, broad and idealistic. You don't have to be a seasoned HR critic to muster a critique. In practice some of the goals may not always sit comfortably together. Pursuing some may be at the expense of others. Outcomes can 'look' different in different contexts – across companies, across continents, across different socio-economic contexts. They gloss over the political realities of mergers, and so on. It is easy to nit-pick. Nevertheless, the goals have three qualities that recommend them.

1. The outcomes are worth aiming for – even if they can never be fully reached.

2. They can be built in as a check upon *every* implementation policy choice. The simple question of any implementation decision is: Will this decision have a *negative* impact upon any of the four goals?

3. They are potentially measurable. They can be benchmarked. Acquirers can set fairly specific targets for what they want to achieve along each dimension and then benchmark progress during a particular implementation (a 'How-well-are-we-doing?' check). Or they can benchmark between deals and compare the effectiveness of perhaps different approaches to implementation.

The big question, of course, is: **what types of policy choices are most likely to realise each of the above goals?** This is what the next two chapters are going to explore. They are not going to say: this is how to bring newly acquired staff into your firm. Nor: here is your blueprint for a M&A HR strategy. What they will do is examine how people act and react on both sides of an acquisition, and also give some examples of implementation best practice. It will then be left to managers to draw upon their judgement and experience (and also the other chapters in the book) to combine the material into an overall HR strategy that fits their own unique circumstances.

CHAPTER 12

Three-Stage Commitment Building

'If they're not fully with you from the beginning, they're ag'in you. There's no middle ground.'

(CEO, distribution)

Many of the behaviours outlined in the previous chapter are unavoidable in acquisitions and mergers. They are natural and stem from the human condition – in particular from two basic emotions: fear and greed. Fear occurring mostly on the target side and greed (or the urge to own and control) on the acquiring side. These emotions are always present in mergers. They cannot be avoided – but a good HR strategy should be able to minimise their destructive consequences.

If we go back to Figure 11.1, a Human Resource strategy for acquisitions and mergers emphasised two things. One was the tight integration of human concerns into implementation planning long *before* the deal is signed. The other was making the most appropriate policy choices that should maximise commitment, flexibility and quality on both sides in the months and early years *after* the deal.

Of these outcomes, commitment is probably the most pivotal. If acquired staff can become firmly committed to the new owners, and if both sides can become strongly committed to what the acquisition is intended to achieve, then other HR outcomes should follow more easily.

However, commitment is not something that can be engineered at lower levels if it does not already exist at the very top. There is a wealth of HR evidence[1] of firms trying to engineer commitment at lower levels with only half-hearted support from senior managers. What they get, almost invariably, is a half-hearted response in return. Staff will go through the motions and *say* they are committed (i.e. there is superficial or behavioural commitment). But what is missing is the attitudinal component, the attitude of mind, that is essential for full mental engagement and involvement.

For full commitment to an acquisition, it has to start at the top during negotiations and it has to be sustained through the often long and difficult process
of implementation and integration. There are three important stages here,
each influenced by different factors.

Stage 1. Building commitment at the top during negotiations.
Stage 2. Reducing fear and securing commitment immediately after the
          announcement.
Stage 3. Winning and maintaining commitment during the months or
          maybe years of implementation.

These are the three essential stages to commitment building. Each step is
different – in terms of time frame, the parties involved and the issues that
have to be addressed. This chapter and the next will take each stage one at a
time and examine some of the key factors that can (a) encourage and (b)
hinder commitment along the way.

Stage 1: Commitment at the Top During Negotiations

Willing Buyer – Willing Seller

What makes for a really willing buyer and an equally willing seller? Popular
accounts of mergers, especially in the American press, often dwell on how well
the two presidents or CEOs get on with each other, whether they enjoy a
personal understanding and not just a business relationship. The word *chemistry*
is often used – a chemistry at the top – which conveys the important idea of a
catalytic coming together with one side inspiring the other. Unfortunately,
popular accounts don't say much about how this actually happens.

The study: *Acquisitions – The Human Factor* (Hunt et al., 1987) looked
more closely at this idea of chemistry at the top – the spark that can turn
exploratory talks into enthusiastic partners. Two types of factors were
identified. First were business factors – like strategy on each side going in the
same directions, having a shared vision of the future and meeting a need the
other lacks. Being in the same industry and talking the same industry
language also helps the chemistry along.

But none of this is very surprising. Most discussions begin around calculations that say, theoretically, both firms might be better off by combining.
Business factors, in effect, do little more than add flesh to bones; adding
strategic context to computer projections.

Far more significant was the second group of factors, the human factors.
In particular, the quality of the relationship that developed between the two

negotiating teams (typically the two presidents/chairmen, the two finance directors, and the relevant CEOs/managing directors from each side). How these parties related to one another in face-to-face discussions and the informal relationships they developed over time were far more important for creating empathy and making the flesh on the bones come alive.

> It didn't matter whether the acquisition was large or small, how these two groups related to each other in an informal, face-to-face way was what really got a spark going. In particular, a shared philosophy, honest talking, solid assurances and a genuine sense of trust – these were the sorts of factors that brought about real commitment to the other side and to striking a deal that would work.

Shared Philosophy

Like deciding to enter serious discussions on the basis of the early impressions made by the other side. 'It felt right; they felt right.' 'They had similar philosophies and values to ourselves.' 'They were the same as us, just speaking a different language.' This came through in many of the deals, from managers on both sides. In fact, the CEO of a major UK company (with many acquisitions to his credit) took it a step further and enshrined it into a principle: 'I would not talk figures until I was satisfied with philosophy.'

Honest Talking

Like being open and transparent about the real reasons for wanting to buy – and equally open about the real reasons for wanting to sell. When target managers freely:

- disclosed the true business condition
- provided detailed financial and performance data over several years
- gave an honest assessment of who were the good executives and what they might do for the acquisition

these all helped the two sides to bond. Similar transparency on the acquiring side also helped. On the other hand, any duplicity or deviousness on either side invariably created distrust. If picked up during the diligence process, it cast a shadow over further negotiations. If picked up later, it soured implementation and created a legacy of distrust.

Assurances

Like giving target managers assurances that were solid and believable.

- Clear plans on what was to happen to the acquired business and to its board and management.

- Honouring all existing contracts and conditions of employment, and guaranteeing pension arrangements especially for the vendor's top management.

- Nobody to suffer as a direct consequence of the acquisition, except in clearly defined problem areas where there were agreements to cut deeply if necessary and maybe to implement the target's contingency survival plan. But to cushion the downsides as far as possible.

- Honourable disposal of surplus businesses – either through management buy-outs or redeployment of staff elsewhere.

Assurances along these lines were often significant in persuading targets to sell – even although many managers took the view that assurances are 'not worth the paper they are printed on' after the deal has been completed. The acquiring company has the right to do whatever it pleases – especially if market circumstances change. Assurances are binding in honour only. Nevertheless, of the companies that took part in the study, some 90% were reported to have stuck to their word.

Integrity and Trust

There is a common thread here – integrity and trust. The integrity of the acquirer on a number of dimensions – financial, technical, human, the way they did business, the way they handled earlier acquisitions – was significant in building trust and commitment. Companies with a reputation as 'honourable people to sell to'; 'solid companies with thoroughly professional management', usually started negotiations with an advantage. The 'wheelers and dealers', the 'cheap and cheerful cowboys' and the asset strippers often had a credibility problem.

It works both ways, of course. Acquirers are just as concerned about the integrity of the people they are sinking their money into – not just the integrity of the business prospect. There were many reported instances of firms walking away from otherwise promising deals mainly because they felt they could not trust target managers to behave honourably during negotiations and in the years ahead.

This emphasis on trust came through in most of the deals investigated, and from both sides. Although the presidents and directors and CEOs in the study were engaged in cold commerce – buying and selling companies – they themselves were seldom cold and detached. Instead, most approached negotiations with the same value system they would wish in their *interpersonal* dealings with one another – straight talking, transparency, and taking their opposite numbers at face value. And most showed a genuine concern about any negative impact the acquisition might have on both sets of staff. Some parent companies disposing of subsidiaries even went further and sought specific assurances from the new owners concerning the longer-term welfare of the staff they were setting loose.

For all this to work lay a deeper value – something that is the eternal basis for doing good business. *A person's word is his or her bond.* That what is agreed in negotiations is adhered to, even if it means some constraints and compromises in the years ahead. It is interesting to note that the vast majority of deals in the study were trustworthy in that what was agreed during negotiations was adhered to. Only a tiny minority of acquirers went back on their assurances or had a hidden agenda that they did not disclose to the target board. These deals ran into trouble from the outset.

Small Company Deals

What about small companies and owner-manager firms that don't have much of a public profile and have few (or maybe no) earlier acquisitions to show as role models? (Remember: mega-mergers grab the headlines but the majority of deals in any year are between small companies.) All the above findings apply – but with some extra considerations in owner-manager companies. Three are worth noting.

'Our Kind of People'

With owner-manager firms, everything is more personal. The psychological bond with the business is much stronger. Often the owners *are* the business.

They have probably built it up. They are accustomed to near-total autonomy and freedom of action. And they imprint the business with their own personal 'stamp' – an ethos that reflects their own mix of attitudes and values and preferences. These factors affect whom they choose to enter discussions with.

Generally speaking, owner-managers seek a more personal relationship with the other side than large companies would want or consider necessary. But what initially attracts them to a prospective partner can be highly subjective – idiosyncratic even – and not always easy to pin down. They might just say: *'They were our kind of people.'* This is a phrase that small firms sometimes use. It seems vague and indefinable. But what it often means is that they saw in a prospective partner a mirror of their own particular values and ethos and style. That's what they feel most comfortable with.

There are several implications for large companies. One is that they cannot assume that small firms will 'buy into' their value systems and ways of operating even if terms are generous. Another is that they may have to spend a disproportionate amount of time trying to get into the mindset, the way of thinking, in a small target before any serious talking begins. 'Wooing' them can take much longer – perhaps with a lot of preliminary socialising around what the target likes doing best. And that in turn has implications for the type of executive the corporation sends in to open discussions. Grey ties and surfboards seldom mix.

Proprietorial Instincts

When owner-managers decide to sell, the negotiation agenda is more complex. There is a business agenda *and* a proprietorial agenda. Leaving aside value systems and matters of compatibility, owner-managers are typically concerned with four on-the-table issues:

1. price

2. succession

3. growing the business

4. resolving family interests (like a partner or brother retiring, or securing the positions of other family members).

Unless there is a pressing need to sell, owner-managers will want to satisfy all these considerations in an acceptable balance. The key point in any discussions is to find out what they really want. A first approach can often meet with a cold refusal – five out of seven Americans say 'No' to the first offer, and that applies in other countries as well. Subsequent approaches may continue to be rejected until perhaps the 'right' figure is mentioned.

Although stalling may appear to be about price, it is commonly a delaying tactic to allow the true intentions of the acquirer to be revealed. It is also to assess the acquirer, especially to get a measure of their trustworthiness and whether assurances can be relied upon. If the deal straddles different continents, there may be a strong fear of the unknown as well as a sizeable culture gap. Neither side may be fully aware of the 'taken for granted' cultural assumptions the other is operating to (see Box 12.1).

Hence the importance of 'no hassling' in small company deals until the owners' needs can be fully established and they in turn can assess the benefits the buyer might be able to bring to them. Global deals also need time for acquirers to understand the social and cultural context they are planning to buy into.

Box 12.1   Asian tango

Suppose the target was a small company in Asia. There could be a network of extended family interests to be taken into account as well as a network of suppliers and associates who would expect to retain a relationship after the deal. Little of this might come through in early discussions. Western managers might negotiate on the assumption that all arrangements post-deal will follow a *business* logic. Asian managers might assume they will continue according to local custom and practice – to the logic of *tradition*.

The two owners might enthuse at length about technical and market synergies – but the mindsets concerning what would actually happen on the ground literally can be continents apart.

Implementation

The third point has to do with implementation. If big firms experience implementation problems in a far-off country, they have plenty of executives who can be sent across to sort things out. Not so for smaller companies. The factors of distance, different environments and difficulty in maintaining a presence in the acquisition mean that the character and personality and mindsets of the target's top management become extremely important in deciding whether to buy and secondly in deciding how to manage the acquisition subsequently.

A business relationship built around *'our kind of people'* means that each side knows most of the taken-for-granted assumptions the other is operating to. That's pretty important in any small company deal, and absolutely essential in a deal spanning halfway round the world. Some quotes from acquiring CEOs can illustrate.

'We trusted them to make the acquisition work, and they did. We had no resources to spare if it had run into problems.'

'From the beginning, I developed a trust in the seller's president. We shared similar values and attitudes and philosophies in all sorts of things. If this had not happened, I doubt if we would have gone ahead.'

'You must have trust. If you are prepared to sink your money into them, you've got to believe in them. You can't do business if you're always looking over your shoulder.'

In Summary and One Danger

All this is a long way from the cold, impersonal, formula-based approach to acquisitions and divestments typified by the BCG matrix (see Figure 4.1). Very little of what is outlined here can be reduced to figures or be computer simulated. Yet it is so important for building commitment at the top and cementing the foundations for two firms to work together.

Some readers, of course, might argue that personal relationships and emotional commitment are important only in small company deals. They might argue that large corporations that buy and sell companies as a strategic routine do so on the basis of hard numbers and with a professional detachment. It is certainly the message in many finance and strategy textbooks.

That would be the wrong conclusion to come to. Numbers only help to narrow down targets. Thereafter, it is the quality of the relationship at the top that is crucial in determining whether a deal – large or small – comes alive or not.

- At a *simple practical level*, both teams of top managers have got to bond if they are to work together in the years ahead. If there are personality clashes or likely power struggles in early discussions, it is usually a sign of difficulties ahead.

- At a *ground-rule level*, each side has to understand the mindsets and value systems and basic assumptions governing business on the other. It is only through informal discussions that these are brought to the surface. Again, major differences usually indicate problems ahead.

- At a *trust level*, it is mostly through the relationship that each side can discern the honesty and integrity of the other in respect of the deal. Targets in particular want to find out: Will acquiring managers go back on their assurances? Do they have a hidden agenda?

However, there is one danger here. At a deeper and less conscious level, there is the danger that too much reliance can be placed on the relationship at the top. *The relationship can become a surrogate for the acquisition itself.* Part of the reason has to do with coping with uncertainty. In any acquisition, managers know that statistically the odds are stacked against them. The outcome is but an idea, a distant possibility, and they may have only the sketchiest outline of how it is all to happen. When deals are really big – like global mega-mergers – these can be so mind-boggling that none of the parties can grasp the full scope and complexity of what they are negotiating. That's a bit scary.

Top managers need reassurance. They need something real and tangible around them to draw comfort from. Numbers are helpful – but the best comfort usually comes in human form. Top managers on each side embody the promise of what they hope others down the line will deliver. If the negotiating team can see people around them who share similar beliefs and values to themselves. If they can see a meeting of minds and a shared vision. If they can detect (even if only at gut level) integrity and honesty and a strong commitment to deliver. Then these will be seized upon as 'go' signals; that the deal should be all right.

There lies the danger. *Familiarity can become a surrogate for performance.* The quality of the relationship at the top can become a surrogate that is *seen as representing* the acquisition and its calculated possibilities. That in turn leads to the simplistic (but quite common) assumption that if the two boards 'click', the two firms will 'click'.

Bonding at the top is necessary – but by no means sufficient. Armies of managers and staff on each side have also to be brought together. It is to this we now turn.

Stage 2: Reducing Fear and Securing Commitment

The Realistic Merger Preview

Getting commitment at the top is comparatively easy because of the small number of people involved and the length of time spent in negotiations. Much harder is securing commitment among the ranks of managers and staff on both sides – most of whom will know nothing about the deal or its rationale until the announcement is made. For acquired staff in particular, the first HR concern is to address their deepest fears at being taken over and to arrest the range of dysfunctional behaviours that typically follow (see Chapter 11). If the acquisition is horizontal or if closures and lay-offs are envisaged, fears on both sides have to be addressed.

There are two schools of thought about how much information to disclose to employees around the time of the announcement.

- One is to tell very little about any reorganisation that is planned and instead give an upbeat message about the benefits of the deal for both firms (synergies, improved competitiveness, repositioning for the future, and so on). The usual justification is that too much detail too early might upset staff even further and create a backlash. In practice, however, it is often an excuse for lax implementation planning and not having answers to questions that both boards know will be asked.

- The alternative approach is to give staff as much information as possible. The realistic merger preview – or better still, the realistic job preview – is to be as open and up-front and specific as possible with all levels of staff about the likely consequences of the acquisition. It also assumes that staff who are typically highly responsible are also mature and responsible enough to handle any news that may be unsettling.

The arguments in favour of the realistic preview are persuasive. Directly after a takeover, acquired management and staff are looking for a clear picture of the future. They want to know where the new owners intend to take the company. They are not necessarily seeking a detailed blueprint. That's sometimes impossible at the early stages. But they are looking for a clear vision or scenario about the future.

In particular, they want to know:

- Will a new management team be taking over or will existing managers stay in place?
- Will business directions change?
- What is the new owner's business philosophy?
- What major changes are intended in the first year or so?
- Will there be changes to contracts and conditions of employment?

These are basic questions in any acquisition.

Being open and up-front with staff in the early days following a takeover directly addresses their deepest inner fears and reduces counterproductive behaviour. It quickly reassures those staff who will be unaffected. And it gives others time to plan options if necessary – either preparing for changes to their existing jobs or moving to new positions elsewhere (see Box 12.2).

Box 12.2   Telling the truth: the realistic merger preview

Should employees be given the fullest information as early as possible about the likely impact of a merger on their jobs and careers? Schweiger and DeNisi (1991) put this proposition to the test in a merger of two *Fortune 500* companies.

Two plants in the same division that was to be merged were given different amounts of information. Employees in one plant (the control plant) got a typical merger communication – a letter from the CEO explaining that the merger would improve the competitive position of both firms by combining product lines and achieving economies of scale. That meant some people and jobs would become redundant. No specific details were given, other than to assure employees that there would be as few adverse effects as possible and that further information would be forthcoming as soon as it became available.

The other plant (the experimental plant) got the same letter – and a lot more. Employees got specific information concerning lay-offs, transfers, promotions and demotions, and changes to pay, jobs and benefits that would take place in their work units. They received a special merger newsletter every fortnight. There was a telephone hotline for specific questions, with answers posted on notice boards and appearing in the newsletter. And each department had a weekly briefing with the plant manager.

Measured differences were significant over a four-month period. In both plants, the announcement triggered significant increases in uncertainty and stress, and significant reductions in various factors including commitment, job satisfaction, and perceptions that the company was trustworthy, honest and caring.

But after a month the differences began to show. In the control plant with limited information, problems associated with the announcement continued to reverberate. After three months, morale declined so rapidly that the plant manager became seriously alarmed. In the experimental plant, behaviour stabilised and most measures returned to their pre-announcement levels. (Schweiger and DeNisi, 1991)

This is a compelling piece of research. It is one of the few empirical studies in the merger field that is rigorous, statistically sound and pursued in the best social science tradition. The control and experimental plants were matched on as many dimensions as possible. They were hundreds of miles apart (in different states) to ensure that neither became aware of what was happening in the other. Eight different measures of employee morale were utilised. And data were collected systematically at key stages throughout the study.

The evidence is convincing. In the weeks following a takeover, giving employees as much information as possible not only reduces individual fears. Collectively, it reinforces morale and commitment and minimises counter-productive behaviours. It also minimises rumour and the alternative scenarios that feed on speculation. And it sends an important signal that the new owners are honest and direct.

Meeting the New Owners

Acquired staff will want to meet the new owners. They want to look them in the eyes and maybe press the flesh and hear at first-hand the new vision and any changes that are to happen. Many firms arrange some sort of social event, a get-together for both sides, soon after the announcement. Sometimes these events are on an impressive scale.

> There is one big problem with such gatherings. They often turn out to be stage-managed ceremonies; one-way good-news theatres. It is not uncommon for acquired staff to come away brimming with vision and strategy and wine – and none the wiser about what is to happen to them and their jobs. Social gatherings are great for social purposes, for meeting opposite numbers. But they are no substitute for the realistic merger preview.

That's why seasoned acquirers often take two approaches. One is to host a get-together as a celebration of the merger – a fun event but with work overtones. The other is to meet and communicate in detail with newly acquired staff as an integral part of the merger preview. And that can take many forms depending on the size and type of acquisition.

- A major UK food company acquired an old established English chocolate manufacturer with over 200 years of tradition behind it. To quote their production director:

    'On the first day, the entire board flew up. They toured the factory and met everybody, from top to bottom. They explained what was to happen (business to be grown but to remain intact; only marketing to move to HQ). It was impressive to see their chairman in a white hat and overalls sitting with the production workers – long question-and-answer sessions. No questions were barred.'

- A UK industrial firm bought out a rival chemical business with distribution depots across the country. On the second day, the divisional MD and his team met all the factory managers then got the production workers together to explain exactly what was to happen and what the changes to their contracts would mean. Then came several weeks of legwork.

  'I went across country and talked to the staff at all their establishments, some as small as five.'

- When two retail chains merged, the acquiring CEO arranged a series of one-day regional conferences for all area managers. These were working conferences with members of both boards attending.

  'They all got the same message – no frills, no job losses and double your profit in three years. "Impossible", they said. We then explained what they needed to do and they spent the day planning how they would do it.'

There are many other ways of communicating in depth to acquired staff. And if acquirers don't arrange it, target CEOs can take the initiative.

'Before the deal was signed, I agreed a series of dates with their chairman for him to visit our main centres – tours, dinners, speeches. His willingness to see everyone and speak of his ambitions for the group was significant … I took steps to enhance the new owner, to build up respect for him.'

Social events bring together a broader mix of people for different purposes. They rarely meet the business and psychological needs that the realistic merger preview fulfils. But social events are important for getting people on-side and winning commitment. In some countries they are *very* important. That's why, when acquiring abroad, it is wise and worthwhile to find the norm and run with it.

In North America, for example, it's often said that business is not just a way of life. Business *is* life. Work and social life are much more closely intertwined than, say, in Europe. Managers and staff expect high levels of social mixing around work and especially after a takeover. If new bosses don't arrange a get-together, acquired staff might feel slighted. They might feel that an important and taken-for-granted aspect of their culture has not been recognised.

'In the States, get-togethers where ranks are broken and everyone is on first-name terms are essential for winning commitment to the new owners.'

'They are intensely committed to *their* business plans, *their* marketing plans … They will talk all night about ambitions, new directions, and where we as new owners might take them.'

Small national differences, perhaps, but important for building commitment – something novice acquirers in the US might overlook.

In Russia and China (and other countries with a history of tight state control) post-merger social functions have a strong political dimension. They are essential for acknowledging and bringing together parties in the wider environment who claim a stake in how the business is run. How senior the guests should be depends on the size and type of merger or joint venture. Apart from top managers, obvious candidates are politicians and government officials, civic dignitaries, and major suppliers and customers (often another branch of the state). Less obvious but worth recognising are the 'shadowy figures' whose influence can make all the difference. Take the example of a German firm acquiring in Russia.

'We knew they couldn't meet their energy bills and were paying in kind to an official who "fixed it" with Gazprom. We didn't know who he was until he introduced himself at the reception and said he wanted to continue helping the company. It was a racket – truckloads of stuff were disappearing from the factory. But given where he was and given what we wanted, we had to work something out … Two years later we ran into a big problem. He smoothed it out – never found out how.'

Two examples from different corners of the world – but they illustrate the importance of finding the norm and running with it. And targets are best placed to help in this respect.

Other Good Practice Tips

Lock the Brains In

This will already have been done for top people as part of the deal – perhaps owner-managers on a fixed-term earn-out or key executives and boffins on special contracts. Further down the firm there are likely to be executives and experts whose capabilities are special and worth making the extra effort to retain. In the first 30 days, identify these people and consider whether any special contracts or silver handcuffs or enhanced budgets and status would be appropriate.

Avoid Acquisition Drift

Even if no job losses or major changes are planned, after a few months good people often drift away. There can be many reasons. It may be that they do not like some aspect of the acquirer's approach or strategy or style. In owner-manager companies, there may be resentment among other managers at the owner selling out and profiting from what they perceive to have been a collective effort over the years. Whatever the reason, it is usually a loss to the business.

If key people have been identified for perhaps special consideration, listen carefully to what they have to say about the takeover and any changes that are planned. Often they have their finger on the pulse of the company and their views are worth listening to.

Move Fast in Critical Areas

There is a popular merger maxim: '*Move fast while they are expecting change.*' Take it seriously – but selectively – especially in the first 30 days. In critical areas it is vital to move fast – like filling key responsibility positions, integrating financial and IT systems and getting all essential controls in place (see Chapter 9). Likewise for dealing with any loss-making parts of the acquired business.

Otherwise, it makes sense to spend time in consultation and explanation with the people involved and to check out points of detail. Change is always easier when those affected are brought on-side and their sharp-end experience is factored into any plans.

Remember also that acquired staff usually know when things are not as they should be. They know when business is slipping away or when administration is slack. If they are expecting change and nothing happens, acquirers often lose credibility. There are numerous reported examples of firms acquiring top-heavy targets in other countries and not slimming them down early out of fear of offending foreigners.

Be Generous

If downsizing or closures are planned, inform people as early as possible and *be generous*. Mobilise HRM on both sides well in advance to plan internal transfers. If redeployment is not an option, bring in headhunters, recruitment agencies and any other support functions to give whatever help is needed.

Have them primed and ready to talk options with each person as soon as the news is given. It costs very little – and is trivial compared to acquisition transaction costs.

Don't Just Walk Away

Closing a plant that is the mainstay of a local economy can impact severely on the wider community. Even if severance terms appear generous, don't just shut down and walk away. Start working early with trade unions and local officials to plan how best to compensate the community and to lay the seedcorn for future enterprise in the area. Managerial expertise is often the scarce resource and large corporations usually have it in abundance. Remember also that everyone's situation is different. In areas of high unemployment, the part-time driver or cleaner who is laid off may be the sole breadwinner for a whole family.

Outpost Problem People

Act quickly and decisively with any managers – on either side – who obstruct integration. One solution (if it is feasible) is to outpost them to a position where they can create less mischief. Don't wait until problems accumulate. Identify the signs early and act swiftly.

30-Day Review

Hold a 30-day review to ascertain whether progress is on target and to assess problem areas and gauge commitment. American companies often use attitude surveys as a routine part of personnel work. If that's the practice, get data on the first 30 days. Otherwise use whatever informal soundings are appropriate.

In Summary

First actions are critical for winning commitment and avoiding many of the problem behaviours that bedevil integration. Even if acquired staff are warmly disposed towards the new owners, first contact can turn them off and subsequently eat into the value of the deal. Some of the most important actions for any acquisition have been outlined. Others will be firm-specific and judgement has to be used on what else is essential.

At the time of the announcement, there has to be an agreed implementation plan in place where strategy, communication and actions are all tightly coordinated. All the left hands must know what the right hands are saying and doing. The integration manager is central for ensuring that this happens.

In most instances, there are few excuses for not having a detailed implementation plan at closure with top managers on both sides clear on what is to happen and how. Target shadowing time is usually sufficiently long for

---

Box 12.3   How not to win friends

Many are the tales about bungled implementation, crude actions and crass communication. Here are just five.

1. A chairman sent a welcoming video to staff at all branches of an acquired business telling them, among other things, how over the years he had been impressed with their honesty and integrity in the way they did business. As staff listened, teams of workmen with security escorts were rushing round every branch changing locks on all the safes and doors.
2. In a media merger, two senior managers went through the target's open-plan offices, ripping calendars off walls and throwing personal effects from desks into black dustbin liners. 'We're the new masters now', they shouted.
3. The first words of a US executive to newly acquired French staff were in English: 'Bet you're all scared you're gonna lose your jobs.' As fear gripped the staff, he stood in silence ... with a big, wide, menacing grin.
4. An old established family firm was acquired by a profit-by-any-means company. On the second day, the chairman laid on a small reception to welcome their new owners. Three not-very-senior managers turned up. They ignored the reception and went directly through all the offices identifying antiques and valuables and labelling them for auction – including the entire contents of the chairman's office.
5. A chain of electrical shops was acquired by a retail giant. The first staff knew they had been taken over was when they arrived for work and found themselves locked out and a new name above the door. A spokesperson for the acquiring side explained to the press: 'We had to keep the customers out.'

capability profiles to be at hand when negotiations begin and for a detailed plan to be in place when negotiations end.

However, if planning is incomplete or if acquirers choose to delay some announcements until they have conducted further audits of the target, the integration manager has two essential tasks.

1. To ensure that the message given in the merger preview process is as accurate, realistic and unambiguous as possible.

2. To exercise tight control over the boundaries of the two firms to keep apart what has to be kept apart until a decision is made otherwise. Managers on the acquiring side often try to intervene with opposite numbers in the target and it has to be resisted. Roving bands of executives shooting from the hip is invariably disastrous (see Box 12.3).

There is one final point about get-togethers that should be emphasised. The more the two sides are brought together in a managed atmosphere, the more likely it is that hostility and suspicion and stereotyping will be reduced. It can never be eliminated, but perhaps its most damaging effects can be minimised. If it is not done, some innovative managers further down will try to do it themselves – and that can have very unpleasant consequences (see Box 12.4).

Box 12.4 Lone Ranger bites the bullet

The difficulties in merging rival marketing staff are the stuff of legend. Here's another example. A marketing executive in a *Fortune 100* firm found himself in a post-merger situation where he was managing a hybrid staff, including his counterpart from the acquired firm. And the two teams were not blending well. There was low morale, jealousies, petty exchanges, poor cooperation and in-fighting – and it was crippling productivity.

This went on for several months until, as a last-ditch attempt to unify his staff, the executive took them to his fishing cabin for a weekend. He had hoped that some frank discussions around a relaxing lake setting would relieve tensions and get rid of some of the hostility that had been building up.

The discussions turned out to be more than frank. Instead of leading to reconciliation and accord, they led to a fist fight! (Robino and DeMeuse, 1985, pp. 33–9)

CHAPTER 13

The Implementation Environment

'When there is a threat – fears for job security – the effect is to forget about the team spirit and worry about Number One. It is disastrous for everyone else.'

(Finance Director, leisure)

Winning over acquired employees in the early weeks is necessary, but not sufficient. Commitment and morale have to be sustained during the many months (and sometimes years) it can take to bring two companies together. This in turn hinges on how acquirers handle the implementation – how they manage acquired staff and how they manage what, in horizontal mergers, can be a long and tortuous process of organisational change.

Stage 3: Winning Long-Term Commitment

Very little is known about how best to proceed here. It is another 'black hole' in management research. However, important insights were gained from the study: *Acquisitions – The Human Factor* (Hunt et al., 1987). In each of the 40 acquisitions under investigation, the insights came from those key managers who had 'hands on' responsibility for integrating the two companies together. They came from both sides and were mostly CEOs, managing directors, vice-presidents, specialist integration managers, former board members with merger experience, or owner-managers.

These acquisitions were all very different. No two were alike. The effectiveness of implementation across the sample (as agreed by both sides) ranged from highly successful through to truly awful. Nevertheless, seven common factors stood out. Seven dimensions of acquirer behaviour *common to all acquisition types and industries* were identified as having a direct impact upon the quality of implementation:

If acquirer actions lay at one end of each dimension, the effect on implementation and on employee morale and commitment was generally positive.

Conversely, if actions lay at the other end of each dimension, the effect was generally negative. Implementation was more troublesome and morale dropped (see Figure 13.1).

Interestingly, there was very little variance between how each side rated the implementation, although acquirers tended to rate their actions higher than targets. However, there was divergence around the question: *would you want go through with it again?* Managers from the acquiring side were usually positive, but many target managers were ambivalent. From a business perspective many said they probably would. But from a personal perspective, the experience of being taken over was so traumatic and destabilising that many had absolutely no wish ever to repeat it.

Honourable Rhetoric

The issue here is *acquirers sticking to their word* – that assurances given during negotiations and promises made during the first few weeks are strictly adhered to. Two acquiring CEOs make the point very clearly:

'Two or three years is nothing in the lifetime of a company. Misleading statements and falsehoods early on, catch up on you and your integrity and credibility are gone. In terms of a medium-term to long-term investment, it can destroy morale completely.'

'Slick, off-the-cuff promises and glib assurances do you no good.'

Target managers would agree. It is often reported that trust and commitment to new owners are enhanced considerably when managers from earlier acquisitions say: 'they stuck to their word' or 'they did what they said they would do'. When acquiring firms come with this sort of reputation and it is evident from the beginning, it can boost confidence at all levels of the acquired management team.

However, failure to keep assurances is not always deliberate. Sometimes there is duplicity, but more commonly the problem is either (a) over-optimistic promises that prove hard to deliver, or (b) weak central control over communications and who does the communicating. For example:

- A corporation assured all acquired staff that they would know of any job losses within six months. When six months came, details had still not been finalised. Fear and panic gripped the company and there was

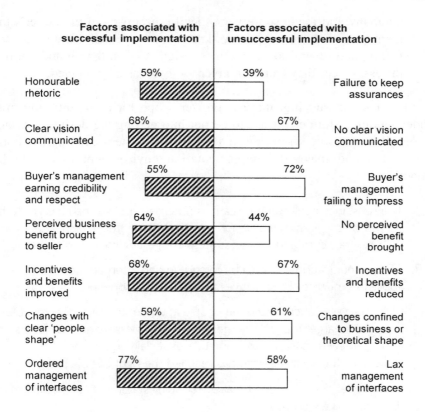

Figure 13.1   Critical acquirer actions that shape the implementation environment

Notes: The acquisitions were divided into two groups: those where implementation was judged by both sides to be Successful or Very Successful (55%), and those where implementation was judged to be 'So-So' or Unsuccessful or Very Unsuccessful (45%). This gives the left-hand and right-hand sides of the figure.

The percentages *on each dimension* indicate the extent to which both sides highlighted the factor as contributing significantly to the quality of implementation. On the left-hand side are the percentages of successful implementations where the factor was singled out as helping implementation; on the right-hand side where the factor was highlighted as contributing significantly to implementation difficulties.

Source: © Reproduced with permission from Hunt, J.W., Lees, S., Grumbar, J., and Vivian, P. (1987), *Acquisitions – The Human Factor*, London: London Business School and Egon Zehnder International, page 79

a visible decline in performance because there had been no communication with managers and staff across the period.

• A UK company was making a further acquisition in the US. An existing US subsidiary assumed that it would have some influence over the new company and made some very specific promises to the target's top management that headquarters knew nothing about. There was bad feeling and several top executives resigned when they found out that the assurances they had been given were not as they seemed.

When mergers are big, there is greater scope for ambiguity and mis-understanding. More effort has to be put into getting the desired message across. But even when firms are small, four simple steps can improve communication and make the implementation environment that little bit smoother.

1. The substance of all communications (internal and external) has got to be *derived directly from a carefully formulated implementation plan.* There must be a central script and a clear strategy for getting messages across.

2. All communications have to be joined up and internally consistent. That applies as much to PR initiatives as to executive briefings for staff.

3. Make sure assurances reach the people at whom they are directed. Don't just rely on target top management to get the message across. Take steps consistent with custom and practice especially in another country, to make sure the right message has reached the right people.

4. Last and very obvious: don't make misleading statements or give promises that are unlikely to be kept.

Clear Business Vision

A clear business vision reduces uncertainty at the time of the announcement. It also provides focus and direction throughout the implementation stage and beyond. When all parties share the same broad vision of the future, it becomes a shared mindset component that pulls together thought and action. It provides a justification for any changes that are to happen and prepares staff to take change on board. And it helps to keep eyes more on the ball, more on the market and competition, at a time when attention is invariably drawn inwards.

That much is pretty obvious. It's what the 'excellence' gurus have been saying for years. But what happens when no vision is put across or just a vague scenario is left in the air? As always, an information vacuum is filled with speculation. Second-guessing goes into overdrive as people create their own visions of the future based on their own interpretation (and misinterpretation) of acquirer actions. Then they compete among themselves on the basis of these scenarios.

Implementation hubris is the result – rumour and counter-rumour, lots of political manoeuvring, interdepartmental conflict, managers on the acquiring side trying to control and maybe destabilising their opposite numbers, and an atmosphere that can make good people jump ship. It can also waste valuable time and resources (see Box 13.1).

Box 13.1   Digging a hole to the future

Take the case of the corporate merger where implementation had yet to be worked out and it had been left to acquired managers in each division to announce the takeover to their own staff. No implementation details meant they got a very loose and general picture of the future. The announcement was typical of many – some meaty projections of future earnings and market shares all topped with a rich sauce of merger-speak (building on strengths, repositioning, cooperation and sharing, synergies, and so on).

Each division 'heard' something slightly different. That in turn led each to enact different views of the future. Over the next year (with nods and winks from headquarter executives) the divisions began to reprioritise their R&D, shelve promising projects and dust off others, recast budgets and move executives around – all in preparation for 'their' view of the future to happen.

When the implementation plan was finalised, it was not as anticipated and none of the divisions were ready for it. Considerable amounts of time and effort and resources had been wasted – digging themselves into holes that made integration that much harder.

Earning Credibility and Respect

A third contributor to long-term commitment is winning the respect of acquired managers, especially at middle to senior levels. That doesn't come automatically. Even if a deal makes sound business sense and early actions are textbook copies, the credibility test is how the management team from the acquiring side conduct themselves on target premises. Integration managers, turnaround managers, project managers and functional chiefs all have to act in ways that *earn* credibility and respect – qualities that cannot be bought.

Wise acquirers recognise this. They ensure that the executives they send across have the requisite mix of personal and business and leadership skills. And that the executives know their reputations are on the line. One CEO put it very clearly:

> 'Irrespective of their past achievements, as far as running *this* company is concerned, our key players start off with *zero credibility*. They must win respect from the start in a personal capacity. This then creates a following that makes change easier.'

This is very different from the typical attitude of superiority by virtue of buying the other company – 'We own you, so we control you and you do as we say.' It's a different attitude – and it pays dividends in the longer term. For example, in more than half of the successful implementations in *Acquisitions – The Human Factor*, targets reported that the factor that particularly won them over was being visibly impressed by the behaviour of the new management team they came into contact with – for example:

- The management team's knowledge of the technology or the industry.

- Their thoroughness and diagnostic capabilities displayed during the post-deal audits. 'They asked a few questions, and were able to look through walls.'

- In former family-owned businesses, the 'sheer professionalism' of the implementation team was often sufficient to win the loyalty that once had been accorded to a founding father.

- In badly managed companies, it was the speed with which the acquiring team identified problem areas and took remedial action.

- Speed of capability transfer and getting it to work.

- In horizontal mergers it was their leadership and social skills in bringing rivals together and getting them working as a team.

Although every deal was different, these were the sorts of factors that shifted mindsets and won them over to the acquirer's way of thinking. And that in turn made change easier.

By way of contrast, in more than 70% of the unsuccessful implementations the behaviour of the management team from the acquiring side was also singled out. Not only did it fail to impress. It often also aroused levels of hostility that made integration significantly harder and performance more elusive. Examples included:

- Conflict within the implementation team with each pulling in different directions.

- Leaving acquired staff in an information vacuum about what was to happen.

- Weak understanding of the industry they had bought into.

- Executives appointed from the acquiring side to run specific functions and being out of their depth or not understanding the technology they were managing.

- Fast-trackers using implementation as a proving ground – and proving they didn't have the requisite disposition and experience.

- Imposing change based on inaccurate preconceptions of the business.

- Relating to acquired managers in a roughshod and cavalier manner.

On the last point, it surprised many targets just how *tribal* implementation can be. When top managers adopt an attitude of superiority, it can extend through the ranks of the acquiring firm. Even when they don't, middle managers can adopt negative stereotypes and a 'them and us' attitude towards the target. Sometimes it is latent, under the surface. Other times it is quite overt (like saying to opposite numbers: *'If you were any good, why did you let yourselves get taken over?'*). Or there can be the rival football team syndrome (*'We're better than you'*). And even denigration (*'That lot couldn't even spell merger'*).

Readers who have been through a merger will no doubt be able to provide other examples. Often we don't want to look at them at all because it is always a little embarrassing that competent and well-salaried managers behave in this way. Yet the behaviours are so prevalent in mergers, especially between former competitors. We can interpret them in various ways – reactions to stress and uncertainty, or inevitable group dynamics, or culture clashes. Whatever the interpretation, they hamper integration and eat into the value of the deal.

That's why it is so important to select managers for the implementation team who understand and can handle these dynamics, and have the appropriate blend of personal, business and leadership abilities to pull the two sides together successfully in the planned way.

That way they earn credibility and respect for themselves and for the acquiring firm. Every acquisition is different. Every implementation is different. But every implementation team carries their firm's culture and reputation with them. They are the visible front.

Bringing Perceived Business Benefits

Way back in 1987, Michael Porter proposed the 'better off' test for mergers. Essentially, it argued that all sides should be able to see that they should be 'better off' as a result of a deal, not just one side. Looking back, it seemed a reaction against the waves of hostile and asset-stripping takeovers of the 1970s where targets often gained little, if at all (Porter, 1987). However, the test is eternally valid. *All* levels and *all* parties with an interest in both firms should see advantages coming from the deal.

Typically, target boards and senior executives can see all the 'better off' possibilities in detail. They've got the big picture – the new strategy moves, the efficiency and synergy possibilities, the new investment programme, the rosy projections. Only some of this detail trickles down to middle levels. And still less makes its way to the lower ranks.

But all levels look for evidence that business prospects are better under new management. It is important that they see 'better off' in real, tangible ways and not just in statements of intention and strategic hope. If lower levels can see visible business benefits, esteem for the acquirer usually rises, as does commitment, and this helps to make implementation that bit smoother.

Clearly, what satisfies the 'better off' test varies with each firm. For neglected businesses, an immediate injection of resources to develop and expand the business may be the answer. For firms in a market slump, delivering new marketing and design and retailing initiatives can be seen right down to the shop floor. Likewise for firms with a capability deficit. Access to new R&D, new technologies and new systems are all visible signs of improvement, as is access to new global markets. When various levels of the target can say: 'They realised our plans and ambitions', it is an enormous boost for morale.

The simple point to note is that levels of the acquired firm that are not privy to the merger calculations and who do not meet the implementation team nevertheless need to see the benefits from being taken over. This can boost morale significantly and make change smoother.

Sometimes acquirers will *say* that they are bringing benefits to the business and may actually believe it, but not all translate into greater organisation-wide commitment. There are two situations where this can happen.

1. Where the benefits are enjoyed by only a small coterie of senior managers. This can be seen as a 'fat cat' syndrome and it is divisive.

2. Where target managers don't feel any ownership of changes that are happening. Psychological ownership of any improvements must reside with target management. They have got to feel that *they* are in charge and that *they* are driving them.

For example, businesses that are 'fat and flabby' usually benefit from initiatives to shake out the cash – but incumbent managers must be allowed to take the credit for improved levels of performance. Likewise when turning round underperforming units. The drive and the ideas come from the new owners. But psychological ownership of the improvements must lie with the target managers. They have got to feel that *they* have turned their business round.

Retaining Incentives and Benefits

Retaining or improving incentives and benefits is central to morale and commitment. It won't guarantee a smoother implementation, but any reductions in the package (incentives, benefits, pension entitlement, career prospects, stock options, etc.) are likely to cause problems. Most managers recognise this. In fact, nearly all acquirers will *say* that the incentive and benefit package offered is an improvement on what existed previously. However, 30–40% of acquired managers will disagree. So what causes the mismatch?

- *Subjective perceptions.* A lot hinges on the *subjective* perception of personally being 'better off'. That usually involves a trade-off between various elements of any new package. Thus, managers from small firms may accept a salary reduction for large-corporation career and pension prospects. Managers already in large corporations may not. Also important is whether new performance targets are perceived as attainable and non-threatening. If managers are told: 'Make X% ROI or be sold off', that is sure to colour their perception – even if incentives are generous.

- *The culture influence.* Most incentive schemes are culture-dependent. They rely upon a particular way of thinking and a particular style of managing. If acquirers try to impose their own formulae on targets, it doesn't follow that they will share the same assumptions about the linkage between incentives and performance. For an incentive formula to transfer across and work, especially at lower levels, it usually requires a similar culture to be in place – similar thinking and priorities and ways of doing things – and that can take time to introduce.

- *Performance criteria.* A popular approach is to retain the *level* of financial incentives on the target side but to try to shift the *focus* more towards performance. In principle, it's fine. But in practice, selecting the most appropriate performance criteria across different levels and functions can prove fiendishly difficult. There are at least three challenges here.

  1. Selecting performance goals that underpin and reinforce the *acquisition strategy* as well as the business strategy.
  2. Choosing the right mix of 'hard' and 'soft' performance criteria, both short and long-term.
  3. Getting the appropriate balance between individual and group incentives, and also setting the respective ceilings for each.

The last point is especially important when companies from highly individualistic countries (like North America) acquire in countries with a more collective or egalitarian spirit (like in the Far East or Southern Europe) or vice versa. For example, top pay-levels in Europe are typically 12 to 15 times the average salary or wage. In the US, the multiple can be as much as 100 times the average (Henzler, 1992).

- *Selective incentives* is another tricky area – like improving incentives at the top but not lower down. It might work on the acquiring side if that is the accepted philosophy. But if thinking is different on the target side, managers might interpret it as a 'fat cat' syndrome. On the other hand when a large corporation acquires perhaps a small knowledge-based firm, letting the owner keep his or her Porsche or Jaguar might breach company-car guidelines. But it can be important for locking the brains in – and also signalling to the acquired business that they are still intact and cohesive (see Box 13.2).

- *Benefit packages* are another minefield. Different bits have a different attractiveness, have a different cultural significance, and are bounded by different legislation in every country. That's why in foreign deals, seeking the best *local* advice is important – and absolutely essential if legislation is subject to change. Acquirers have got to find the norm and *understand* it before making any changes.

Box 13.2   Big hat, no throttle

What happens when a lean-and-hungry company takes over a fat-and-flabby company and decides to standardise company car sizes downwards? According to one acquiring HR director, some astonishing compensation.

About a year after the merger, the HR director was visiting one of the acquired factories when something odd struck him. The car park seemed to have far too many high-capacity cars. He checked the records but all seemed to be in order with the new car policy. So he scratched his head and had a think.

Then all became clear. Many of the managers whose engines had been downsized had also felt personally downsized. So they hit on a simple and symbolic way to restore their egos to size. They went down to the local car dealership and purchased engine-capacity badges to stick on their cars that were more in line with what they had previously.

Take a simple example. For North American managers, an equity stake in the business – no matter how small – is an important symbol of involvement and commitment. UK companies in particular often fail to recognise its significance and remove the option post-deal because it is not company policy at home. Acquired managers see it as an act of exclusion.

As a general rule, if a firm is doing well it is often wise to leave incentives and benefits alone and wait until there is a downturn in business or some other significant event before making any changes – even if it means living with extravagance for two or three years.

Most important of all is communicating the rationale for any alterations to incentives and benefits. Managers have got to know clearly and unambiguously *why* changes are happening and *what* they are intended to achieve. Don't leave them to guess the meaning and intent of any changes. They have to be crystal clear about what the alterations expect them to deliver.

Change with a Clear 'People Shape'

The last two items are about how organisational change is implemented. First is the phrase: *Change with a clear 'people shape'*. It has a particular meaning.

Any major process of organisational change has to start by recognising how people make organisations 'happen' and in particular how managers make structures 'happen'.

Central to this is the idea of 'organisation in the mind' – that organisation structures are essentially *subjective* entities and not the reified and supposedly objective entities typified by organisation charts in change manuals.

Managerial psyches are the fundamental components of structure and not appendages to structure as depicted in so much of organisation theory.

This is not mainstream thinking so it needs to be explained.

When managers are going about their jobs and pursuing their various goals and coordinating with one another, they navigate around their enterprises with mental maps – maps 'in the mind' – of their own bit of responsibility space and how it relates to adjacent responsibility spaces. These maps are internal representations of bits of structure, and can be thought of as having a whole series of pathways or action routes that lead from problems to solutions.

Putting it very simply: depending on the problem to be solved there are some action-routes that are direct and unobstructed (*My problem; I solve it*). Some routes belong to other people (*My problem; he solves it*). And there are fuzzy routes (probably the majority) that meander in and out of other responsibility spaces where action is negotiable (*Let's decide who does what*) depending on the problem in question.

Managers create their own maps of action routes with themselves at the centre. That's what managerial autonomy is all about. Obviously, there are features on the maps. There are invisible blocks (like the influence of culture). There are 'no-go' areas – some with high walls; others with peep-through fences. And there are constraints (like budgets and the 'dos and don'ts' from on top and from peers).

But there are also many choices (like management style and selecting the limits of individual responsibility and ways of manoeuvring around constraints) that make each manager's action map quite distinct and personal. However – and this is the vital point – each map must have sufficient overlap and sufficient points of dovetail into adjacent maps for an organisation to work with a coordinated smoothness.

These individual mental maps when all joined together are the *real* organisation structure; the organisation structure in action; the structure that really enables the enterprise to function as it does.

Implicit in this description are a myriad of invisible relationships and taken-for-granted understandings and negotiated arrangements that insiders share but outsiders can barely glimpse.

Major change (like structural merging) throws all this in the air. Psychologically, it is like the aftermath of an earthquake. Familiar landmarks disappear. Action routes are blocked. There is a new landscape with new features, and managers need time to develop new maps and new ways of managing – renegotiating boundaries with other managers, letting go of some responsibilities and connecting up to others, sorting out reporting lines, getting controls in place, establishing new understandings, and so on.

For all this to happen smoothly, the most important precondition is that *managers have got to see themselves in any new structure before they can act*. This is vital – yet often overlooked in practice. New structures regularly get imposed on targets (or sometimes on both firms) that turn out to be impenetrable from an action perspective.

It doesn't matter how obvious a new structure might seem. Even if it works well on the acquiring side, even if business schools have convincingly demonstrated its superiority – if managers can't see themselves in it and see how to navigate through it, the structure will have a 'theoretical shape', 'a shape that exists only on paper', disconnected from the day-to-day reality they work with.

Hence there are six important requirements for structural change to retain commitment.

1. Managers have got to 'see' themselves in any new structure. From their own 'inside-looking-around' perspectives, they have got to see how to move about and take action to make the new structure 'happen'.

2. Managers have got to know the *rules* by which they make the transition from where they are now to the new structure. For example, in horizontal mergers where only some managers are to survive, all need to know well in advance the final selection criteria. They need to know the rules of the race for getting from A to B.

3. New reporting lines must be clearly defined.

4. New career paths must be identifiable.

5. Networks of organisational relationships need to be substantially preserved.

6. Time and space must be allowed to develop new action maps and establish new understandings with other managers and scenario-test how critical contingencies will be handled, *before* the changes come into effect.

If these six conditions are satisfied, commitment to the new structure and smoother implementation should follow. Otherwise, protracted integration and manoeuvring are the most likely consequences as managers resist and try to reshape the intended structure into something they are more familiar with.

These behaviours often get labelled 'obstructive' or 'political', but they are not always deliberately so. They are natural psychological reactions to the frustration of sense-making – managers trying to make sense of how they fit into a new structure and how they are to make it 'happen' *from where they are at present*. Until some sense is made, everything gets slowed down.

Ordered Management of Interfaces

The final influence on commitment is the way the two organisations are brought together. It underscores yet again the pivotal role of the integration manager.

> Interfacing has to be tightly centralised with *one* senior person on each side having overall responsibility for bringing together what has to be brought together and keeping apart what has to be kept apart.

Interfacing is about *how* elements of each organisation are brought together – how the structural relationships described in Figure 10.1 are made to 'happen'. At its simplest, interfacing can involve little more than harmonising financial controls and IT systems (as when the target is to remain autonomous). At its most complex, it can involve full organisational merging (bringing together and harmonising structures, manufacturing systems, procedures, controls, management styles, HR practices and all the variables that typically get bundled together as culture – values, beliefs, priorities, assumptions, and similar).

The important finding from *Acquisitions – The Human Factor* was this. Regardless of what interfacing actually involves, in every acquisition where implementation was judged to be successful, two practices stood out.

> First, a clear policy decision was made about interfacing and unambiguously communicated to *all* senior and middle managers on *both* sides.

> Second, the policy was rigorously enforced by a senior person on each side.

- If the acquired company was to remain autonomous and separate, *one senior person* on each side had responsibility for ensuring that functions on one side did not attempt to control their opposite numbers. But when boundary regulation was lax, intervention in target management was commonplace. It had a destabilising effect, even although managers were mostly acting in good faith and believed their actions were beneficial.

- If a decision had been made about which functions and systems were to be merged, *one senior person* on each side was given overall responsibility for bringing it about. Their task was both to merge what had to be merged and to keep apart what was to be kept separate.

  Central coordination was especially important when much of the detail got delegated to a variety of individuals and committees. When there was no single overall authority in charge, integration tended to go off in different directions and according to different timetables – further complicating an already complex process.

- If there were to be no changes to the target until an integration plan had been worked out, again this was communicated to both sides and *one senior person* on each side ensured that premature changes were not attempted. But in the absence of a regulating authority, different functions began to anticipate the eventual outcome and started competing among themselves for supremacy.

The evidence was convincing. Lax management of the interfaces confounded and protracted the integration process and led to commitment problems – political manoeuvring, interfunctional conflict, uncertainty and 'both sides playing footsie under the table'. One HR director summed up his own experience thus:

> 'We had two management teams resenting each other during the first year. Each was trying to get the measure of the other before any changes were made. There were far too many of our people "sniffing around" the other side to see whom they would integrate into the company. Nobody had the job of picking up the ball and running with it.'

Note that the preventative aspect of interfacing (keeping the two sides apart) and the boundary regulation task (acting as a channel between both sides) are just as important as the enabling aspect (bringing the two sides together).

The skills outlined here are essential in *any* implementation team. They are absolutely crucial when the success of a deal depends on some capability transfer – especially R&D or 'know-how' – between the two firms. The ability to bring selected boffins together and weld them into a team while at the same time preventing their respective cultures getting in the way, is a very special skill.

Likewise in cross-border deals. Bringing together managers from different national cultures who are accustomed to different management styles and practices and getting them to work effectively as a team, again requires very careful boundary regulation and interfacing. It is another compelling argument for the specialist integration manager being involved early in acquisition planning (see Chapter 6). The skills required are highly specialist and very different from the usual finance and market skills that dominate acquisition planning.

In Summary

This and the previous chapter have discussed the factors that influence commitment – one of several goals that a merger HR strategy should be aiming to achieve. It is probably the most important goal to pursue because, if realised, other HR outcomes (reducing uncertainty, minimising post-merger conflict, improving flexibility, retaining quality staff, etc.) should follow more easily.

Commitment is a multidimensional concept and building it is a multistage process, involving both personality and situational factors. It is not something that can be engineered as an afterthought – it has to be integral to the entire acquisition planning process. Here we took a three-stage approach. First were some of the factors that can influence commitment at the top during negotiations. Then what needs to be done to reduce fears and secure commitment at the time of the announcement. And finally the factors that can be critical during the implementation period.

The three stages are not a blueprint for action. They contain only a compilation of research findings – although probably as good a compilation as any currently available. Taken together, they represent important elements of best practice – with as many of the elements to be aimed for *within the specific context of each merger*. If all are taken on board, there is certainly more than enough here to get any implementation off to a good start.

Part 5

Culture

CHAPTER 14

The Culture Concept

'Looking back, the closer I thought I was getting to their culture, the more it seemed to slip away. Even now, I'm not entirely sure what it was I was managing.'
(HR Director, pharmaceuticals)

Culture is one of the loosest terms in the management vocabulary. It is a word that rolls off the tongue – but definitions stick in the throat. People use culture in a wide variety of ways to capture different aspects of organisational and national life, often with little in common. That's one reason why the C-word has not been used much in earlier chapters.

Yet culture is prominent in merger thinking. Culture clashes are a common explanation for acquisition failure. Culture meshing is said to be the most difficult aspect of integration. Analysts who used to value mergers solely on figures now downgrade a deal if they think the cultures will be incompatible. So what exactly do the terms *culture* and *culture clash* really mean? And what does *meshing cultures* really involve managers doing?

These sorts of questions will be explored in the remaining pages. This chapter will explore the culture concept. The next will focus more on organisational culture in a national setting. The final two will have an international flavour. Across all four chapters some of the most important things an integration manager needs to be aware of will be outlined. But remember – as with the rest of the book – there are no 'how to do it' prescriptions. The emphasis is on how to *think* about doing it – ways of thinking about the culture concept that are useful in a merger context.

The Culture Concept

Grappling with the culture concept is not easy. Kluckholn and Strodtbeck (1961) identified 164 definitions of culture in anthropology, all of them different. More have been added since culture became a management buzzword. So starting with definitions may not be the best way forward. More helpful is to get a general flavour from the many ways the concept is used.

- For some management writers, culture is about *collective doing* – the acquired habits and behaviours and customs of a social group. In Deal and Kennedy's (1982) popular definition: 'It's the way we do things round here.'

- For others it is about *collective thinking* – about shared values and beliefs and assumptions and mindsets. In Gregory's (1983) phrase, culture is 'a system of meanings'.

- For many anthropologists, culture is a dark, multilayered world of myth, ritual, tradition and social heritage – so deep and mysterious that we can barely penetrate it. The best we can do in our lifetime is get a glimpse of how much we are prisoners of our own culture.

- Management writers (especially American) often take a simpler view. Culture is just another organisational variable, the last frontier of management – something objective and tangible that managers can rise above and control. If some gurus are to be believed, the possibilities for 'culture management' appear endless. Take the right approach and – *zap!* – vast reservoirs of untapped energy can be released inside a firm, galvanising employees and grinding rivals into the ground!

- In everyday use, culture is the civilisation or the historical development of a people as expressed in material and social form. Artifacts (such as art objects or architecture or technical achievements) and social features (styles of government, ceremonies, theatre and dance, patterns of greeting and meeting, use of language, gender roles, etc.) are looked upon as expressing something deeper about a country and how its people think.

- The parallels for *organisational* culture are artifacts (such as logos and office layouts and distinctive products) and prominent social features (such as management style, patterns of organising, get-togethers, dress codes, in-house jargon, levels of camaraderie, etc.). Again, these are seen as expressing something deeper about the firm – how its managers think and what they value and prioritise.

- Finally, culture is sometimes used as an explanatory term of last resort. If some aspect of a firm or a country can't be explained, we often fall back upon saying 'It's *because* of their culture' – as if that was a sufficient explanation and somehow said it all.

This is only a thumbnail sketch, but it shows some of the major ways culture is used – and how different they are in so many respects. That's why the concept is so slippery and hard to pin down. But several things stand out that should be noted.

Culture as Shorthand

The first point to note is that **culture is essentially a shorthand term**. It is shorthand for a whole range of social processes and attributes, all of them interrelated. Pick up the culture concept and a whole baggage of associated terms comes with it – myth, ritual, values, belief, religion, custom and practice, law, heritage, language, symbolism, and so on. And they are all linked together.

It's a bit like a compressed programme on a computer. Click on the icon and lots of seemingly different (but internally related) files burst forth. Or like the knots on a fisherman's net. Pick up one and all the adjacent knots come with it.[1] That's why a crowd of people will all nod that they understand roughly what culture means when someone asks them, but they are probably thinking about very different aspects.

Lenses

The lenses we look through to 'see' and interpret other cultures are important. We all carry our cultures with us and that shapes how we see other cultures. This has been a perennial problem in anthropology – Western researchers looking at primitive societies and projecting Western explanations into what they observe.

It is also a perennial problem in mergers. Managers from one side tend to interpret behaviours on the other side in terms of their own values and assumptions and not those that are actually driving the behaviours they see. Or seeing a similar procedure or practice on the other side and assuming that it has the same justification and significance as at home.

And it is a common problem in international management. Managers sometimes go into a foreign posting with the expectation that they will manage and be managed much the same as at home – then find themselves not fitting in and losing control.

Icebergs and Onions

The simpler and more superficial our view of culture, the easier it is to believe that culture can be controlled and managed. We often home in on the most superficial aspects, forgetting the iceberg metaphor. Only about 10% is visible – the other 90% is invisible, floating below the surface. Or the onion metaphor – that there are deeper and deeper layers of culture that have to be peeled away in order to get closer to an understanding.

In recent years there has been a flurry of popular books on cross-cultural management, in particular comparing US and Japanese styles of management. These identify the most obvious differences (some of the *whats* of each culture) but not always the *whys* – the history and tradition and thought processes that have made each what it is. The best we usually get is a Western (functional) interpretation of what lies beneath the Japanese iceberg – but not the indigenous (symbolic) view. With simple cross-cultural comparisons and non-indigenous explanations, the unwary can be seduced into believing that one side can be transformed into the other with relative ease.

Sometimes culture-management writers give the impression that an organisation is a self-contained universe in which all-powerful managers and business leaders not only can manage culture. They have near-total freedom to create – in an almost Genesis-like way – a tailor-made set of values, beliefs, rituals, myths and meanings that are solely in the interests of strategy and the bottom line. And all this can happen without any reference to the wider social and cultural environment of the firm. This obviously is not the case. So can we talk about managers *managing* culture in any meaningful way?

Managing Culture

Climate and Culture

The best way to start exploring organisational culture is to see organisations as subcultures of national culture. More accurately, to see each organisation in a country as a technological subculture of national culture, with visible points of distinctiveness and vast chunks of invisible sameness.

This allows us to separate out (analytically) the two parts of organisational culture – **organisational climate** (the superficial technological part, the 'sub' part) and **national culture** (the deep 'culture' part) (see Figure 14.1).

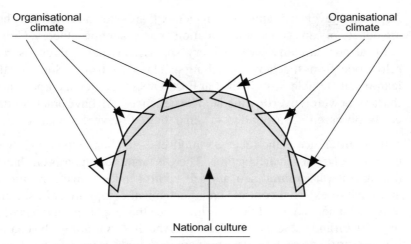

Each organisation in a country is a subculture of national culture with
visible points of distinctiveness and deep chunks of invisible sameness.

Figure 14.1   Two components of organisational culture

Managing Organisational Climate

Organisational climate – the superficial part – is the part that managers can
manage in a direct-and-control sense – just as they have done across the
decades. It's called social engineering of the workplace. That's usually what
is meant by the phrase *managing organisational culture*. Unpack the phrase
as popularly used and lots of familiar themes and practices come tumbling out
– leadership styles, flexible structures, redesigned jobs, decentralisation and
devolved autonomy, empowerment, human relations styles, and much more.
All the old chestnuts are there.

In the 1960s and 1970s, it would have been called managing organisational
norms – engineering the human side of the enterprise to maximise output
from a technical core. Now there is a new title and emphasis – managing
organisational cultures in the pursuit of a global mission. But at heart it is
still engineering the norms of the workplace in the interests of strategy and
the commercial imperative.

That – in a few sentences – summarises the vast bulk of what has been
passed off as culture management during the last two decades. However,
three differences are worth noting:

1. The Culture-word gives the process more gravitas and underscores its
   strategic nature – that the engineering is aimed at the whole organisation and not just at lower levels.

2. Aspiration levels for 'culture management' are real and tangible. They are not simply an accountant's creation or an academic's theory. Cross-cultural comparisons (even if very superficial) have given us *real* role-model firms that have something special to latch onto. Some are the lean-mean-flexible firms in the Far East. Others are global corporations that are (or were!) overflowing with 'excellence'. All have practices that can be observed and aspired to – even if they can never be reached.

3. A third difference is the focus on mindsets – to change the *thinking* of managers and not just their actions. There is far more emphasis on change through internal commitment and self-control and less on the traditional approach of external controls and mechanical compliance. In simpler terms, Skinner is out and Freud is in. Hence the emphasis on *internalising* mission and values across all levels. And *understanding* why change is necessary. And seeking commitment in *thought* as well as in action.

These differences apart, managing the *climate* part of organisational culture has a long history (i.e. managing the thinking and behaviour in a firm that is predominantly a product of a core technology). And there is plenty of evidence of new technologies and new systems and new structures transforming firms and industries. The manufacturing industry is a good example. New artifacts (automated production, desktop computers) and new social behaviours (delayering, outsourcing, etc.) have changed organisational thinking dramatically compared to how it was in most countries 20 years ago.

So changing thinking and practice in the *climate* part of organisational culture is perfectly possible provided, of course, that the changes are within limits permitted or legitimated in the wider environment. But what about going beyond these limits? What about trying to manage the other part of organisational culture (the larger and deeper part) that is a product of national culture? In short, can a tail wag a dog?

Managing National Culture

The national culture component in organisations cannot be managed in a direct-and-control sense. Organisations are microcosms (or technological subcultures) of the wider culture in which they are embedded and from which they draw their personnel. A Russian firm is fundamentally Russian; an American firm fundamentally American; a Chinese firm fundamentally Chinese, and so on. In practice, it is simply not possible to separate out national culture from organisational culture and proactively manage it in the same way as climate.

In every country, beliefs, attitudes, values, customs and practices, and a whole host of basic assumptions that exist outside the firm, exist inside the firm. Some are imposed by law. Some by powerful societal expectations. The rest are carried in, often unconsciously, by managers and staff. All the components of national culture are in national organisations and managers cannot rise above or step outside them. Nor can they direct and control the cultural inheritance of managers from other countries.

But it is possible to manage *aspects* of national culture if (a) management is redefined more modestly as interfacing and harmonising and bridging across differences, and (b) the focus is on the effects rather than the substance of culture. The key thing to remember in mergers is this:

> Culture only becomes a problem when there is a mismatch of values or beliefs or priorities or assumptions on each side *and the difference impacts upon performance.* If there is no impact on performance, there is no significant management problem.[2]

This holds true at the *organisational* level (between what are often called departmental subcultures); at the *national* level (between organisational cultures of merging firms in the same country) and at the *international* level (between firms in different national cultures).

> Culture clashes in a business context are almost always at the *edges* of culture. The corollary is that when foreign firms work together smoothly and their national cultures appear to bond, again it is at the *edges* of culture. On each side there is a massive core that remains distinct and separate.

Hence, in global mergers – but also in international management in general – managing national culture is mostly about managing friction points and major points of disjuncture, and figuring out how best to interface them.

- If two firms are to remain autonomous and separate, managing national culture is largely a HR issue. The first priority is to develop and select executives for key boundary positions who can mentally bridge the differences and build cohesive teams around them. Also important are reward packages tailored to context – like rewarding smooth implementation and team building and specific elements of acquisition strategy.

- If the firms are to merge structurally, the additional agenda is to design a new organisation – designing new structures and systems and practices that are acceptable to both sides. Or in other words, creating a new organisational climate within parameters legitimated by two different national cultures.

Developing Managers

Going Native

All this requires managers with a special type of understanding and experience. Global mergers need managers with sharp insights into how culture mentally programmes people from birth. In particular, they need insights into the taken-for-granted assumptions they carry with them and which govern their own thinking and behaviour. And they need similar insights into the other side. They need to understand the special meanings each side attaches to what they do.

Little of this can be gleaned in the hectic months of negotiation. Nor as executive tourists cocooned in airport Hiltons. It has to happen long before and very differently.

The best insights come from going native for a period and living another culture – from stepping out of familiar surroundings and mindsets and being immersed among a people who think and act differently. The insights come from living the daily routines in a foreign land and learning the language and managing foreign staff and discovering the thousand-and-one subtle ways in which they are the same and where they are different. Then gradually being taken into their sacred worlds of private thought, of religion and mystery and wonder and explanation, and learning what is totem and what is taboo and *why*. And then returning home to the familiar – and seeing it in a very different light.

That's the best way to learn about another culture, including one's own culture – stepping out and stepping back in again. It is risky and can be discomforting, and some managers might feel psychologically vulnerable. For a lot of the time there is no office or figures or targets to hide behind.

But armchair anthropologists have never liked it either. They have never liked it when one of their number went native and saw the world through the eyes of preindustrial tribes – and produced indigenous explanations of culture that turned upside down paper-based Western assumptions about tribal behaviour. And that's perhaps the most powerful lesson of anthropology. *Real* culture understanding and *real* culture experience go hand in hand.

A Definition of Culture

Finally, we need a snap definition of culture that goes beyond the hackneyed: 'The way we do things round here.' It has been around too long and anyway it's indistinguishable from a definition of a norm.

If you delve into social anthropology, three domains of interest stand out. First is artifacts (i.e. physical and tangible objects of culture). Second is social behaviour (ranging from everyday interactions through to major ceremonies). And the third is patterns of thinking (again ranging from day-to-day sense-making through to deep systems of belief and meaning). Combining all three gives us a working definition of culture acceptable to both anthropology and management.

Culture is the artifacts, socifacts and mentifacts of a people.

A bit unusual, perhaps, but it seems to say it all in one line. It is a definition that has already taken us a long way – and will take us further as we shall see in the following chapters.[3]

CHAPTER 15

Mergers and the Dynamics of Culture

'The cultures were very different. We had a HR director who set out to humanise the company – make it less oppressive, more like us. He damn near destroyed the business.'

(Managing Director, manufacturing)

The introductory notes to culture in the previous chapter are perhaps longer and more detailed than usual. However, with such a slippery concept as 'culture', detail is important – as much for clarifying how the term is being used here as for benchmarking how other writers use the term. Certainly, when we dip into the merger literature, culture understanding can be – shall we say – somewhat elastic! Box 15.1 provides a not untypical example.

Box 15.1   Cock-eyed culture

A few years ago, a management consultancy firm produced a report on merger management. It contained helpful tips for would-be acquirers in several areas – on restructuring targets and integrating divisions; on turning round troubled companies; on putting controls in place quickly; and tactics for getting the new business philosophy and style across to acquired managers.

The report was well written and fairly convincing – until the final section on culture. There in bold letters was a warning: *Whatever you do, don't touch the culture!*

If you think about it for a moment, this is nonsense.

Why is it nonsense to say *don't touch the culture*? One reason is that culture cannot be *touched* in the way that systems or controls or procedures can be touched – in the sense of being examined objectively and changed around. The culture of any organisation – whether the superficial climate part or the deeper national part – can only be inferred after lots of probing and ferreting around.

Culture is not 'up front'. Culture manifests itself *as a consequence* of what people do; its many components have to be deduced.

The beliefs, the values, the meanings, the basic assumptions and the logic that *really* drive the business (i.e. not the PR or the manufactured mission statements or the gloss in annual reports) can only be inferred from what managers do; from examining their actions and listening to what they say and then trying to piece together the mindsets and meanings that lie behind it all.

A second reason why the warning is nonsense is that to make any significant changes to a company is to change some part of its culture. Restructuring is to change the responsibility behaviours of managers and their thinking about why change is necessary. Changing controls is to change priorities and ways of pursuing them. Adopting a new philosophy means adopting new beliefs and values and assumptions about how business is to be conducted.

All of these changes seek to alter managerial behaviour and thinking, and that adds up to attempting to change at least part of the culture of the target. That's why it doesn't make sense to advocate change yet say: don't touch the culture. Nor does it make sense (as some other advisers suggest) to set up committees to plan the merging of the cultures irrespective of strategic logic of the deal or the degree of structural integration.

A common oversight is to view culture as comprising just the 'soft' or expressive elements in a company (like values or beliefs or basic assumptions) and not those aspects that are considered to be 'hard' (like structures or controls or procedures). This is to overlook how managers make both structures and cultures 'happen'. By their thoughts and actions managers are the agents – the enactors of structure and the bearers and perpetuators of organisational culture. A second (related) oversight is to overlook the connections, the dynamic interrelationship, between artifacts, behaviour and thought – the three essential components of culture.

A Working Model of Culture

The insights of Schein and Smircich are helpful here. These two authors have made perhaps the most significant and enduring contributions to our understanding of the dynamics of culture. In Schein's (1985) model, which should be familiar to many readers, culture is seen as operating at three levels:

- *visible artifacts and behaviour* (easy to identify but difficult to interpret without understanding their underlying logic)

- *espoused values* (the *stated* whys – the values people *say* they are following when they act as they do)

- *basic assumptions* (the *real* whys – the deep, taken-for-granted (perhaps even unconscious) assumptions that determine how members of a collective perceive and think and feel).

Schein's argument is that to really understand a culture it is necessary to probe down through all three levels. Likewise, to intervene in a culture, it may be necessary to tackle not just the public thinking but also the deepest basic assumptions that drive thought.

Smircich (1983) is more complex but amply repays careful reading. She identifies five fundamental ways of looking at culture – five sets of academic 'lenses' – each of which (being different) highlights different aspects of culture and leads to different interpretations. To understand an anthropologist's interpretations of culture, it is first necessary to examine the 'lenses' he or she is wearing. To get a fuller grasp of culture (and especially the many positions in anthropology), *all* the perspectives have to be taken on board.

The perspectives range from the objective to the subjective, from the visible and superficial through to the deeply psychological and unconscious. What is especially interesting about Smircich is that she covers broadly the same ground as Schein, but in five stages rather than three and in far more depth and detail. Adapting both frameworks gives us a working model of culture that is especially relevant to mergers (see Box 15.2).

Level 1: Artifacts and Creations

These are the most visible and tangible expressions of the thinking and values in an organisation's culture. They include the organisation's architecture and design (especially public areas), office layout (open plan through to monastic cells), core technology and production layouts, and public documents. Also important are market outputs – especially products or services that are either leading-edge or distinctive statements in their field. All are visible testimony. All say something about the thinking in the firm. But to understand why, we have to probe deeper.

Level 2: Structures and Behaviour

Again, the most visible behaviour patterns include the leadership and management styles, the organisation structure and degree of centralisation,

---

Box 15.2   Five levels of culture

Level	Examples
1. Artifacts and creations	An organisation's architecture, office layout, technology, public documents, and products – especially those that are either leading-edge or distinctive statements in their field. (*Artifacts*)
2. Structures and behaviour	An organisation's structure, leadership and management styles, degree of centralisation, size of budget-holding, levels of risk-taking, reward systems, dress code, in-house jargon, gender and ethnic mix of staff. (*Socifacts*)
3. Justifications and values	Shared logic and explanations about the world, about competitors, about own strengths and weaknesses; espoused (stated) values and beliefs, and justifications (or 'becauses') for action and non-action. (*Public mentifacts*)
4. Meanings and symbols	Shared meanings known only to organisational members. Meanings of logos, budget sizes, car sizes, office locations, perks and similar; the personal significance of mission and values and myths and heroes; meaning of action and what action signals. (*Private mentifacts*)
5. Unconscious assumptions	Taken-for-granted assumptions that have been learned and so habitually reinforced that they slip out of conscious recognition; some national, some organisational. (*Unconscious mentifacts*)

(Adapted from Smircich, 1983; Schein, 1985)

---

the attitude to risk and level of accountability given to managers; the level of informality and camaraderie and dress code, and perhaps the gender and ethnic mix of staff.

Some of these are not as immediately obvious as artifacts but are fairly easy to detect. But as with artifacts, they are difficult to interpret without understanding the underlying logic of the thinking that supports them. Two merging firms can have very different characteristics – one lean and flexible, the other highly centralised – and an observer might say that their cultures are visibly different. But *why* each is the way it is may not be so obvious.

Level 3: Justifications and Values

Here we find the stated (or espoused) whys – the public justifications people give for the organisation being as it is and people behaving as they do. For Schein, this level is all about shared *values* that govern behaviour. Other authors (e.g. Argyris and Schön, 1978; Weick, 1995) go further to include shared cognitions or frames of reference – like shared interpretations of the environment and shared perceptions of strengths, weaknesses, opportunities and threats (SWOTs) and shared ways of reacting to competition.

This is the domain of **public thought** – highly cognitive and rational and well articulated. Perhaps the most useful diagnostic probes are around the *'becauses'* that people give for what they choose to do and what they choose not to do. 'We do this *because* …'; 'We avoid that *because* ….' *Becauses* are excellent clues to culture and shed a lot of light on the pattern of rational thinking in organisations – why rules and procedures are there and what justifies the scripts that people appear to follow at work.

The limitation at this level is that justifications are usually impersonal and functional. Often they are couched in strategic terms, in business language and priorities, rather than in personal preference terms. So we have to dig deeper. We know that behind every *because* there is another *because* … and that opens the door to private thought and private meaning.

Level 4: Meanings and Symbols

The domain of meaning is the domain of **private thought** – shared by members of a culture but mostly unspoken. At this level, symbols and associations and beliefs and myths and mission and purpose all become interconnected in ways that are difficult to disentangle. It's a cobwebby world but of enormous cultural and personal significance. The underlying idea here is that organisations are maintained through shared meanings and shared realities known only to organisational members.

The meaning that members attach to particular events and to what they and others do is tacitly understood but difficult for an outsider to penetrate. Belief and vision are one part of it. But most is derived from a shared past – part organisational, part national, and sometimes even part personal if there is a particularly strong shared experience.

Here the boundaries between organisational history, national history and personal history become fuzzy. But they all combine to shape managers' shared concepts of themselves and the meaning and significance they attach to their lives and their work. At this level, more than any other, a lot of personal psychology and ego is at stake.

The essential tools are deciphering and decoding. For example, the Japanese practice of *kaizen* (continuous improvement) can be justified rationally *because* it is good for business. But to a Japanese manager it is also loaded with historical and symbolic significance. Likewise for rugged individualism in the US. That too can be justified as good for business. But to an American manager the full significance is an association with the struggle of the early settlers and the mythology of folk heroes along the way. A third example could be rewarding excellence with a banana. Most people would feel insulted – but not at Foxboro where, Peters and Waterman (1982) tell us, the banana apparently has a special significance.[1]

These are simple examples to illustrate the point. In practice, it can be fiendishly difficult to penetrate the mindsets in another company or in another country and decipher the real meaning and significance behind what people say and do. Published material on large corporations and national cultures obviously can help, but in most instances managers have got to rely on their own diagnostic skills and judgement. For starters, two useful probing questions are:

'If I was a new member here, how would I decipher the organisation and know how to think and act appropriately?'

'What meanings will be attached to me if I think or act in particular ways?'

These are not easy questions – in any context. Yet most managers have gone through this exercise at some time in their careers (like when joining a new firm) and should have some idea of what is involved.

Level 5: Unconscious Assumptions

This is the domain of **unconscious thought** – taken-for-granted assumptions that drive conscious thinking. Some assumptions are organisational in origin. Others are national in origin. But all are basic ways of thinking that have been learned and then *so habitually reinforced in a particular context* that they drop out of conscious recognition. They slip into the unconscious and become, literally, taken-for-granted ways of thinking in a company or a society.

One big problem here is that unconscious thought is, by definition, unconscious, so it usually takes an outsider with a different mindset (from another company or another country) to bring assumptions to the surface. But probing any deeper into the unconscious – to Freudian levels of analysis

---

Box 15.3   The ethics of debt

GE Capital (a subsidiary of the General Electric Company) has reached its considerable size (over 50,000 employees worldwide) mostly by hoovering up credit agencies in every corner of the globe. That has given the company a wealth of acquisition knowledge and experience – but knowledge doesn't guarantee tact or sensitivity.

According to a recent article in *Harvard Business Review*, one of the first things GE does is introduce new companies to its integrity policy. And we are told, very clearly, that integrity at GE is not just embodied in some corporate policy statement. It is a detailed requirement that is meant to ensure that every employee understands what constitutes proper and improper ways of conducting business.

The routine approach after every deal was to do a mass reprint of the integrity policy and distribute copies at the dozens of meetings that are mandatory for all acquired employees. This was standard practice until, in one acquisition, the integration manager took another tack. He first asked some senior managers on the other side how they would react to receiving GE's policy.

The response apparently came as a surprise. If the policy was sent out, he was told, it would be like saying to the acquired business that they had no integrity until GE came along. This is the *meaning* that would get read into it. So it was left to acquired managers to tactfully introduce the GE policy – wrapped up in a non-offending form of words.

In a company brimming with integrity, it's funny nobody had thought of that before! (Ashkenas et al., 1998)

---

or exploring Jung's (1964) concept of a 'collective unconscious' at the root of all culture – is highly specialist and beyond the scope of the layman. So for our purposes here we have to stay close to the surface and be selective.

Twelve areas of taken-for-granted thinking that give a firm its distinctive character and ethos are listed in Box 15.4. Differences in these basic areas are commonly at the root of culture clashes in mergers – both national and global.

Note that the twelve basic assumption areas overlap to a certain extent – they are not mutually exclusive. Also worth noting is that post-merger conflict can have other causes. There can be personality clashes. There can be competing market scenarios based on different sets of rational calculations. There can be political conflict driven by ego and face-saving and protecting territory. However, these aside, most integration problems that attract the label *culture clash* usually centre around one or more basic assumption areas.

Box 15.4   Twelve basic assumption areas of organisations

Basic assumption areas	Exploratory starter questions
1. Business drivers	What *really* drives the business? Is it technology/manufacturing driven? Is it market driven? Is it finance driven? Or do a few key people drive the business on a contingency basis?
2. Style of governance	How is corporate governance practised? What is the management style? What are the leadership expectations? What is the relationship between the centre and the periphery? How much transparency is there at the top? In whose best interests does the board operate?
3. Time orientation	Are mindsets in the firm locked mainly in the past, the present or the future? What is the balance between short-term and long-term considerations?
4. Market relationship	Is the firm a market leader or a market follower? How close is the firm to its customers?
5. Margin environment	Does the firm operate in a high-margin or low-margin environment? Does it have to squeeze margins to survive or are margins generous? Is the firm 'fat and flabby' or 'lean and mean'?
6. Power structure	Is power highly centralised (as in owner-manager firms – sometimes called the 'person culture')? Is power vested in hierarchical positions (as in typical corporations – the 'role culture')? Or is power in the hands of professionals and experts (as in the matrix structure of an engineering consultancy – the 'task culture')?[2]
7. Risk and uncertainty	Is risk always pinned onto individual managers or is it allowed to circulate? Do managers contain uncertainty at their own level or do they delegate upwards – and on what issues? Is decision-making quick (low facts/high intuition) or ponderous (high facts/high procedure)?
8. Human Resources	Are employees regarded mainly as a short-term cost to be minimised or as a long-term resource to be maximised? Are they perceived as trustworthy (high autonomy/loose control) or fickle (low discretion/high direction)?

9. Deviance	Are mavericks and eccentrics tolerated or shunned?
10. Team orientation	Do structures and rewards emphasise individualism or team-orientated behaviour? Are incentives individual or group-focused?
11. Reward System	What actions does the reward system encourage and discourage? How flexible and error-tolerant is the system? Are surpluses retained at the top or distributed through the ranks (for example, employee shareholdings)? Is promotion time-linked or performance-linked?
12. Race and Gender	What is the gender and racial mix in the company? What is the balance between male and female values? Is there a track record of equal opportunity at all levels?

In Summary

To get a fuller understanding of culture, it is necessary to probe far below visible artifacts and visible structures and visible behaviour (socifacts). These are important. They describe a lot – they are the visible and immediate *whats* of culture. But to understand *why* they are there and what sustains them, the domains of thought – public, private and unconscious – also need to be explored.

This is the major limitation of many writers on culture – both organisational and national. They describe the most visible aspects without getting below the surface to identify the various types of thinking that give rise to what they describe. How thought shapes visible culture needs to be scrutinised. But so does the converse – how visible culture shapes particular kinds of thought. This two-way dynamic lies at the heart of culture.

In the above analysis, unconscious thought has been limited to basic assumptions – learned values and preferences – *at the organisational level*. And to the extent that assumptions are organisation-specific, they potentially can be changed.

However, basic assumptions are also *national* characteristics. Readers familiar with the culture literature may have noticed that four of the areas listed in Box 15.4 have close parallels with Hofstede's four dimensions for analysing national culture (see Chapter 16). And that at least two of Schein's basic assumptions have been taken on board (*relationship to the environment* has been interpreted at the market level, and the *nature of human nature* has been interpreted as Human Resource attitudes). And that at least three of Kluckholn and Strodtbeck's (1961) six dimensions of culture are also incorporated.

So the above frameworks can be used to explore culture at both an organisational level *and* a national level. That can be helpful in global deals. However, one important caveat has to be stressed.

> Suppose that in a foreign target a particular way of thinking is identified as a cause for concern. Working out the extent to which it is organisationally determined (potentially changeable) and the extent to which it is nationally determined (welded-in and difficult to change) may not be easy.

Mergers and Culture Change: Using the Frameworks

That is more than sufficient on concepts and theories and frameworks. What do they mean for practice?

Clarifying Culture

First, and very obviously, the frameworks *clarify*. Typically when people are talking about culture and culture clashes and culture change, it is seldom clear which level(s) they are referring to. Is it all levels, or some, or just one? Precision here goes a long way to making analysis more rigorous and change more focused. Note that the problem is not confined to popular literature.

> In the strategy literature there are numerous well-respected papers that deal with culture in one form or another – for example, polarising 'culture' versus 'the market'. It would be invidious to name them, but note that repeated reading still does not clarify precisely what the writers mean by 'culture'.

Predicting Culture Clash

Second is *predicting culture clash*. The frameworks can be used to construct a tool for capability profiling or for pre-deal culture audits. The twelve basic assumption areas listed in Box 15.4 cover the most common areas of culture clash in mergers. Remember that the starter questions are highly compressed – ask them and a whole set of supplementaries pop out. There are many possibilities when the frameworks are read into context.

In Buono et al.'s (1985) much-cited account of a merger between two banks – one rigid and centralised; the other more flexible and devolved – a quick glance at the basic assumption areas would have led to the prediction of serious culture clashes ahead ...

Constraining 'Gung-Ho' Integration

Third is *constraining 'gung-ho' integration*. Typically, merger planners and financial analysts think either integration or non-integration. Full integration is usually favoured because of the theoretical synergies that are believed to follow. However, Figure 10.1 showed there are many degrees of integration (from substantially autonomous through to full merging) and that *acquisition strategy must determine the type and extent of structural merging*. That in turn should determine how closely the two cultures are brought together.

The greater the level of integration, the greater is the potential for culture clash and the greater is the intervention effort needed to achieve some form of harmony. The complexity of what that can involve should underscore caution.

Note that this should also cap the tendency to talk about culture integration in isolation from strategy (e.g. Nahavandi and Malekzadeh, 1988). Acquisition strategy, structural change and culture change must be tightly integrated and coordinated, and it is unhelpful to think otherwise.

Explaining Culture Change

The frameworks help to *explain* the psychological mechanisms for changing organisational culture – especially the relationship between the visible (objective) culture and the invisible (subjective) culture. **Changes in artifacts or visible behaviour have got to be accompanied by changes in thought, and vice versa**. The three levels of thought – public, private and unconscious – need to be incorporated in any explanation of culture change.

Suppose (a common example) that a sleepy target is reorganised with a flatter structure, better control systems and a more flexible operation. None of this will change the target culture unless there is a *collective change in thinking* at three levels.

- At the level of *public thought*, there must be a logical acceptance of *why* change is necessary (i.e. new '*becauses*' like market pressures, or a new vision of a grander business, or demonstrated superiority of a new way

of operating). The intrinsic logic behind any new structure has also to
be accepted.

- In *private thought*, managers have got to *believe* in what they are being
  asked to do (i.e. not just accept the logic) and they must *believe* that the
  changes are necessary and that new targets are reachable, and *feel*
  comfortable operating with new mental maps. They have to gain inner
  meaning from it all and a collective sense of ego-enhancement.

- If both of these happen, it should be easier for managers to raise into
  consciousness the taken-for-granted *basic assumptions* that governed
  how they managed before (like, in this example, attitude to risk,
  timeframes, responsibility levels and market relationship).

These three psychological steps have to happen for there to be inner
commitment to the structural and operating changes. If not, the changes
simply won't deliver.

Protecting Target Culture

Equally important is *protecting the target culture*. A common problem –
especially when large corporations acquire small innovative firms – is
destroying the culture components in the target that deliver value. Usually
it is unintentional and it can happen in any basic assumption areas. Most
frequently it is in the areas of management style (too formal), attitude to
risk (too conservative), decision-making (too ponderous) and controls (too
constraining).

Large firms will say that change is necessary *because* they have to know
what is going on and exercise cost control (i.e. they operate according to their
own basic assumptions). But acquired managers often see things differently.

- They don't accept the new *whys*, the logical justifications for the
  changes. What they see are changes that destroy old ways of operating
  that – in their view – were tried and proved to be successful.

- Their collective sense of who they are and what makes them special –
  their identity – gets eroded. If, for example, much of the meaning of
  work lay in taking on the big boys and beating them at their own game,
  that meaning lay as much in what they produced (outputs) as in how
  they bonded and worked together (process). Challenging process
  undermines one of the twin pillars of mission and purpose.

- And when basic assumptions come to the surface, they often get reinforced rather than changed. They get reaffirmed because, after all, they worked. Sometimes the thinking goes: 'If *their* systems were any good, why didn't they do it themselves instead of buying us out?'

Then can come the all-too-familiar 'acquisition drift' factor. Knowledge and value get up and walk away.

Hence the importance of boundary management. In particular the integration manager and his or her team understanding the basic assumptions that create value in the target and, where necessary, ring-fencing them. This is a highly skilled operation – way beyond what one would expect from financial planners and merger analysts. Having capability profiles to hand helps enormously. Thorough pre-deal organisational audits are absolutely essential.

Using Human Resource Practices for Culture Change

How best to reinforce culture change? Popular literature says that leadership and communication are essential. It sounds plausible – except that leadership and communication are almost universal panaceas. They have been offered as the staple reinforcers of almost every management practice since the First World War! So it's not very helpful. We need to know what *types* of leadership and what *methods* of communication are most appropriate in different contexts.

Culture change can be a long, difficult and tedious process – often with disappointing results. Pettigrew (1985) reminds us that ways of thinking that are soldered in with the heavy hand of history can be difficult to change. As are ways of thinking that are interconnected with other organisational systems or reinforced by organisational politics.

Culture change *at the level of thinking* has to start at the top. The acquired CEO and top management team have got to be brought over to learn in detail how their new masters think. And new masters must learn how the target thinks. *It is a two-way learning process across both top management teams.* Even if there are to be few changes in the target (i.e. it remains substantially autonomous), each side still has to understand the expectations and the thinking of the other.

Thereafter, Human Resource practices, *if focused towards integration and acquisition goals*, can contribute significantly to culture change – especially the four core practices of selection, appraisal, reward and development (Fombrun et al., 1984). Targets are expecting change, and that can work in the acquirers' favour.

Two facts about HR practices are worth noting here.

1. HR chiefs put far more time and effort into worrying about whether and how to harmonise their respective HR systems than they do on focusing existing systems towards acquisition goals and especially integration goals.

2. Most merger advisers say: *If you want integration to go smoothly, don't meddle with HR systems – especially reward systems.* And they are right. Early attempts at standardisation often backfire and are usually counter-productive. Changes especially to pay and benefits take time and require a lot of negotiation and consensus.

But the advice is right for a more fundamental reason. There is no hard empirical evidence that one HR practice is more effective than another in delivering performance. Everything depends on context (see Box 15.5).

Box 15.5   Personnel sings the blues

Human Resource consulting is a multi-million-dollar industry that loves mergers. Most deals attract a queue of advisers wanting to harmonise HR practices or trying to install a brand new system for both firms.

Here's a sobering thought. Over half a century's personnel management practice has taught us that *there is absolutely no proven relationship between any HR practice and bottom-line performance.* Each decade has brought us new approaches, new techniques and new promises – in selection, training, reward packages, appraisal, management development, and many more – but no clear link to performance.

All we have is assertion and perception and belief that one practice may be superior or more likely to succeed than another. What works in one firm may not work in another. What is acceptable in one country is often rejected in another.

So if the target's HR practices ain't broke ... don't fix them – ride them!

If the target's personnel/HRM procedures are adequate (and in most medium to large firms they are), they are best left alone during the first year or so unless there are obvious areas of weakness or major sources of discontent.

Post-deal is *always* a time of high stress and uncertainty. Often it is a time of upheaval and change and reorganisation as well.

The primary task of HR chiefs is not administrative tidying or competing over whose procedures should dominate. It is focusing the four core personnel practices – selection, appraisal, reward and development – to assist integration and any planned culture change.

Selection

Having the right people in key positions is crucial in any acquisition. However, most firms think in terms of job or functional competence rather than personality characteristics. Managers with particular psychological qualities can be invaluable for changing culture.

- *Bridge builders*. Managers with a history of successfully bridging across cultural divides (no matter where or when) are useful. It doesn't matter which side they come from or what level they are at. If they have done it before, the chances are that they can do it in a merger and take others with them.

   Both sets of HR chiefs – if they are on the ball – will have lists of such managers to hand as a matter of course during integration planning. If capability profiling has been attempted, any managers who contributed significantly to the exercise or showed particular insight will be on the list.

- *Walking the talk*. Sometimes the best form of communication is behavioural – people who can *walk the talk* in a persuasive way. Every firm has managers like that at all levels – role-model managers who are good at their job and also able to articulate what they do and build effective teams around them.

   Moving such managers to boundary positions or to selected positions in the target can bring the two sides closer together. As can bringing target role-model managers over for periods of time then exporting them back.

- *Deviants and mavericks*. Deviants can be useful in some situations – for example, when ways of thinking are politically reinforced. Parachuting an original mind into the centre of a power bloc to say the unsayable and think the unthinkable sometimes breaks the mould. Likewise for mavericks. They're more risky, but usually they can show how to make the break from convention.

- *Headhunting*. Buying in *process* competence is sometimes necessary – e.g. managers with integration experience or with a history of turning round departments or functions in similar situations. With early integration planning, new managers can be in place and ready to take charge in the first week.

- *Personality Profiling*. Personality profiling for boundary positions is sometimes helpful. It can't predict how a person will perform but it can identify traits that might get in the way of cooperation.

  For example, a quality often found in effective boundary managers is a strong task focus that is not distracted by differences in culture or status differentials – like opposite numbers enjoying higher salaries or benefits. Profiling for these sorts of qualities in boundary roles seems sensible.

  Another aspect is the composition of capability transfer teams – like two knowledge teams brought together to develop joint R&D. Belbin (1981) has shown that teams composed of a particular mix of personality types usually perform better and work more smoothly than would otherwise be the case. Profiling is essential here.

Appraisal Systems

Appraisal systems can be excellent channels for communicating to individual managers what they need to do to make an acquisition deliver. The two pre-requisites are (a) a working appraisal system (which doesn't have to be top-notch), and (b) a bottom-up business plan for the acquisition.

If these are in place, new performance targets can be set, culture-change behaviours can be explored, and benchmarks for assessing progress put in place – *all at the level of each individual manager.* And it can start very quickly – often during the first weeks.

Starting quickly is important. Vision and strategy statements around the time of the announcement are usually fuzzy at the edges – and that's probably for the best. It allows lots of 'buy in' and that eases uncertainty, especially on the acquired side. Thereafter everything has to become more focused.

Appraisal systems provide a *coordinated* and *integrated* platform for each manager to explore two questions in detail.

'What changes are to happen to me and my job and the jobs of the people around me?'
'What do I need to do *that is different* to make this acquisition deliver?'

In other words, each manager has to explore the changes that are to occur in terms of how he or she *performs, acts and thinks.*

Performance Targets

The process commits each manager to a specific part of the business plan and allows specific targets to be set. It also allows the business plan to be explored. How attainable are the targets? Will additional resources be required? Will extra insourcing or outsourcing be needed? Will there be any changes to methods or procedures?

Dealing with these sorts of *process* questions is as important as *output* considerations. When all this has been worked through, it should be possible to set new targets and put some benchmarks in place for assessing progress. In other words, all the usual things an appraisal system should do. But there is more.

Culture Change

The appraisal process can help in exploring and coordinating what each manager must do to make culture change 'happen' – at both visible and invisible levels.

- Restructuring, for example, involves individual managers negotiating with those around them (horizontally and vertically, and maybe with opposite numbers on the other side) exactly what each is now responsible for. Where do the new boundaries lie? Then each has got to develop new mental maps of how to manage in their responsibility spaces and they've all got to make sure their maps dovetail together.

- Likewise for decentralisation and downsizing. Usually these mean bigger jobs with decision-making and risk moving downwards. So basic assumptions have to change – timeframes, style of decision-making, uncertainty carried, and similar. New maps, new relationships and new ways of thinking all have to be sorted out.

None of this is easy. In practice, it can be a difficult and protracted process with resistance, political manoeuvring and self-interest often getting in the way. An appraisal system is a good platform to start from because:

- it ties everything to what managers are currently expected to do and the criteria they are being appraised against

- it provides focus that can defuse some of the politics and tensions

- it allows coordination and integration with other levels and functions.

Implementation Review

Finally, an appraisal system – if used sensibly – can be an excellent upward communication channel for how implementation is progressing.[3] Collecting the responses and reactions of managers and feeding them upwards can be prime data for progress reviews (starting at the 30-day review) and can test the climate in different functions and levels and indicate where particular difficulties lie or whether timeframes need to be adjusted.

Reward Systems

Tying some component of reward to culture shift can be an incentive to change. If, for example, particular behaviours or basic assumptions have been identified as needing to change – like higher risk-taking, more networking, more team-orientation, tighter customer bonding or whatever – then rewarding improvements seems sensible.

For this to work, there has to be coordination through all levels and consensus on how progress is to be gauged. *This can be tricky and has to be carefully thought through.*

- The need for culture change might vary across the acquired company. Faster progress might be expected in some areas compared to others, and measures of progress might 'look' different in different functions. Guidelines on interpretation and on reward distribution would be necessary.

- Would some proportion of target top management remuneration be tied to how effectively they brought about culture change? Before this was attempted, the principle and the percentage at stake would have to be agreed with the target board during negotiations, and also the criteria to be adopted.

Note that this isn't breaking the rule about leaving reward and benefit packages alone. It's just another example of directing existing reward systems more towards integration goals and acquisition goals. The principle outlined here has got to be read in context and tailored accordingly. Sensitivity to context is essential.

Another situation where intervention may be necessary is when cultures are *not* being merged (when two firms are being kept autonomous and separate, for example) but managers from each side are seconded to work on project teams. Differences in reward and compensation sometimes become status issues that actually push the two sets of managers apart. Again, sensitivity to context and selective intervention can stop money getting in the way of performance.

- If two R&D or project teams are brought together each with their own reward packages, making adjustments to obvious areas of disparity can usually prevent one side from feeling aggrieved and having a sense of inequity. More effective, of course, is to have significant performance bonuses. These keep eyes more on the future and less on looking at what the other side is getting.

- If managers from both sides are flying off to a conference, don't have one lot in executive class at the front of the plane and the others stashed away at the back. Or one lot staying in a comfortable hotel and the other down the road in something inferior. It may be consistent with each side's expenses policy – but it creates bad feeling and is often seen as a public humiliation.

In other words, foresight and flexibility – not to mention a large dose of common sense – usually prevent issues of reward and compensation from getting out of hand and amplifying cultural differences. Sometimes levelling up is appropriate; other times levelling down. It all depends on context. Yet it is surprising how many HR chiefs overlook the obvious.

The other thing to remember – regardless of whether reward systems are being used to bring cultures together or stop them going further apart – is that *it is not the rewards* per se *that matter.*

What matters is the meaning (Level 4 in Box 15.2) that managers attach to them. Understanding the significance of different kinds of rewards – money, benefits, recognition, social rewards – is the real key to using rewards effectively at both the national and the international level.

HR chiefs (if they are on the ball) will have thought these through – but so often they don't.

Management Development and Training

In the longer term, all the usual mechanisms of management development and training can be used to bring two cultures closer together. Merging fast-tracks, broader career development, secondments, project-based management development, action learning on the other side – all can help. Training in all forms can get the new assumptions right through to the heart of the target.

CHAPTER 16

Culture and Global Mergers

'Oriental managers aren't inscrutable. We just don't know how to scrutinise them.'
(CEO, electronics)

In one sense, foreign acquisitions are no different from national acquisitions. Everything that has been covered in earlier chapters applies to the global scene – the detailed planning; the need for skilled integration managers; the careful bringing together of people, structures, controls and cultures; the linking of integration to acquisition strategy. Merger planning and merger implementation on all five continents follow exactly the same principles – and in practice are subject to the same mindset blocks and practical misfortunes.

In another sense, international acquisitions are literally a different world. So much that is taken for granted and invisible in national deals suddenly becomes an issue that *cannot* be assumed and often becomes awkward or incomprehensible and a source of problems and concern.

Factors of distance, differences in law, language, political context, ways of doing business, management styles, ways of thinking, values and basic assumptions (to mention but a few), all make foreign integration a far more complex endeavour. And if acquisitions are truly global (across all continents), the complexity can be mind-boggling.

This chapter will look at some of these issues. Once again, the usual reminder. It is *not* about global merger strategy nor about the international management of foreign subsidiaries. It is about how to *think about* national differences when acquiring and integrating foreign companies. Obviously it is not possible to cover every country in one short chapter. But examples will be given from different parts of the world to indicate how the frameworks in the chapter can be used in various contexts.

Thinking About National Differences

Most people start with the culture concept when thinking about national differences in mergers. It's obvious why. National organisations are packed full of national people, and people carry their cultures with them. Ways of thinking and behaving that people in any country have learned since birth get carried into the workplace, and they give national organisations their distinctive characteristics.

On the surface, of course, all organisations look different. In any country, a steel mill looks different from an electronics plant from a food-processing plant (i.e. they have different superficial features or organisational climates). But underneath there are common national characteristics in terms of mindsets and characteristic behaviours.

Hence the point in Chapter 14 that national organisations are subcultures of national culture – with visible points of distinctiveness (due to technology and leaders) and vast chunks of deeper, taken-for-granted or invisible sameness. It's that deeper level that we will focus on here – and that's not always easy to grasp.

When managers look at a foreign organisation, the two big integration questions to be asked are:

1. Which characteristics of the organisation are products of leaders and technology (and hence potentially changeable) and which are products of national thinking and hence almost immutable?

2. Of the many points of difference – organisational and national – can we identify those that will be major friction points that will impact upon performance?

These are not easy questions. But this chapter will provide some helpful ways of *thinking* about how to approach them.

Starting with Culture Writers

A good place to begin is Hofstede's (1980) work on comparative culture. It is a landmark study and a useful starting point because of its global geographical spread. Most managers should be familiar with the basic constructs. Hofstede proposed that cultural differences between nations could be described along originally four (then later five) *bipolar dimensions*. The position of a country on each of the dimensions should allow predictions to be made about the way in which each society operates, including its management processes and the kinds of theories that management draws upon. These dimensions of culture give five major areas where we can start identifying differences that can impact upon integration and styles of acquisition management.

Power Distance

This refers to the degree of power inequality in a country – in its institutions and organisations – and the extent to which people in the country accept the differences. All societies are unequal, but some are more unequal than others. Highest power-distance scores were found in countries that included the Philippines, Mexico, Venezuela, India and Singapore. Lowest power-distance (greater equality) countries included the Scandinavian countries, Ireland, New Zealand, Austria and Israel.

As a general rule, management styles in low power-distance societies are more participative and interactive and consultative. Employees expect superiors to be accessible and will bypass their boss if they have to in order to get their work done. In high power-distance societies it is the opposite. Management styles are more autocratic and centralised and there is a general reluctance to question or challenge directions from above. Subordinates consider superiors as special kinds of people. Privileges accrue to rank in a heavily disproportionate way.

Individualism

The individualism–collectivism dimension refers to the degree to which people in a country prefer to act as individuals rather than as members of a collectivity. In highly individualistic societies, life is often depicted as a race, a contest, in which people must take part to get a share of the rewards. People are generally expected to be self-sufficient and take care of only themselves and their immediate families. That often engenders the social attitude '*me* **versus** *you*'.

In collective societies, people are born into extended families or clans that protect them in exchange for loyalty, and there is strong emphasis on fitting in harmoniously and face-saving. The prevailing attitude is '*me* **with** *you*'. Hofstede found individualism to be highest in North America, Australia and the UK; moderately high in mainland Europe; and considerably lower in the Far East and Latin American countries.

Management styles reflect this polarity. In highly individualistic societies there is a strong emphasis on competition, on individual performance, on managers versus other managers. In collective societies, the emphasis is more on group targets and performance, on consensus, and on preserving harmony and a cooperative spirit. Notions of a *collective* greater good prevail over *individual* personal gain.

Uncertainty Avoidance

This dimension emphasises the extent to which people in a country prefer structured to unstructured situations. Structured situations are those with formal and often ritualised rules about how to behave – sometimes written down; sometimes imposed by tradition. Countries with high uncertainty-avoidance are generally depicted as formal and rigid with an attitude that *'what is different is dangerous'*. Low uncertainty-avoidance countries are the opposite. They are more easygoing and flexible. There are fewer rules about how people should behave; ambiguity is less threatening. The general attitude here is *'what is different is curious'*.

Management styles in high uncertainty-avoidance countries (typically Greece, Spain, Portugal, Japan and across South America) are usually highly conservative. There is a heavy reliance on rules and procedures, low risk-taking, and a strong need for certainty and approval before taking action. In low uncertainty-avoidance countries (lowest scores in Denmark, Sweden, Singapore, the UK and Ireland), management styles are more flexible and spontaneous; there is greater tolerant of deviance, and change and innovation are more accepted.

Masculinity

The masculinity–femininity dimension captures the extent to which 'tough' values like assertiveness, performance, success and competition (which in nearly all societies are associated with the role of men) prevail over 'tender' values like quality of life, maintaining warm personal relationships, service, solidarity and care of the weak (values typically associated with women's roles). Gender roles differ in all societies, but the differences are more pronounced in masculine societies than in feminine societies – and it is that difference that the dimension tries to capture. As Hofstede defines it, Scandinavian countries are the most feminine; Japan and Austria the most masculine, followed not too far behind by Venezuela, Mexico and the English-speaking countries.

Management in highly masculine societies emphasises achievement, advancement, getting greater power and responsibility, and stretch targeting.

Feminine societies place more emphasis on camaraderie at work, physical working conditions, job security and perhaps the quality of working life.

Time Orientation

Hofstede later introduced a fifth dimension – long-term versus short-term orientation – to examine whether a society's time orientation was located predominantly in the past or in the future. It was based on research conducted in the Far East and nearly all of the values around this dimension were heavily influenced by the teachings of Confucius. Long-term (future-referenced) values included thrift, persistence, and a sense of shame. Short-term (past-referenced) values included personal stability, respect for tradition, protecting face, and a strong emphasis on reciprocal greetings and favours.

   In general, past-oriented people believe that plans should be evaluated in terms of the customs and traditions of a society and that change and innovation are justified only according to past experience. Future-oriented people justify innovation and change in terms of future economic pay-offs, and have less regard for past societal and organisational customs and traditions. From a business perspective, there are parallels here with pursuing short-term profitability versus long-term growth; and also the pursuit of static efficiency versus dynamic efficiency.

These thumbnail sketches barely do justice to the issues that lie behind each of the dimensions. But they are sufficient to highlight important areas where transnational integration commonly runs into difficulties. Time orientation is especially relevant to strategy. Differences at the top about time horizons can cripple an acquisition and how it grows. Table 16.1 summarises the culture dimension scores of over 50 countries in Hofstede's original (1980) IBM sample, with the fifth (time orientation) score added subsequently for as many of the countries as possible.

   Note that the five dimensions do not constitute culture. They are offered as probes or tools for comparing important aspects of culture – aspects particularly important for management. Note also that while each dimension is revealing by itself, it is how the dimensions combine that gives the deeper insight into each country and how its institutions and organisations are managed.

Table 16.1 Culture dimension index scores and ranks for 52 countries and 3 world regions

Country	Power Distance Index	Power Distance Rank	Uncertainty Avoidance Index	Uncertainty Avoidance Rank	Individualism/ Collectivism Index	Individualism/ Collectivism Rank	Masculinity/ Femininity Index	Masculinity/ Femininity Rank	Long-/Short-Term Orientation Index[1]	Long-/Short-Term Orientation Rank
Argentina	49	35–36	86	10–15	46	22–23	56	20–21	–	–
Australia	36	41	51	37	90	2	61	16	31	22–24
Austria	11	53	70	24–25	55	18	79	2	31[2]	22–24
Belgium	65	20	94	5–6	75	8	54	22	38[2]	18
Brazil	69	14	76	21–22	38	26–27	49	27	65	6
Canada	39	39	48	41–42	80	4–5	52	24	23	30
Chile	63	24–25	86	10–15	23	38	28	46	–	–
Colombia	67	17	80	20	13	49	64	11–12	–	–
Costa Rica	35	42–44	86	10–15	15	46	21	48–49	–	–
Denmark	18	51	23	51	74	9	16	50	46[2]	10
Ecuador	78	8–9	67	28	8	52	63	13–14	–	–
Finland	33	46	59	31–32	63	17	26	47	41[2]	14
France	68	15–16	86	10–15	71	10–11	43	35–36	39[2]	17
Germany	35	42–44	65	29	67	15	66	9–10	31	22–24
Great Britain	35	42–44	35	47–48	89	3	66	9–10	25	28–29
Greece	60	27–28	112	1	35	30	57	18–19	–	–
Guatemala	95	2–3	101	3	6	53	37	43	–	–
Hong Kong	68	15–16	29	49–50	25	37	57	18–19	96	2
India	77	10–11	40	45	48	21	56	20–21	61	7
Indonesia	78	8–9	48	41–42	14	47–48	46	30–31	–	–
Iran	58	29–30	59	31–32	41	24	43	35–36	–	–
Ireland	28	49	35	47–48	70	12	68	7–8	43[2]	13
Israel	13	52	81	19	54	19	47	29	–	–
Italy	50	34	75	23	76	7	70	4–5	34[2]	19
Jamaica	45	37	13	52	39	25	68	7–8	–	–
Japan	54	33	92	7	46	22–23	95	1	80	4
Korea (South)	60	27–28	85	16–17	18	43	39	41	75	5
Malaysia	104	1	36	46	26	36	50	25–26	–	–
Mexico	81	5–6	82	18	30	32	69	6	–	–
Netherlands	38	40	53	35	80	4–5	14	51	44	11–12
New Zealand	22	50	49	39–40	79	6	58	17	30	25–26
Norway	31	47–48	50	38	69	13	8	52	44[2]	11–12
Pakistan	55	32	70	24–25	14	47–48	50	25–26	0	34
Panama	95	2–3	86	10–15	11	51	44	34	–	–
Peru	64	21–23	87	9	16	45	42	37–38	–	–
Philippines	94	4	44	44	32	31	64	11–12	19	31–32
Portugal	63	24–25	104	2	27	33–35	31	45	30[2]	25–26
Salvador	66	18–19	94	5–6	19	42	40	40	–	–
Singapore	74	13	8	53	20	39–41	48	28	48	9
South Africa	49	35–36	49	39–40	65	16	63	13–14	–	–
Spain	57	31	86	10–15	51	20	42	37–38	19[2]	31–32
Sweden	31	47–48	29	49–50	71	10–11	5	53	33	20
Switzerland	34	45	58	33	68	14	70	4–5	40[2]	15–16
Taiwan	58	29–30	69	26	17	44	45	32–33	87	3
Thailand	64	21–23	64	30	20	39–41	34	44	56	8
Turkey	66	18–19	85	16–17	37	28	45	32–33	–	–

Table 16.1 continued

Country	Power Distance Index	Rank	Uncertainty Avoidance Index	Rank	Individualism/ Collectivism Index	Rank	Masculinity/ Femininity Index	Rank	Long-/Short-Term Orientation Index[1]	Rank
United States	40	38	46	43	91	1	62	15	29	27
Uruguay	61	26	100	4	36	29	38	42	–	–
Venezuela	81	5–6	76	21–22	12	50	73	3	–	–
Yugoslavia	76	12	88	8	27	33–35	21	48–49	–	–
World Regions:										
Arab countries	80	7	68	27	38	26–27	53	23	–	–
East Africa	64	21–23	52	36	27	33–35	41	39	25	28–29
West Africa	77	10–11	54	34	20	39–41	46	30–31	16	33
Additional index values[3]										
China	80	–	60	–	20	–	50	–	118[4]	–
Russia	95	–	90	–	50	–	40	–	10	–

Notes:
1 Other LTO ranks: Bangladesh 15–16; Poland 21. 2 Based on consumer survey data.
3 From Hofstede (1993). 4 Highest rank.
Sources: © Hofstede (1993, 2001). Reproduced with permission.

The Limitations of Culture Comparisons

Hofstede's work has been highlighted for international and global integration purposes because it is visually accessible and covers a good spread of the world. But there are other writers we could cite. For example, Trompenaars (1993) has done some interesting work on cross-cultural differences, particularly on time orientation across a range of countries, exploring how people in each country see the relationship between the past, the present and the future.

Child (1981) looked at cross-cultural difference from a slightly different angle. Are national cultures becoming more similar (as some scholars claim) or are national cultures retaining their dissimilarities (as others claim)? It's a fascinating question in itself – and it's important for global integration. Child concluded yes and no. Yes, there was convergence across countries at the visible, superficial levels of culture – mostly around the structure and technology and systems in organisations. But at deeper levels, divergence persisted. People within organisations continued to think and behave in their own national ways.

It's not our purpose to review these works here. Many readers will already be familiar with them and with other cross-country comparisons that are available – both academic and commissioned. Most multinational firms and global consulting houses and business schools have a wealth of detailed comparative data for any two countries in the world. The far more important task here is to identify the limitations of any cross-cultural comparisons based on a handful of dimensions.

Probe Limitations

Universal dimensions can only probe so far into a country. They can only tell us so much. Hofstede is very clear that only about half of his findings in each country could be classified according to his dimensions. The other half is specific to factors in individual countries. That reminds us of the danger of attributing *all* differences between countries to socio-cultural factors (i.e. the danger of culture becoming a catch-all term for national differences).

Dimensions Don't Explain

Dimensions don't explain anything. They are *tools for describing and classifying* the most visible and superficial aspects of national cultures. They don't explain either the deeper levels of thinking about why particular behaviours exist, nor do they explain the thought-processes in each country that justify what people do. Dimensions don't explain mindsets.

Subjective Perceptions

Objective measures don't reveal the subjective feelings of people of one country to another. Two countries can have broadly similar ratings on comparative scales – but it doesn't mean that companies in these countries will integrate easily.

For example, Sweden and Finland are two Scandinavian countries that share a border and have a lot in common. On Hofstede's scales they have broadly similar ratings on power distance and individualism. Finland is more uncertainty-avoidance than Sweden (59 versus 29 on an 8–112 scale). On masculinity, Sweden is the most feminine country (a score of just 5 on a 5–95 range). Finland comes in just slightly higher at 26.

On this basis, the unwary might conclude that merging companies from each side should not be too difficult. But that would be to ignore the effect of history and national stereotypes (see Box 16.1).

Spread

Single-point scores don't reveal the spread of characteristics among a given people. All national behaviours exist on a continuum, a normal distribution,

Box 16.1   Steel and fudge, Scandinavian style

Eero Vaara at the Helsinki School of Economics tells a delightful tale about a Swedish-Finnish steel merger that began life in 1986 and fizzled out in 1991. All the classic *how-not-to-do-it* ingredients are there.

The merger happened at a time when the European steel industry was going through major restructuring. Tough decisions had to be made about shutdowns and modernisation of production plants in each country. The Swedish and Finnish steel owners ducked the issues and decided to merge their plants instead.

Each side had different reasons for hopping into bed – and these they also ducked. Neither side wanted total control, nor did they want to invest any money in the creation of the new company. So they settled for another Nordic fudge – the symbolic 50–50 joint ownership.

A new top management team was appointed with more Finns than Swedes and with the chairmanship rotating annually between the two owners. From the outset, the new company was plagued with internal dissent about where product and production responsibilities should lie, and about the future of the main units – which to invest in and which to shut down. With corporate management firmly divided along national lines, it wasn't long before each side championed its own national interests.

Attempts to build a new corporate culture proved disastrous. National identities and national hang-ups and historical stereotypes all got in the way. The Sweden–Finland, '*big brother–little brother*' syndrome (a residue of history) plagued decision-making. Some managers behaved true to type – more dominant on one side; less so on the other. Others went in various directions. Some Finnish managers took the attitude: *I'm a Finn and historically inferior to a Swede so now's the chance to redress the balance.* Some went further and behaved more Swedish than the Swedes.

Other managers deliberately rejected the stereotypes. They reasoned along the lines, *I'm a Swede so I must* not *behave like Swedes usually do to Finns.* Or: *I'm a Finn so I must* not *behave like Finns usually do to Swedes.* But by repressing themselves, they sometimes let important decisions go through without sufficient challenge.

Vaara's account of the merger gives an unusually rich insight into a near-tribal set of merger relationships. Of managers on each side collectively insecure about their identities and preoccupied with how they came across to their opposite numbers. Implementation became a political arena where decisions were driven as much by rational calculation as by historical stereotypes and false conceptions of the other side. Task and ego and face and nationality all blurred inexorably.

The tie-up lasted five years – not bad for Scandinavian bedfellows! (Vaara, 1999)

from strongly committed to weakly committed. And it is the *spread* along the distribution that is important, especially for knowing how far deviation and change will be accepted.

So, there are obvious limitations to comparative cultural dimensions. However, there is another significant aspect to Hofstede's work that seldom gets attention. It is especially relevant to international mergers. *Comparative dimensions should force managers to look at the cultural assumptions behind their own styles of management.*

> The way in which you, the reader, and I, the author, are conditioned to see strategy and organisation and management is shaped largely by where our countries lie on each of the five dimensions. If we live in the same country, there is probably a lot we share unconsciously and take for granted. If we live on different continents at opposite corners of the world, our basic assumptions are likely to be poles apart and we will see management very differently.

That's the implicit – and all-important – message behind Hofstede's work. *Every management approach is a cultural product – a product of a particular time and place and way of thinking and set of circumstances.* That is something that many managers – especially in America – find difficult to accept. One reason is that the vast bulk of what is known as 'Western' management practice is American – taught in American business schools as near-universal truths for universal application rather than ways of thinking that are time and circumstance and culture dependent.

Managers are seldom taught the idiosyncratic basis of national management thinking. But that's something that international and global integration managers know well – or have to learn very quickly!

The National Determinants of Management

We need something much broader than cross-cultural dimensions to capture the complexity of integration on an international or global scale. Figure 16.1 gets closer to what is required.[1]

Essentially, what the model in Figure 16.1 is saying is that management thinking and practice in any firm are shaped by five major features of a country:

1. The *political characteristics*, most notably the way national leaders are selected and deselected and the way they exercise power. These act as highly influential role models for others to exercise power.

2. The *nature of the economy*, in particular the economic prospects and material well-being of the population.

3. The *legal context*, which governs how people relate to one another and conduct their affairs, and how business is to be conducted.

4. The *socio-cultural background* of the people which includes values, beliefs, myths, religion, attitudes to time, relationship with the environment, and the other factors that typically get classified under the *culture* label.

5. The *national history* of the country, particularly in relation to other countries.

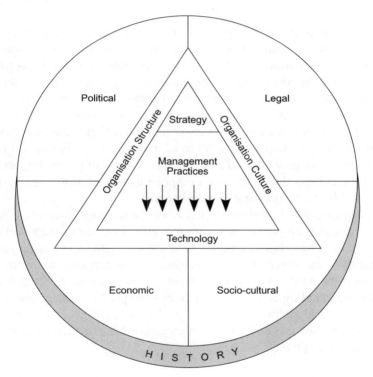

Figure 16.1 The national determinants of management practice

Source: Adapted from Lees (1996)

These five national features all interrelate and shape the vast bulk of what happens inside companies. The way people in a country think – their mindsets – and the way they perceive choices and constraints, the way they act, react and don't act, are predominantly products of these five factors. Indeed, it is probably true to say that these five factors have been the most fundamental influences on thinking and action in *any* society – right back to the earliest of times. Note that only one of the factors is truly 'soft' – the socio-cultural aspect.

> When integrating firms across different countries, it is not just the socio-cultural differences that need to be examined. It is how *all five factors* shape strategic and management thinking on each side that needs to be understood.
>
> It is not sufficient to know where the other side is coming from. Managers on each side have got to know where they themselves are coming from – how all five factors have shaped their own management mindsets.

A second feature of the model (perhaps of more interest to academic readers) is that it reminds us that national culture is neither static nor completely deterministic. *All cultures evolve*. This is an important point for foreign integration and something that many culture writers overlook. People carry their cultures with them – but they are not totally locked into customs and practices that have gone before. *Each generation reinterprets the past in the context of what they need in the present and what they want in the future*. Most people want to improve the material and social conditions of life and to experiment with new ways of living and new ways of producing essential goods and services. Hence the two components – continuity and change – are essential for understanding culture in action.

Japan, for example, is routinely cited as a most traditional society – but the country has also been one of the most innovative in terms of manufacturing. That innovation has changed Japanese society and Japanese organisations significantly in the space of two generations. What happens inside Japanese factories can be partly understood in terms of socio-cultural factor. A much broader understanding comes from including the political and economic and legal and historical factors that gave rise to Japan's particular form of export-led industrialisation and how these factors all combine to shape management thought and action today.

> Two important ideas are implicit in Figure 16.1. One is that all cultures evolve. The other is that economic, political, legal and historical factors are powerful forces for culture change.

To illustrate the model in action, we will start with Western management thinking then make some broad-brush comparisons with the former Soviet Union and East Asia – three areas of the world where management thinking has distinctively different characteristics.

Probing Around Western Management Thought

Western management thinking and practice (broadly North America, Western Europe and Australia) is embedded in a context that most Westerners take for granted. But if some of it is brought to the surface, the influence on management thinking can become clearer.

The Political Influence

All Western countries are social democracies with a common background of:

- Challenging and replacing elected leaders with free and contested elections.

- Constant scrutiny of the executive by an empowered population.

- Belief of freedom of information and encouragement of freedom of thought.

- Government being 'hands off' with respect to business – limiting its role to creating what it judges to be the most appropriate conditions for business to operate under.

These four features are common to the governments of all Western countries, and they are ingrained into Western thinking about how power *ought* to be exercised. There are, of course, many variations and imperfections. The political process in each country 'looks' slightly different. Historical influences and socio-cultural factors give national governments their distinctive shape. Levels of transparency also vary across countries – some countries are more 'open' than others. And there are the usual imperfections that accompany the exercise of power – like withholding some types of information and discouraging scrutiny that might be uncomfortable. But that is to get into fine-tuning. What is important is the broad picture. As a general model of how government *should* be practised, what is outlined here is welded into Western minds.

And it is substantially reflected in the way companies are managed. One obvious consequence is that *corporate management in the West is a professional process that is largely free from political control.* Top managers are selected and rewarded on market-efficiency grounds, and they have enormous freedom to drive their firms in directions they choose and to acquire and utilise resources for strategic purposes independent of political control. There is a history of challenging and displacing business leaders on objective (market) grounds, to the point of the hostile bid to unseat underperforming boards.

At the same time, there is close public scrutiny of corporate affairs – some of it imposed by law; the rest by numerous stakeholders and pressure groups. Management style (or style of corporate governance) *must* be collaborative to balance the expectations of multiple constituencies. Shareholder and market interests predominate, but not exclusively. Notions of corporate responsibility to a wider public prevail.

In other words, there are many parallels between the national political model and how national corporations are managed. But Western managers seldom ponder over it – it is just so taken for granted.

The Economic Influence

Western economies are tightly managed organisational economies with distinctive features:

- Good infrastructures and stable currencies.

- Affluent societies (by world standards) with high levels of social provision and high levels of education and training.

- Freedom of movement within countries and high levels of labour mobility. Labour markets are well developed and operate at a sophisticated level.

- Concepts of *the market* and *market forces* are ingrained into the population – especially the idea of markets as arbiters in resource allocation.

Again, each national economy has different characteristics; different strengths and weaknesses. But the general features outlined above feed directly into how management is thought about and practised in the West. For example, stable economies and stable currencies allow for predictability in strategic planning and greater certainty in day-to-day management. That in turn spawns the enormous range of forecasting and planning and control practices that are modelled on mathematical rationality. Add good infrastructure (transport, communications, etc.) and that allows for efficiency in distribution and permits practices such as Just-In-Time (JIT) manufacturing.

Affluent societies and flexible labour markets reinforce one another. *In fact, virtually all Western leadership theories and HRM practices are predicated on empowered populations and freedom of labour movement – and also upon psychological contracts with employers that are mature and calculated.* But, again little of this ever gets spelled out. It is just taken for granted.

The Legal Influence

Western legal systems are *secular* legal systems that remain independent of political control. They vary from country to country but draw broadly on common Judeo-Christian foundations. Consistency in the evolution of law across the centuries is another feature – but most important is the independence of the judiciary from the executive.

Three features of Western law appear to have particularly significant influence on management thought and practice.

- First is the inviolate nature of legal contracts and especially the banning of inducements or favours to further a contract.

- Second is human rights and employee rights. These concepts are highly articulated in the West and are taken-for-granted underpinnings of employment contracts and the employment relationship.

- Third is that trade union opposition to management is firmly and effectively enshrined in law.

In Summary

The above are only thumbnail sketches, but they are sufficient to capture three very important *sets of influences* on management thought and practice in the West. Almost all the management theories in Western textbooks – on planning, control, leadership, people management, and so on – are predicated on these three foundations, but are so taken for granted that they are almost unconscious, invisible.

Obviously, there are wide variations on each of these factors across countries. Economies differ in strength and profile. The laws in each country differ. Styles of government differ. There are socio-cultural variations between countries (and often within each country), and there are multiple influences of history. These, however, are points of national detail. They should not be allowed to blur the more general picture.

However, one larger point of detail is worth noting and is especially relevant to transatlantic deals. **The North American management model is *not* the Western management model**. There are many points of similarity, but also many points of difference. Hofstede (1993), for example, singles out three features of the model that don't fit comfortably in mainland Europe.

- First is the stress on the individual – European thinking has more of a collective flavour. Social market thinking is stronger in mainland Europe than in North America.

- Second is the emphasis on managers rather than on workers or other professionals. In America, the manager is portrayed as the cultural hero – but not so across Europe. In Germany, for example, the engineer probably comes closest to filling the cultural hero role.

- Third is the overemphasis on the market – that somehow market processes are more efficient than organisational processes. The American model holds that organisations are more efficient when, internally, they resemble markets and not the institutional structure of a country. And when managers relate to one another on a competitive market basis rather than on a cooperative and national-traditional basis. Again, these nostrums do not hold as strongly across Europe.

Some aspects of the American model can be explained in terms of the history of a young country with few traditions and populated by *individual* immigrants. When a country has no institutional heritage, the *market* becomes king – more by default than by deliberate choice. Then when industrialisation gathered pace and America's industrial might was forged during the first great merger wave at the end of the nineteenth century, it was *managers* who did the industrial integration from coast to coast that made possible the dream of America's greatness. Managers made the dream happen.

In other words, America's historical profile is reflected in its management nostrums. And it's that type of broad picture we need to keep our eyes upon – the idea that management thinking in a country is shaped by the five elements in Figure 16.1 and that the validity of a theory of management is bounded by national borders. It is an absolutely essential idea when integrating firms across continents or at opposite corners of the world. What is taken for granted as working in one country simply may not work in another.

Russia and the Former Soviet Countries

The breakup of the former Soviet Union into independent republics and the introduction of some Western-style economic disciplines have led to some rose-tinted views of the changes. Various writers have suggested that some of the new Russian business leaders are really not very different from the pioneering American business leaders in terms of their vision and ruggedness and drive and persistence. This may well be true – but that's where any resemblance ends (see Puffer, 1994). Business and management are two very different concepts.

Russian businessmen may have embraced market forces and possess similar business drives – but their management mindsets are very different.

The media gives disproportionate attention to Russia, so it is worth remembering that Russia is only one of 15 independent states that comprise the former Soviet Union (now the CIS – Commonwealth of Independent States) and what happens in Russia is not necessarily representative of the other countries. Russia still retains a powerful central influence especially over military matters – but otherwise the states are very different and do not always sit easily together. Since its creation, the CIS has been plagued with infighting about its purpose and direction and several states have had civil wars during the last decade.

Some states have strongly embraced the notion of market forces. Other states remain highly socialist. The ethnic and cultural backgrounds are also highly diverse – roughly 40% Christian and 60% Muslim. Although the Soviet Union was nominally atheist, western republics have a Christian Orthodox tradition. Those to the east and into Central Asia are predominantly Muslim.

The contrast between the political and economic and legal contexts in CIS countries and the West is stark. We will outline these first and then explore their influence on management thought and practice.

The Political Influence

Until the 1990s, the Soviet Union was governed by a one-party non-democratic political system operating under enormous secrecy with state controls and censorship extending into all corners of society. Freedom of thought and freedom of information were forcefully discouraged. A generation further back, most families had living memories of horrific abuses of power – mass executions, forced movements of swathes of the population, mass terror and fear.

Recent changes have seen a fledgling democracy in Russia, but not in other states, most of which remain one-party but which have elected parliaments. However, the extent to which elected representatives in *any* of the member states can scrutinise the executive remains questionable. Also questionable is the extent to which the military, especially in Russia, is under full political control.

Controls over freedom of thought and information have been relaxed, but over-scrutiny of government or business can provoke a backlash. Intimidation of investigative journalists is fairly commonplace and assassination is not unknown. To Western eyes, CIS countries still convey the impression of quasi-military states but now with a more human face.

The Economic Influence

All CIS states are weak, labour-intensive industrial economies with weak currencies and poor (almost Third World) infrastructure, especially in transport and communications.

Removal of state subsidies has led to the collapse of indigenous manufacturing and a near-total dependence on imports of all sorts – foreign goods, foreign capital, foreign management and foreign knowledge bases. One enormous centrally planned, state-directed *production* economy has given way to many state-directed *rescue* economies.

Inflation to world prices has left most people in state employment needing one or two additional jobs to survive. There are extensive black economies and a massive drift of professionals (doctors, nurses, teachers) into lower-skill jobs in the alternative economy that pay closer to a living wage. Enormous divisions now exist between rich (a tiny minority) and poor (the vast majority) in what were nominally egalitarian societies.

Soviet notions of comprehensive social provision (full employment, state housing, high-quality education and tight restrictions on travel) have resulted in populations that are highly educated, poorly skilled and unfamiliar with Western notions of labour mobility and self-provision of a home near a chosen job in a chosen geographical area.

Notions of *the market* as a sophisticated regulator of industrial policy and management practice are unfamiliar – and here the learning process has been painful for the majority. But notions of *the market* at an individual, barter level are ingrained.

The Legal Influence

Legislation in CIS countries is in a state of flux. Each of the 15 states began drafting new national legislation on gaining independence, not always consistently. Laws are often ambiguous and rewritten frequently. Hurried drafts of new business legislation appear regularly for reasons that often seem political or opportunistic. Old Soviet law and new state law sit uneasily together. Case law is thin on the ground.

Current law-making is set against a backcloth of the CIS, from its creation, showing a strong disregard for written declarations. And, further back in time, of Soviet law-making being a heavily politicised endeavour with tight legal restrictions on private enterprise. By Western standards, the CIS countries have a poor record on human rights and on regulating health and safety at work.

Post-Soviet Management Style

If we add to the above the collective nature of the Russian people, their legacy of poverty and hardship, and Stalin's attempt to gatecrash through history with rapid industrialisation along a particular ideological basis, we get the full picture. It created a distinctive Soviet style of managing that operated up to about a decade ago – centralised and rigidly bureaucratic management of a centrally planned economy with very little challenge to authority. It is still the only model most ex-Soviet managers know – welded into their mindsets. But now the old certainties have disappeared and there is no new management model to follow.

Instead, lots of different models are competing for attention. Hopes for economic and industrial recovery are vested not just in the West – but in the South and the East and wherever firms have come from and acquired or joint-ventured in former Soviet lands. All are bringing their own management techniques (that have evolved out of different economic and political and cultural and legal and historical contexts) and are trying to graft them onto ex-Soviet mindsets.

So, what would be the major points of difference, particularly friction points, in acquisitions and joint ventures? From a Western perspective, six are worth noting.

Management as a Political Process

Compared to Western management which is essentially a *professional* process, former Soviet management was predominantly a *political* process. In a state-controlled, centrally-planned economy, senior managers were appointed politically; their targets set politically; their resources were allocated politically; the methods of production decided politically, and evaluation was carried out by more senior political appointees. There was no independent market to act as arbiter.

To a very large extent, strategic management is still a political process across the CIS. Industrial rescue and renewal is still politically controlled. Vast chunks of industry have been sold or joint-ventured by governments to foreign firms with the state retaining a significant stake. And that's the first friction point in mergers or joint ventures.

Western managers accustomed to rapid head-to-head negotiations and autonomous action often find the rounds of political negotiations and the delays in getting decisions both time-consuming and frustrating – as is the range of non-business agendas that state officials introduce and expect the deals to satisfy.

Dependence on the Centre

Delegation upwards and dependence on the centre for resolving problems is another feature that goes back in time. With no independent market to act as arbiter on managerial performance, Soviet performance criteria were politically determined. Managers pursued *hierarchical* evaluation, meeting the performance expectations of more senior political appointees, not the evaluation of a neutral and independent *market*. Loyalty to superiors and espousing the 'correct' ideological (i.e. Communist Party) principles were at least as important for promotion as talent and ability.

This residue persists. CIS managers now espouse 'market' principles because that is the new official ideology – but they still depend heavily on hierarchical approval for decisions rather than relying upon independent reasoning and critical judgement. This is more than just a collective way of thinking. It is partly because they are unfamiliar with autonomy as understood in the West. And partly because they don't have a firm enough grasp of Western management techniques. Managers will apply Western-style techniques but lack the background and training to follow through in detail. They wear a new uniform but often lack the inner substance.

> Western managers involved in joint ventures will tell of ex-Soviet managers and senior government officials ritually working with Western planning and risk analysis techniques – but not following calculations through in necessary detail and not being able to exercise critical judgement over the implications of the figures they produce. But if approval for the calculations comes from a higher authority as a basis for proceeding, the figures are accepted uncritically – sometimes on the flimsiest of calculations.
>
> Or firms adopting the full package of Western selection techniques including psychological testing – but not conducting any prior job analysis and not having local norms to score the tests. Then perhaps selecting a perceived least suitable candidate because of that person's connections with the political centre.

Rigid Boundaries

The Soviet doctrine of full employment meant massive overmanning and tiny rigid job boundaries. When jobs are tiny, everybody can get one. Structure was politically determined and authority was not challenged. Initiative was not only discouraged; often it was punished severely. Any notion of managers driving a firm – formulating a competitive strategy or utilising resources to the full or managing beyond the boundaries of the firm – were alien.

> This has left another legacy. Western notions of autonomy, experimenta-tion, job enrichment, individual performance-related incentives, psychological ownership of work (the American 'that's *my* goal' syndrome), to name but a few, are all predicated on an empowered population.
> Westerners growing up in market-referenced and efficiency-driven societies are familiar with the concepts from childhood and take them for granted. To populations that have grown up in a command economy, they are alien concepts that go against the grain of tradition.

These notions are being introduced slowly by entrepreneurial managers, but the Western idea of giving a manager full responsibility for a task and leaving him or her to get on with it doesn't always work. There is still enormous reluctance to challenge boundaries without higher approval.

Socialist Pride

People right across the former Soviet Union have enormous pride in their achievements under a socialist regime and many still find capitalist ideas unattractive. High levels of educational achievement for all was always a state priority and that has left a population educated to standards higher than in some Western countries. But living standards are much lower. Most people would like material improvements to their way of life but their ideology remains collective and socialist. The legitimacy and morality of private enterprise is still hotly debated in the media.

All of which can present a dilemma for people employed by international firms operating in CIS countries. The material rewards they receive are sig-nificantly higher than they would otherwise get, but that does not guarantee commitment if contracts are less secure and career prospects are less favourable than those the firm offers in other countries.

> The patronising Western view often is 'You're much better off than before.' The post-Soviet view often is 'We're being exploited.'

This is especially the case among highly educated doctors and scientists and academics who of necessity have abandoned their professions and entered management for a living wage. They know their capabilities and their market value on the world stage. Hence a sensitive and flexible approach to each individual case is important if long-term commitment is really being sought.

Box 16.2   Decoding Soviet management

The former Soviet management model was different from Western styles of managing. Yet aspects were slightly familiar. For example, some management behaviours could be predicted from an understanding of bureaucracy operating in its most rigid form. Other behaviours were consistent with what we know about the effects of highly centralised power.

Industry also had a distantly familiar look to it. Anyone who visited Soviet factories in the 1990s might have noticed a resemblance to descriptions of American industry in the 1920s and 1930s – a time warp waiting for F.W. Taylor and his stopwatch team to arrive; a snapshot of pre-war Fordism. To the analytical eye, quite a lot of Soviet management had a recognisable but distant ring.

Western industrial efficiency evolved across the twentieth century. Soviet industry mostly stood still. It's a tall order to expect former Soviet mindsets to gatecrash through more than half a century to catch up with Western thinking. Narrowing the gap will take time, perhaps a generation or more.

Community Links

Soviet industrial chiefs always enjoyed higher status and exercised more power than their Western counterparts – almost a cross between a company president and a city mayor. Part of the reason was that they lived side-by-side with their employees and were embedded in the same community.

Western top managers are usually disconnected from the communities where the workforce lives. They live in more affluent areas; they enjoy a superior environment; they concentrate almost exclusively on strategy and the bottom line; and they make their contribution to the community *in money* through taxation of various sorts.

Soviet enterprise chiefs lived in the same towns as the workforce, often in similar (but perhaps roomier) flats, and they experienced the same communal exigencies as everyone else – food shortages, power disruption, polluted water and other infrastructure breakdowns. But because of their position, there was enormous pressure on them to fix problems when they arose. Their contribution to the community came in a different form. They were caught up in detail and made their contribution *in kind*. This expectation still remains – and has grown even stronger in recent years as industrial decay has blighted entire communities across the land.

Western managers often fail to recognise the political and social roles senior CIS executives and managers are expected to play in maintaining the wider environment of the firm. They regard them as distractions, non-core activities, time wasted away from goal-directed performance and chasing the bottom line.

Fixers *Par Excellence*

Logic tells us that a centrally planned command economy cannot deliver to plan if plant managers on the ground have no control over what resources they receive and when they receive them. So what held the Soviet system together? One answer is barter and fix. To reach targets when supplies failed to arrive on schedule or when production problems arose or other misfortunes hit their plants, Soviet managers demonstrated enormous ingenuity in persuading and bartering and negotiating to their own advantage. *Whom they knew and what they could exchange were the critical resources.*

This highlights another difference.

In Western firms, if supplies don't arrive or there are production breakdowns, managers instinctively ask: *Where can I buy a solution?* They go to markets – to the markets for alternative supplies, for technical assistance, for new machinery. And if they are short of cash, money markets are awash with money they can borrow.

In non-capitalist economies where there are no markets as such and few alternative sources of supply, managers ask: *Who do I know who can fix the problem?* Personal contacts and the capacity to network and barter and exchange are the essential qualities.

This difference extends into whole societies, not just in factories. *Where can I buy it?* versus *Who can get it for me?* is a distinctive division. In poorer societies where money is scarce, all sorts of other currencies are used instead – barter, gifts, compromise, favours of all kinds. What matters is the subjective judgement of the value that is exchanged – not the objective monetary value. The exchange cements a bond, an ongoing relationship, that may well lead to further contacts. In the West, the preferred approach is to buy a solution in a market and terminate the relationship with a monetary payment. This puts a very different complexion on what are often called *questionable payments* (see Box 16.3).

Box 16.3   A raft of graft

East Asian philosophy teaches that compromise is often necessary to achieve a goal. Confucius says it, of course! He is often cited as preaching moderation in all undertakings – and that justifies a raft of graft. Baiting an opponent with a small prize to gain a much larger prize is a common stratagem. Consequently, gift-giving, lavish entertainment and bribery are common practices in East Asian societies.

More generally, research has shown a strong correlation between high-context cultures (characterised by implicit communication and extensive networks) and the use of questionable payments. An estimated 70% of the world's population belong to high-context cultures, including East Asians, Arabs and Mediterraneans. Low-context countries include the US and most of Northern Europe. (Tung, 1994)

In Summary

These are six significant areas of difference that managers will experience in acquisitions and joint ventures in former Soviet lands. There are other differences, of course, but these six are probably the most important. And they go deep. They are fundamentally different ways of thinking and of managing. They are rooted in the national inheritance managers on each side carry with them, and that inheritance cannot be changed.

It is just as hard for a Russian manager to think like an American as it is for a Canadian manager to think like a Kazak or an Uzbek. But understanding where the other side is coming from and the meaning each side attaches to what they do is the all-important first step to bonding and working together more effectively. The five areas in Figure 16.1 can offer some helpful starting points for probing.

Also worth remembering is that *there is no post-Soviet management model*. There *was* a distinctive Soviet model of management but now each of the governing variables is in a state of flux. The political context in each state is variable and sends out different signals. The economic context across the region is only just stable although some states are comparatively richer than others. Legislation in all states is still evolving and often inconsistently. And there is the big cultural divide between the Orthodox Christian tradition in the north around Russia and the Muslim tradition in the south and east. With a new world order polarising around a broad Christian–Muslim axis, this divide is especially significant.

So all the major influences on management thought and practice are fluid. There are few fixed markers for navigation. To some, this represents anarchy (and there is certainly a sense of lawlessness across the region – an attitude that says: *Do what you want and fix the law afterwards*). But fluidity is better thought of as opportunity – opportunity to build *firm-specific management approaches* provided each side can understand the background each is carrying into the acquisition or joint venture.

Asian Management Thinking

The third area of the world we will look at, briefly, is Asia – a vast continent, the largest on earth, comprising over 60% of the world's population (20% in China alone). Asia spreads across 45 countries from central Asia (where much of the former Soviet Union lies) through the Middle East, the Indian subcontinent and through to the Far East and the Pacific Rim countries. Moving across Asia is to move across countries where, *in each country,* fundamental thinking can be completely alien and sometimes incomprehensible to the Western mind.

A few years ago, a founder of the Honda Corporation made an insightful remark:

> Japanese and American management is 95% the same and differs in all important respects.[2]

This is the all-important cue for Asia in general, not just Japan. Management looks pretty much the same in most corners of the world, but it's the subtle variations in thinking that make the critical difference. In recent years, the Southeast corner of Asia has been the main focus of attention because of the high levels of economic growth in the region. Japanese industrial efficiency and management styles in particular have attracted a lot of interest, and one result is that many people equate Japanese management with Asian management. That is a big mistake.

Across Asia, there is an enormous diversity of cultures and philosophies and economies and historical influences.

> There is no Asian model of management in the sense that there is a general Western model or there was a general Soviet model. There are many different Asian models of management. Most are country-specific.

The major influences on management thought and practice are different in each country. Styles of managing in the Arab world are different from the Indian subcontinent and different again from either China or Japan.

Influences on Asian Management Thought

Again, Figure 16.1 helps to highlight the factors that shape management thought across Asia. The five governing forces – economic, political, legal, socio-cultural and historical – all vary considerably across the continent.

The Economic Influence

Asia embraces the full spread of economic development – First World and Third World together. Most Asian countries are regarded as underdeveloped, low productivity, labour-intensive economies. However:

- Japan is a longstanding exception and more recently is China (which achieved the fastest growth rate in Asia in the early 1990s and could be on target to be the world's largest economy by the year 2025).
- The four Asian Tigers (Taiwan, Hong Kong, Singapore and South Korea) are also exceptions and may claim to be on a par with Western economies.

The economic models these countries work to are very different, and hence the economic influence on management thinking varies considerably. Japan's export-led industrialisation proceeded (and still proceeds) on fundamentally different economic assumptions from China's centrally directed privatisation policy, and different again from India's protectionist public-private model.

Across Asia, economic policies in each country create very different commercial environments for managers to operate in, and dictate different ways of construing and pursuing strategy.

The Political Influence

The range of governmental models operating across Asia include:

- the absolute monarchy of Saudi Arabia
- the constitutional monarchy of Japan
- the democratic republic of India, shaped around the British constitutional model

- the People's Republic of China (a socialist dictatorship with a Communist Party apparatus largely beyond constitutional and legal control)

- the constitutional democracy of Thailand (following periods of military control).

These are just five styles of government to be found across Asia, but sufficient to highlight a second issue:

Each style of government puts different constraints on top managerial autonomy and acts as a different role model for the exercise of power.

The Legal Influence

Across Asia there is a diversity of legal systems, both secular and religious. For example:

- Islamic law features across much of the Middle East – sometimes strictly enforced (as in Iran)

- Hindu law (mediated by a British colonial heritage) is found in Pakistan, India and Burma

- Shinto religion underpins much of Japanese law

- Confucian philosophy underpins Chinese law and more generally across all Far East countries.

This is a breathtaking spread of philosophies and religions influencing management thought. And it's not just the substance of law that varies across Asian countries. The independence of the judiciary from the executive – freedom from political interference – and the honesty and integrity of those administering the law, also varies from one country to another.

The assumptions behind legislation, the rigour with which it is enforced, and the penalties for law-breaking, vary far more across Asia than in Western countries.

Contracts provide a good example. In the West, written legal documents are considered sacrosanct, with terms that are inviolate. Across much of Eastern Asia, signed contracts are regarded as *organic* documents that can be altered as circumstances change. This often confounds Western managers trying to conduct business in the area.

The Socio-Cultural Influence

Asia is the cradle of civilisation. When Europe was still a collection of warring tribes, China and India had flourishing civilisations – at least as far back as 2000 BC and 1000 BC, respectively. Their influence spread to surrounding countries, mostly through philosophy and religion and social organisation, and the legacy endures. Ways of thinking that are centuries old continue to shape day-to-day action.

For example, Confucian philosophy underpins thinking throughout China and adjacent countries. Central doctrines include the family as the prototype of *all* social organisation, and that the stability of society is based on *unequal* relationships between people (i.e. ruler–subject, father–son, etc.). Also emphasised is the importance of moderation in all things – for example, patience, not showing emotion, not spending more than is necessary and rigorously avoiding conspicuous consumption. (In passing, it is worth noting that such values are polar opposites to North American ways of thinking.)

Confucian philosophy spread to adjacent countries and intermingled with other philosophies, giving each country a distinct historical legacy. We know virtually nothing about these legacies *on a comparative basis*. The best we have is, for example, Hofstede's comparative dimensions of culture. These are simple constructs that perhaps distinguish one country from another but explain very little. They shed little light on ways of thinking that lie behind the measured differences.

However, one of Hofstede's dimensions is highly significant for high-lighting strategic mindset differences in acquisitions and joint ventures.

The five countries with the highest long-term orientation (LTO) score all lie in Southeast Asia – China, Hong Kong, Taiwan, Japan and South Korea – with China way out ahead (see Table 16.1).

A further significance is that high LTO scores (which includes Confucian values such as working hard, acquiring education and skills, thrift and persistence) appear to be correlated to economic growth in the region. The proposition is that East Asian entrepreneurship *predicated on Confucian values* was responsible for the significant economic growth in the region.[3]

The Historical Influence

A historical dimension runs through each of the areas examined – economic history and industrial development; political history; philosophical and religious history, and cultural evolution. History is implied in them all. There is also the turbulent history in Asia during the Second World War and subsequently. How people in each country interpret what they did and what happened to them is another enormous area of enquiry.

So it is not always easy to make a direct link between national history and a *particular* management practice. Often it is a matter of conjecture. But in one area – East Asia – and in one management practice – strategy – the historical link with ancient times is evident.

Tung (1994) identifies four historical books that are widely read in the Far East and which are highly influential in shaping business philosophies. Two are regarded as absolutely essential bibles for commercial success. Three draw upon Chinese history – in particular military history – while the fourth is Japanese and based on samurai swordsmanship and Zen philosophy (see Box 16.4).

Running through all four books are principles for competitive success that were successful centuries ago and are still commonly practised in East Asia. For example, showing endless patience. Making compromises while also striving for total victory. Never revealing emotions or true intentions. Using deception to gain strategic advantage. Transforming an adversary's strength into weakness. And always grasping the *interdependence* of situations.

The last point is especially important because it follows from taking a long-term perspective. The longer the time horizon envisaged, the more likely it is that connections will be seen between situations and events which, in the short term, appear disconnected and isolated. Seeing such connections is an integral part of Far Eastern strategic thinking.

In Conclusion

The national influence on management behaviour in three major areas of the world has been examined in this chapter – the West (Europe and North America); former Soviet countries, and Asia (mostly China and Japan). The overview has been brief and superficial, but sufficient to highlight two issues that are vitally important for international or global integration.

1. Cross-cultural comparisons are excellent starting points for *illuminating* differences in management behaviour between two or more countries.

Box 16.4   Oriental strategic thinking

Rosalie Tung, in an eye-opening article in *Organisational Dynamics,* highlights four ancient books that are seminal in shaping East Asian strategic thought and business philosophies – and how different it all is from Western strategic thinking.

The Art of War (purportedly written by Sun Tzu (or Zi) around 500 BC for a military audience) is now considered the 'bible' or handbook for business people in East Asia. So influential has this book been across the centuries that it is reported that Napoleon used the principles in the book to conquer Europe – and that his violation of some of the principles led to his defeat in Russia.

Six major principles for military (or competitive) success are given. Four are straightforward but two are worth highlighting. One is moral cause. To get troops to perform at their best, leaders must present to them a moral or righteous case for going into battle. The other principle is the use of spies and other forms of espionage. Without these it is impossible to obtain adequate information and insight into an adversary.

The Book of the Five Rings was written by Miyamoto Musashi, a late-sixteenth-century samurai, who sought to unravel the connection between swordmanship and Zen. He identified nine principles for competitive success – including endless patience, an iron will to discipline the inner spirit, disguising emotions and intentions, using diversion to distract opponents, and always grasping the multiple perspectives in any situation.

The Three Kingdoms, written by Lo Kuan-chung in the fourteenth century, is a 120-chapter semi-fictional account of the struggle for control of China after the collapse of the Han dynasty (China's longest and mightiest) in AD 220. Military strategies, ploys, intrigues and alliances are all included, plus (according to Tung) an incisive analysis of human nature – good, bad and ugly.

This book is considered essential reading for anyone who wants to survive and succeed in East Asia's highly competitive marketplace. The Sanyo Electric Corporation gives each executive a specially bound copy of the book when promoted to senior management.

The Thirty Six Stratagems is distilled from military strategies presented in 24 volumes of Chinese history and draws upon the basic tenets of Taoism. The stratagems have widespread use in military and business settings. Each can be used on its own or combined with others to give an almost infinite array of stratagems. Hence, in a confrontation, all parties may know the basic 36 stratagems, but the winner is the person who shows the most ingenuity in mixing and blending them into an effective, winning strategy.

Tung then shows how these four classic, historical writings shape Oriental approaches to business. In an intriguing analysis, she identifies twelve themes or principles that run through the writings. Then, one by one, shows how the principles shape the way East Asians do business on a daily basis – and succeed.

Western managers reared on a diet of generic strategies, 'excellence', '7S's' and two-by-two matrices, must surely jaw-drop at the insignificance of what they've been taught. (Tung, 1994)

But to *understand and explain* the differences, economic, political, legal
and historical influences need to be examined in addition to socio-cultural
influences.

2. All approaches to management are idiosyncratic – a product of place,
time and particular circumstances. Managers have got to understand the
factors that shape their own thinking – the inheritance they bring into the
new company – as well as understanding the thinking on the other side.

These pages have been written from a Western perspective – in full awareness
that most of the world does not operate to the Western model of management.
For Western managers, six factors are worth restating as they are especially
relevant to acquiring and joint-venturing in non-Western countries.

1. *Management as a politically controlled process* is a reality across much
   of Asia, especially in China, and in other countries with a history of
   state control. Highly autonomous Western managers used to rapid head-
   to-head negotiations with equally autonomous counterparts often get
   perplexed and frustrated at the way political agendas get intertwined
   with business agendas.

   Negotiations through state officials can be ponderous and time-
   consuming, with long delays over matters that appear either trivial or
   totally unrelated to the business. The skill is in knowing which of the
   supplementary agendas to concede and which to reject. It requires considerable insight to work out their possible long-term implications for
   the business side of the deal as well as their potential political implications for future collaborations.

2. *The more collective a country, the slower is decision-making*. This holds
   true as a general rule, but for different reasons. In former Soviet
   countries, delegation upwards was more of a learned or indoctrinated
   process, largely because initiative often was severely punished. In other
   countries especially across Asia, delay has more to do with getting
   consensus. Or it has to do with assessing prospective partners and their
   true intentions. Western managers accustomed to ballpark figures and
   quick decisions can find this frustrating.

   Patience is valued in most of Asia – especially in the Far East.
   Collaborations are usually entered into as long-term relationships where
   the other side must be thoroughly divined and scrutinised and trust
   established – and that takes time. There's a big difference here. The
   Western view is often to see a tie-up as essentially a business contract
   where everything hinges on detail that has been rationally worked out
   on paper. Buying-in an expertise from another country is approached

impersonally, in pragmatic or cost-effective terms. But in parts of Asia, and especially in Japan, managers sometimes have a sense of shame if they have to buy-in an expertise that they were not able to develop in-house. That's something Western managers often find difficult to understand.

3. *Respecting hierarchy*. The Western view of hierarchy is narrow and functional – an authority structure for industrial and commercial efficiency. In other parts of the world, hierarchy is a symbol of heritage and tradition, invoking feelings of duty and honour and obligation. Western managers sometimes dismiss these attitudes as old-fashioned and inefficient, and post-deal may attempt insensitive restructuring around Western notions of how organisations work. Often they don't have a mindset that understands how tradition can be the invisible fabric that holds an organisation together and makes it deliver.

4. *Community links*. The idea that organisations make their contribution to the wider community *in kind* rather than in money is a feature of many Asian countries and more generally across the Third World. The contribution can take many forms. In CIS countries, industrial chiefs are often looked upon as 'fixers' for the community when major problems arise. There is also tolerance of 'leakage' from firms into the community – for example, petty theft for personal use.

    More generally across Asia, patronage is commonplace. At top levels, kinship ties create loyalty bonds to other firms with tacit expectations of cooperation that outsiders barely recognise. At other levels, kinship bonds can create an expectation that family members will always have an association with the firm – for example, through employment or sub-contracting.

5. *Family or contract. The family* is still the basic economic unit across much of the world and family loyalties are the primary bonds that hold people together. With that come all sorts of unspoken and unwritten expectations about loyalty, duty and obedience on the one hand, and protection and patronage on the other. It is never in writing. It is just taken for granted. Across much of Asia, the family (or extended family or clan) is the basic model that shapes social organisation. Grasping this point is central to understanding employment and interfirm relation-ships across much of the Asian continent.

    By way of contrast, in Western (rational-legal) societies, there is far more reliance on legal contracts. Atomised people and atomised firms are brought together by contracts that specify in precise detail what each party shall and shall not do, and how relationships will be terminated.

There is little notion of an enduring relationship or that the other side is already under a taken-for-granted obligation to a family or clan.

Many East–West organisational and management differences hinge around these two basic concepts – whether people are bonded together by legal contract or by extended family bond. It is a crucial distinction.

6. *Gifts, favours and 'questionable' payments* are all taboo in the West but not so in many other parts of the world. They have to be viewed in context. In poorer countries, the tradition of using 'alternative' currencies as payment is one that will continue. Gift- and favour-giving can also be part of a process of building up a relationship to see if long-term trust can be established. In many parts of Asia, legal documents are more flexible and less binding than in the West, so assurances are sought by other means.

This is about as far as we can go in terms of general conclusions. No two deals are the same. No two countries are the same. There is such a diversity of national differences in every global deal that there can be no general prescriptions.

So we will end the chapter, not on tips for working with foreigners, but on a different note. Something that is consistent with the idea of self-reflection – that Western managers (and indeed all acquiring managers) should examine their *own* styles of managing and the factors that shape their own thinking. We will take a look at how Japanese managers see Americans. It's an insightful mirror on the West (see Box 16.5).

Box 16.5   How Japanese see Americans

The famed short-sightedness of American management can be very frustrating and disappointing to the Japanese. Americans seem unable to appreciate how business relationships can grow over time. Too often, companies provide lacklustre service and sell products of insufficient quality. Too often, blasé or inattentive sales personnel fail to treat customers as 'honoured guests'. Instead of working with people they know well, Americans will do business with almost anyone. But they are too quick to make deals and too untrusting to engage in business without a brigade of attorneys to navigate through potentially catastrophic legal traps they imagine might be set for them.

In Japanese eyes, American work settings lack a spiritual quality. The feeling of 'collective specialness' carefully bred in Japanese organisations is largely absent in US business. People are more concerned with personal job performance and compensation in narrowly defined jobs than in overall mission and success. The Japanese are also surprised by the lack of loyalty in American institutions. Their experience has taught them that effective management depends on a richly woven, internal network of trusted relationships that takes years to develop.

Among Japanese people, many things are left unsaid. Elaborate rituals of social reciprocity build trust and 'institutionalise thoughtfulness'. People are taught to be indirect in conversation, carefully editing their remarks to reflect both good form and the concerns and status of their listeners. The Japanese language richly affirms social hierarchy through an elaborate system of verb conjugations that communicate distinctions of rank. Ideally, superiors don't give orders. Subordinates are sensitive enough to understand exactly what is wanted and to act accordingly.

Americans violate this order regularly. Rather than subtly reading interpersonal cues, Americans are forceful in their interactions and routinely speak their minds. They generally appear to be noisy, disruptive and confrontational, often airing views that are best left unsaid. They pursue personal agendas and engage in political confrontations to protect their own interests, producing nasty turmoil and dissention in the ranks. In Japanese eyes, it is tragic the way harmony is so wantonly violated.

Americans may even walk out of a door at a moment's notice. Such conduct is acceptable – even entertaining – among Americans, but to Japanese eyes, socially unruly Americans must be dealt with cautiously and sometimes excluded from the group altogether. Since they are non-Japanese, such treatment is acceptable in Japanese eyes.

American assertiveness and whimsy confuse the Japanese. One Japanese executive described his confusion this way: '80% of Americans are wonderful, but 20% are not, and I cannot tell the difference.'

That's a nasty nip at Uncle Sam's ego! (Adapted from Linnows, 1993)

CHAPTER 17

Global Integration Managers

'Export a manager and you export your firm's culture, warts and all. Things we turned a blind eye to or didn't even recognise were mirrored back to us – writ large on the other side. It gave us a lot of trouble.'

(Managing Director, electronics)

Finally, we come back to base, to people – to the managers who make organisations 'happen' and make acquisitions 'happen'. The concepts and frameworks in the previous chapters can be useful – very useful – for thinking about what is involved in integration and for planning purposes. But they are just what they are – abstractions. They've got to come alive, be made to 'happen', and it's managers who do that – spanning across a country or between countries. In global mega-mergers, managers literally have to span the world.

The Realities of Global Integration

International and global acquisitions need acquisition managers *willing* to go abroad and *able to operate effectively* in foreign contexts – to negotiate the deal, perhaps to liaise with governments, to investigate the target, to integrate the firms, to troubleshoot if necessary, to head-up specific functions and business areas, and maybe even to run the acquired operation(s).

Then, as integration proceeds, operating managers at various levels in one country will take up positions in another. Project teams from several countries will come together – maybe in yet another country. Experts in various fields will join up to collaborate and to share knowledge and capabilities. And there will be short-term and long-term secondments of varying kinds from subsidiaries on both sides.

In any international merger, an enormous amount of cross-cultural competence is required *with most of it directed at integrating the two firms*. As mergers approach global proportions (i.e. embracing most countries on most continents) the amount of cross-cultural competence needed for integration increases *exponentially*.

Implementing truly global deals requires truly global managers who

- can grasp the massive complexity of integration on a global scale

- can think and act in truly multicultural terms (not just in terms of a handful of cultures)

- are comfortable and competent living a global existence, perhaps with little notion of roots

- can assemble teams of operating managers with specific cultural experience from different corners of the world to handle specific aspects of integration.

A moment's thought should indicate the sheer mind-boggling enormity of what is involved here. What we are describing is a very rare and extremely talented species of manager – absolutely vital if globalisation through merger continues and particularly if corporations wish to quickly realise the value and operating efficiencies of the deals they enter into.

Yet there is little evidence that large corporations have fully grasped the need to systematically grow such managers to support their talk about *acquiring to go global.*

In recent years, all the talk has been about developing global markets, not about developing global managers to sustain the markets.

Global competence grows out of international experience. This seems fairly obvious – but not always to large corporations. When we look at what multi-national firms have been doing over the last 20 years, particularly in North America, many have been *reducing* the number of expatriates they send overseas to gain international experience (Kobrin, 1988; Lane et al., 1997).

One reason for this is the cost of expatriate packages – especially the higher salaries and the expense of relocating managers and their families. Local managers can usually do the job without any additional expense. Another reason is the movement towards developing host-country managerial and technical expertise, especially in Third World countries. Short-term accounting considerations and national political pressures both work against the development of international and global expertise.

However, *merging* multinational corporations is a different ball game from *running* multinational corporations. A different way of thinking is needed. In any global merger, the short-term consideration is having teams of highly specialist integration managers in place to create the new higher efficiency or synergy conditions in operations around the world in accordance with the merger plan. Generating the cashflows from greater efficiencies as quickly as possible is the accounting priority. That can take several years – even with the best teams going at full speed. If a global merger starts life with insufficient multicultural competence and experience in the combining firms, integration is either botched or delayed and there is a cost – far greater than the cost of developing the managers in the first place.

National political pressures also need to be looked at in a different light. After integration is completed and higher-efficiency conditions prevail, local nationals will continue to run the various parts of the businesses in each country just as before. That part won't change much.

What is likely to change is the attitude towards multinational corporations in different countries. For example, anti-globalisation feelings around the world are still embryonic and are likely to grow. Any international merger in the name of globalisation will become a focus of attention, especially when (as is usual) the justifications are economic and efficiency benefits flowing to the merging firms.

A possible scenario – especially in Third World and economically deprived countries – is that some national governments will want a parallel set of benefits to flow to them – perhaps those that local constituencies are pressing for. And they may use cooperation with the merger as a pressure lever on the multinational firms. The bottom line is that merger implementation around the world may well get hijacked by country-specific economic or social policy agendas.

Predicting such events requires managers with an intimate knowledge of the political undercurrents in every country where subsidiaries are located. Handling them requires managers with deep levels of culture understanding and high levels of culture competence stretching right across and into the heart of the business and political and administrative circles in the countries concerned.

That is the integration challenge in any global merger. There are two agendas to be addressed: an economic efficiency agenda *and* a political/legitimacy agenda.

One is to integrate the various businesses across countries and continents in a way that generates projected efficiencies and synergies, both internal and external. In other words, to create the *conditions* for greater efficiency in the operations in each country which local managers will then deliver.

The other task is political. To integrate or align the merger around the economic and social policies in each country where the combined firm operates, in a way that satisfies the political constituencies in each country.

Of course, most international acquisitions and mergers are not of that magnitude. Globalisation for most firms is about presence and visibility on the world stage – international firms getting bigger, smaller firms going further overseas, domestic firms acquiring abroad perhaps for the first time.

Nevertheless, regardless of size, the two agendas have to be addressed. The *efficiency agenda* (creating integration efficiencies for the parent company) and the *legitimacy agenda* (acting in alignment with cultural expectations and political constraints in each country) are common to *all* international acquisitions. It's just the scale and complexity that vary.

Most of the earlier chapters have addressed the efficiency agenda – how best to bring merging firms together and how to recognise barriers to efficiency in strategic and implementation thinking. The legitimacy agenda has been touched upon in the section on culture.

In this chapter we will look at the managers who make it all happen and do the cross-country bridging on the international stage. We will stay at the international (not the global) level and probe around two questions:

1. What do acquiring firms need to know about performance and culture adjustment when sending managers abroad?

2. How best to select and develop managers to integrate international mergers?

Ten Insights into International Managers

Generally speaking, *willingness* to work abroad and acquire or increase cross-cultural experience is seldom a problem if expatriate packages are favourable. Career-driven managers often jump at the possibility. But the *ability* to operate effectively in foreign countries is another matter.

Research gives us some revealing insights into how managers cope and perform on the international stage. Ten such insights are given below. They rarely figure in any merger calculations. But they are essential food for thought for any firm – large or small – sending managers abroad to integrate or drive mergers across countries or continents.

Expatriate Failure Rates

Failure to adapt to an overseas posting is far more common than is realised. Estimates of expatriate failure rates (either summoned back or voluntary early return) run between 20% and 50% (Mendenhall et al., 1987). Some studies put the figure higher – Lane et al. (1997) suggest a range of between 30% and 70%. But it varies across continents. North American managers are many times more likely to return early than European or Japanese managers (Tung, 1982).

Spouses

The most pervasive reason why expatriates return early is failure of their spouses to adjust to a foreign country (Black and Stephens, 1989).

Culture Shock

All managers who go international experience culture shock (more accurately: *acculturative stress*) – even seasoned globetrotters. Those who repeatedly move to new countries are likely to dampen their emotional swings and have a shorter period of adjustment. But they still experience disorientation, stress, and that sense of not having mastery over the situation – especially when moving to another continent with an unfamiliar language.

Adjustment

The period of adjustment to normal or above-average levels of performance usually takes from three to nine months – depending on previous experience, degree of culture difference experienced, and individual personality (see Figure 17.1). Those who don't make the adjustment often display a range of symptoms including withdrawal, severe anxiety or depression. In extreme cases, excess use of drugs or alcohol is reported (Lane et al., 1997).

A Man's World

International management is predominantly a man's world. Although firms strive for equal opportunity, in practice many factors work against the principle in overseas postings. On the supply side, there is the number of women willing to work overseas. On the demand side, there can be situations where sound business reasons dictate a male preference. For example, in some countries (like in the Middle East), local managers may find it

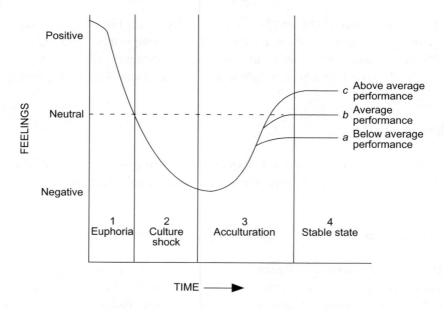

Figure 17.1   The four stages of cultural adjustment

Source: adapted from Hofstede (2001)

unfamiliar and uncomfortable relating to a woman as an equal or organisational superior.

More generally, outside of work, leisure facilities in most countries are geared more towards male comfort. A man in a foreign city can wander into a bar and sit alone if he chooses – something many women might feel uncomfortable doing. Of course, lots of women willingly rise to the global challenge and take everything in their stride – but they usually have quite special coping and defence mechanisms.

Dual-Career Families

Not all firms take into account the unit they are sending abroad. In dual-career families, if the spouse puts career 'on hold' and goes abroad, there are financial and psychological costs – as well as the stress of adjustment overseas. On the other hand, if the spouse stays at home to retain career, there can be loneliness and apprehension on both sides. The qualities of a spouse/partner in these circumstances can be crucial for the expatriate's adjustment and performance.

Training

The training given to managers prior to departure appears to be insufficient – even in multinational corporations. Roughly 70% of all US expatriates receive no pre-departure cross-cultural training apart from language courses and basic survival tips (Black and Mendenhall, 1990). Only a tiny minority of companies arrange a comprehensive package of pre-departure training and post-arrival training and support for the manager – and where appropriate for the entire family.

Psychological Lifeline

Less well documented but absolutely vital is a *psychological lifeline* to base – someone at headquarters (*not* a line manager) who keeps a watchful eye over managers abroad and who visits them regularly and keeps them in touch with what's happening at home. Most important of all, that person is someone they can turn to – day or night – if things get bad.

This provision is non-existent in many firms. Where it does exist it is often the HR chief or a deputy who maintains the link – but job title is less important than the ability to build trust and empathise with managers abroad and get sufficiently close to sense when something is wrong.

What is being described is the sort of person who understands the human condition and knows expatriate life and is trusted sufficiently for managers to turn to in their darkest of moments – when they have blown their mind or in severest hangover; if compromised or when a marriage is disintegrating; when struggling to cope or losing control or – worse – when decisions are going horribly wrong and likely to torpedo a treasury or wipe out the value of a deal.

Whatever the issue, there can be times – dark, horrible times – when managers abroad need to unload to someone *early and in confidence* if they are to get on top of bad situations and ensure that performance doesn't suffer. Likewise for women managers abroad. They need a lifeline to a *female* confidante at base – to someone who has the experience and knows what it is like to be a woman taking charge and managing in a foreign land.

Soft evidence says that this is not always provided. And even if nothing traumatic happens, the lifeline is an essential source of continuing reassurance. That, for a small cost, is important.

Loyalty

Loyalty and commitment cannot be assumed when managers go overseas. Even with generous expatriate packages, various factors can work against the parent company. One factor is distance – it is much harder to exercise control over a person halfway round the world. Another is the pull of local priorities – managers sometimes go solidly native and champion the local operation against headquarters. But even if they don't, getting the balance right between commitment and allegiance to the local operation *and* to the parent firm is always difficult.

A third factor – for some – is the attraction of life overseas on a good package (generous salary, private school fees, high status, lots of freedom). Some managers make the discovery on their first posting and want to remain abroad in a particular country. Others can be more blatant. Going abroad is a gravy train with an entry ticket into the market for free-agent global managers. They have little intention of staying with their company once the assignment ends. And that – almost invariably – means short-term commitment to the task they were sent out to do.

Repatriation

Reintegrating managers after a foreign assignment has also proven to be a problem. There is North American evidence (Black and Gregersen, 1991) that about 25% of managers who return from an overseas assignment leave their companies within one year – taking with them the valuable experience they gained in the overseas subsidiary.

These ten research findings are stark and go straight to the heart of global integration because it is expatriate managers who do the integration. The findings are critical for situations where a high premium has assumed early realisation of efficiencies and synergies. All are strategic Human Resource issues, so we will briefly examine possible HR solutions around the themes of who should run an overseas acquisition and the selection and training of international managers.

Who Should Run an Overseas Acquisition?

This is not an easy question to answer because there are so many variables and because the little research that exists is inconclusive. Some countries seem to favour their own nationals. Others prefer to leave locals in charge. But basically there are three options – retain the incumbent CEO, send out an expatriate manager, or appoint someone new. A lot depends on context and concerns at home.

- As regards incumbent managers, the advice from seasoned acquirers is simple. *If the acquired business has a good CEO and management team at the top, leave well alone.* Try to retain them and work through them. Likewise for smaller companies. If an owner-manager is selling out, try to keep the person on for a couple of years on an earnout. That locks the brains in.

- If there are still worries about monitoring an acquisition that is perhaps halfway round the world, again the advice is straightforward. *Put one of your own people in somewhere near the top – on the board or to head up a weak function or business area.* That gives a watchful pair of eyes and ears.

- There also has to be an *integration manager* located overseas – even if there are no changes to the top management team. *This is absolutely crucial.* Depending on circumstances and the job to be done, there are various options. It might be the home-side integration manager who is sent out on a one- to two-year posting. Alternatively, it could be an executive from the acquired side – a local national (bilingual if necessary) with experience of managing change.

  Whatever the choice, there has to be someone out there whom the home side works through – to bring together what has to be brought together, to keep apart what has to be kept apart, and to regulate the interactions between the two sides.

That's the basic starting position in any acquisition – national or international. However, there are other considerations. For example:

- If the success of the acquisition hinges upon a specific capability transfer from the parent company, some firms might wish to have one of their own nationals at the top who is intimately familiar with the capability and the internal culture that supports it.

- If the acquired business has a major weakness or has to be transformed, putting someone at the top who has the particular expertise may be essential. If the weakness is technological, the person could arguably come from anywhere in the world provided he or she has the requisite background and experience to transform and run the business. But if it is a marketing weakness, and especially if the acquisition aims to penetrate further into an overseas local market, a skilled local national at the top with an industry-specific marketing background might be preferable.

- Language can also be an issue. If there is a significant language difference, some acquiring CEOs might want someone at the top speaking their own language (and thinking with the same mindset). Sometimes they may want a very personal relationship with someone that they know and trust, and that usually points to sending out one of their own people – the expatriate choice.

Selecting Managers for Overseas Placements

Choosing which managers to send overseas is often a dilemma for acquiring firms, especially smaller companies with limited managerial resources. The best managers are needed at home – and they are needed abroad! But irrespective of whether it is to run the acquired business, to head-up functions or business areas, to join project or R&D teams, or as part of career development through the other side – it's a safe bet that shortlisting will start with each manager's domestic track record. That's the first mistake:

Domestic track record is no predictor of overseas performance.

Or firms might say: we'll send out the most senior people we can. That's the second mistake.

Rank is no predictor of overseas performance.

The research findings (above) have got to be addressed. Do the managers have the requisite mix of cross-cultural understanding and experience? Do they have the capacity to adjust and fit in? Are family circumstances supportive? Will their commitment overseas be balanced? Will they remain loyal and return at the end?

These are the *real* questions to ask. Some are selection questions; others are training questions. But all have to be worked through to minimise the chances of overseas appointments failing and managers getting recalled prematurely. It is especially important for smaller companies. Most don't have a pool of overseas competence to draw upon. If a manager fails, there might not be anyone else who can be sent out. There are no failsafe prescriptions to prevent this happening – only some guidelines that are worth keeping in mind.

The 'Warm-Neutral' Test

Some of the selection criteria for culture-change managers (p. 210) might be appropriate for overseas postings. For example, managers who have successfully built bridges across cultural divides (no matter where) might also have the potential to do it abroad. Passing the 'warm-neutral test' was how one multinational HR chief summed it up. *Managers who connect positively to culture difference, national or international, but whose emotional reaction is stable and neutral – neither embracing nor rejecting, just positively curious and productively engaging.* It's a crude rule of thumb but indicative for starters.

Personality Profiling

Personality testing is of limited use. Contrary to popular belief, personality profiling *cannot* predict managerial performance or how managers will react in unfamiliar circumstances. (The best it might do is predict operative performance in clearly defined jobs – e.g. train drivers, receptionists.) But profiling can be useful for discriminating more systematically between candidates and giving perhaps a different insight into their personalities – *provided always that tests are administered and interpreted by a trained psychologist.*

Career Plateau

Managers whose careers have peaked or reached a plateau need to be scrutinised carefully. If they have a special capability that integration needs, then they may be the right choice. Going abroad can get them out of a rut and give their career a boost. On the other hand, the factors that were responsible for constraining career at home can get transferred abroad and constrain performance. That may be significant if a lot of value is at stake.

Loyalty and Commitment

There is always a risk that managers will not return home after a period overseas – that they will discover their market value and go native and offer themselves to other firms. Or that commitment between the two sides will not be balanced appropriately. That's why some companies will not send anyone younger than 35 abroad, preferring managers with the longest career history and with more invested in the parent. Giving indicative re-entry positions before sending a manager abroad is also wise.

Free-Agent Expatriates

Recruiting free-agent expatriates is sometimes considered instead of sending managers from the acquiring side. These are often former employees of multinational corporations who have gone freelance in a particular region of the world. It is an option that can appear attractive especially to smaller firms wanting one of their own nationals in a particular position but unable to spare anyone.

On the plus side, free-agent expatriates are usually less expensive than sending a home manager overseas. They know the region well and have the language and the contacts and other specialised skills. And they have a demonstrated ability to succeed in an international setting. But there are at least two downsides. They are unfamiliar with the acquiring side's organisational culture. And there is the risk that they may pursue their own career objectives at the expense of the job they were recruited to do. Again, when a lot of value is at stake, the risks have to be carefully calculated.

Cross-Cultural Training

Whoever is selected – and sometimes there may be little room for choice – preparatory cross-cultural training is *absolutely vital*. (Remember Black and Mendenhall's (1990) estimate that roughly 70% of all US expatriates receive inadequate pre-departure cross-cultural training.) It is usually the last thing on merger planners' minds, yet it is essential to start early.

Multinational corporations have extensive experience of expatriate training. They don't always do enough and they don't always get it right, but some of the lessons they have learned over the years are especially relevant to international and global mergers.

Level and Depth of Training

As a general rule, training has to be tailored to

(a) the depth of immersion into a foreign culture

(b) the degree of cultural difference exposed to

(c) the length of stay abroad.

Two years of immersion in a foreign country requires much more preparation than a one-month troubleshooting assignment. Drawing on Mendenhall et al.

(1987), we can identify three different levels of training that are appropriate for different lengths of stay. They are indicative of what cross-cultural training can involve (see Figure 17.2).

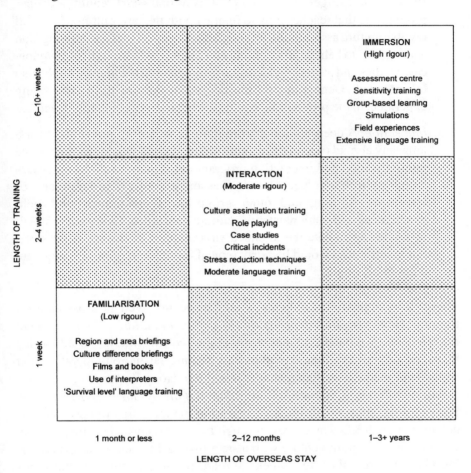

Figure 17.2 Cross-cultural training approaches

Source: adapted from Mendenhall et al. (1987)

1. *Familiarisation.* This level is low rigour, essentially information-giving that is probably sufficient for short-stay assignments (one month or less). It will include business and social briefings on the area or region; basic culture awareness training using films, videos and books; how to use interpreters to best advantage, and rudimentary language training. It is a very basic survival programme that is normally sufficient for a

short-stay visit (but see below) and can typically can be covered in a week or so.

2. *Interaction*. Longer stays (two months to one year) require a deeper programme that teaches how to interact with the new culture. This will involve culture assimilation training, much deeper language training, and leaning how to behave appropriately on a daily basis through role playing, case studies and critical incidents. Stress reduction techniques might also be included. Depending on the degree of culture difference being experienced, the programme could take between two and four weeks.

3. *Immersion*. A deep immersion programme is intense preparation for a long stay abroad (one to three years or longer) and would build upon the familiarisation and interaction programmes. There would be extensive language training, periods at assessment centres, programmes of sensitivity training and other group-based techniques, and field experiences with nationals of the culture concerned. Every attempt will be made to simulate the intended environment as closely as possible. Six to ten weeks would be fairly typical for this sort of programme, but it could be longer.

These three approaches indicate what can be involved in cross-cultural training. However, *a lot depends on the degree of culture difference being experienced*. A Japanese manager moving to North America or a German manager moving to China would usually require far more preparation and adjustment than a Brazilian manager moving to Hong Kong.

Also worth noting is that *short stay does not always mean short training*. For example, suppose an Italian integration manager had to negotiate the details of how R&D was to flow through from a Malaysian acquisition that was in a research joint venture with a state-owned Taiwanese company. The job may require only a few weeks abroad, but in that time an enormous amount of cultural context has to be understood and navigated through.

Spouse and Family Programmes

If a spouse or an entire family are moving abroad, they need training to prepare them. (Remember Black and Stephens' (1989) finding about spouse adjustment being the most pervasive reason why expatriates return early.) The depth of training would obviously depend on respective ages and circumstances and the degree of cultural difference to be experienced. But note there is more to family programmes than language training and learning to be socially competent in a different culture.

Spouses putting careers 'on hold' usually bring skills that can be applied in the host country – if they know how to go about it. Likewise for portable careers – help is usually needed to get them up and running. Children in general are more flexible and spontaneous than adults, but they too may need language training and some understanding of perhaps a very different culture if they are going halfway round the world. Children who go to an expatriate school will enter a peer group of similar others and that can act as a 'halfway' house. But if their language skills are sufficient to allow them to go to a national school, the adjustment process might be difficult.

Post-Arrival Support

Post-arrival support is also important for adjustment. Note that *psychological and culture-understanding support* are the most important – help in interpreting and understanding real-time issues as they happen to the manager and spouse and family. Many international firms provide material support in the form of, for example, company housing and a car with a driver. These are usually welcome, at least initially, but in the longer term they can create psychological problems by insulating a manager and a family from the local culture.

Management Development

Finally and very obviously, one manager adjusting and coping in an alien culture is raw material for other managers to learn from. Any overseas acquisition is a long-term relationship with one or more countries, so whenever managers or boffins are sent abroad for extended periods, send more junior managers over for, say, six-month postings as part of their career development. It's an excellent way of building up a pool of cross-cultural experience.

In Summary

International and global integration managers are no different from other international managers in terms of probability of failure in overseas postings and difficulty of adjustment to foreign cultures. Hence the importance of selecting merger managers on the basis of their cross-cultural competence and giving them (and if necessary their spouses and families) the most appropriate depth of training and support both before and after their posting abroad.

These matters rarely figure in a merger planning agenda – but sharp HR chiefs who are on the ball will be dealing with them during negotiations (or even before) and addressing the major research findings on expatriate adjustment. If, for example, deep immersion training is required, sure it will have a cost and take managers away from where they are also needed. But when value is at stake in integration, any costs and inconvenience become insignificant.

Remember also that some of what has been covered in this chapter is routine knowledge for large firms. They are familiar with the international scene and know where to turn to if they have a problem. Small companies making their first international acquisition may be unsure how to proceed. The standard recommendation, as always, is to seek good-quality professional advice but keep control of your own agenda. Another helpful suggestion – anywhere in the world – is to talk to the senior HR people at a multinational firm and get some distilled wisdom. It is disarming just how helpful some can be.

CHAPTER 18

In Conclusion

'People, structure, processes and culture are like a four-legged stool. If you don't pay attention to all the legs in a merger, it falls over.'

(Finance Director, oil)

This has not been a book about strategy – yet it has gone straight to a question at the heart of strategic thinking: *How best to make strategy happen*? It began by highlighting two of the biggest concerns in the merger strategy field. One was the overwhelming conclusion from decades of research that mergers and acquisitions on average fail to deliver intended value. The other was the underwhelming dearth of research into merger implementation and integration.

Both concerns have been explored with a view to improving practice but with an important proviso. There have been few how-to-do-it prescriptions. The emphasis has been on how to *think* about doing it. To provide managers with a mental toolkit for implementing acquisitions or mergers in ways more likely to deliver strategy and intended value. All the concepts and models and frameworks have to be tailored to each situation and enriched with context – national or international.

Strategic mindsets have been explored – in particular, some of the taken-for-granted North American ways of thinking that have driven merger activity across the twentieth century. Some chapters have challenged conventional wisdom. Others have suggested alternative ways of looking at issues. Some sections (like the section on culture) have tried to move thinking to a deeper level than is commonly found in strategy writings. Others (like the section on integration) have provided some benchmark frameworks for integrating companies under different strategic circumstances.

Note that 'global' has been used in a broad sense. The basic proposition has been that strategic integration in global or international deals differs from strategic integration in national deals in only two fundamental respects. There is the bringing together of two or more national cultures. And there is the need for managers with cross-cultural competence.

Otherwise, integration has to be thought about according to the same principles. A global deal has to follow the same preparatory logic as a national deal. In practice, of course, factors of distance and size and geographical spread all make integration on the ground a far more complex exercise. But in terms of *thinking about* how to approach strategic integration, the frameworks should be applicable to *all* deals – to global mega-mergers, to domestic firms making their first international acquisition, and to national deals in any country.

The core ideas behind the chapters all have been quite simple, and six in particular are worth summarising.

Acquisition Performance is a Function of Strategy and Implementation

The early chapters began by examining strategic thought across the decades as it related to acquisitions.

> We saw the dramatic lurches in strategic thinking across decades especially during the latter half of the twentieth century – strategy as applied economics; strategy as applied finance (or just opportunistic accounting); strategy as marketing; strategy as competitive capability.

> And we saw how some of the thinking that drove acquisition activity – and especially the merger waves – appeared simplistic and often dubious. So it seemed reasonable to conclude that a sizeable chunk of reported under-performance can be traced back to weaknesses at the level of strategy and strategic thinking.

There was another reason for dwelling on strategy at the beginning. The best implementation efforts will not deliver value if it was not there to start with; if it was a figment of fashion and imagination. So the value assumptions that were implicit in strategic thinking across the decades were scrutinised – and again some appeared to be highly suspect.

Bringing all this to the surface was important because many elements of early merger strategic thinking are still alive. Some are to be found in textbooks and business school courses. Others are still lurking in dark corners of managerial minds (especially in the West). Leave them unexorcised and they will continue to swell the statistics on underperformance.

Two Sources of Gain in Mergers – Markets and Hierarchies

Emphasis was put on both. A common imbalance in merger calculations is to focus on combined market efficiencies – and just assume that combined hierarchies will also be more efficient. The points we made were:

- A combined product market usually needs a bigger hierarchy to sustain and grow it.

- Considerable costs and effort and time get diverted inwards to create the bigger hierarchy – usually far more than is required to combine markets.

- The more that attention gets focused inwards, off the market, the greater is the risk of rivals stealing the value.

- There are inefficiencies of size. In large corporations beyond a certain size, bigger hierarchies are often less efficient and less flexible than either was prior to combining.

- Combining markets is largely a rational process that follows well established rules and is easier to put into effect. Combining two organisations is a much more judgemental process that is highly dependent on managerial skill. There are few rules about how to do it (hence sections in this book).

In recent years there has been a lot of talk about efficiencies to be had by being a global player operating in global markets. Buying markets is easy. Relatively small international firms, if they wish, can buy one another's markets and rapidly become global players. Finance is seldom a problem if equity is used as capital.

But the ability to sustain and grow and develop global markets needs globally efficient organisations with global-calibre managers. These cannot be bought and can take years to put into place. Vague phrases like 'operating efficiencies' and 'synergies' and 'rationalising' and 'streamlining' cannot disguise the complexity of organisational integration on a global scale.

Integrating Two Organisations (or Hierarchies) Means Integrating Two Sets of People, Structures, Controls and Cultures

This is the most basic model of organisation but it's the way managers and textbooks typically dissect and analyse organisations. We took each component in turn.

1. On people, we looked at the range of human reactions on both sides of an acquisition, and especially the fear that can run unconsciously through the target side. Then we examined what a HR strategy for acquisitions should be trying to achieve, and focused on commitment as perhaps the most critical HR outcome to pursue.

2. On structures, we looked at varying degrees of structural integration most appropriate for acquisition goals. The argument was that the extent of structural integration had to be driven by acquisition strategy and goals, not political preference or administrative tidiness.

3. The section on controls outlined only some basic essentials – 'hard' controls (financial and information and IT systems) as well as 'soft' controls (key responsibility holders and reporting relationships and expectations at the top).

4. On culture, we examined the concept in some depth and then the dynamics of culture at five different levels. In practical terms, these provide a convenient starting point for analysing organisational culture and predicting where culture clashes might occur.

These divisions are, of course, arbitrary and fuzzy at the edges. For example, a deeper model of organisation might see culture as embracing *all* of them – structure, controls, systems, people, their mindsets and much more (i.e. along the lines of the definition of culture as artifacts, socifacts and mentifacts).

Nevertheless, sticking to the four areas, they provide a convenient basis for *thinking about* how to build up capability profiles of potential targets or rivals, for pre-deal organisational audits, and for planning integration.

But note that they will never say it all. How these components combine around a core technology is different in each firm and this is what gives each its special character and competitive edge. This is the secret of any organisation – how the various components combine to deliver performance – and that's usually hard to penetrate and figure out.

Organisations are Technological Subcultures of National Culture

This is an important concept, especially for international and global acquisitions. Organisations are microcosms of the wider society in which they are embedded and from which they draw their personnel. Ways of thinking about strategy, organising, leadership, control, people management and much more, are often culture-specific. How a North American manager interprets them is likely to be very different from a Japanese manager and different again from a Russian manager.

Some reminders that came with the concept included:

- Only some aspects of organisational culture can be managed in a direct-and-control sense, and these are the most superficial aspects.

- To really understand the organisational culture in a foreign target, acquirers first need to understand the national culture.

- Culture change has to be consistent with the spread of expectations in the wider society.

- As a general rule, organisational cultures don't export and transplant easily.

Strategic calculations often assume value will be delivered through a particular kind of organisation (i.e. an organisation operating to home assumptions). It is an unwise assumption, especially in foreign deals. Technical processes from different countries usually can be combined with relative ease, but not always the management and organisational processes that surround them. This is a core difficulty in integration across countries or continents.

Managers and Their Thinking Make Organisations 'Happen'

Managers with shared mindsets make each organisation 'happen' in its own unique way. And managers with shared mindsets make each acquisition 'happen' in its own unique way.

This theme has run through many pages because it lies at the heart of what is meant by the *human factor*. All strategy and all organisational abstractions (structures, frameworks, theories of managing, etc.) come alive *through* complex managerial psyches that are culture indoctrinated and emotion-driven and self-protecting. These are psychological and cultural realities that cannot be avoided.

But they can be recognised. The argument here – applied to M&A but widely relevant – has been for managers to learn how to step out of their taken-for-granted and familiar ways of thinking and then step back in again. To try to figure out how much of their thinking – thinking that they will *claim* is rational and without bias – is either culture-specific or emotionally driven or ego-protecting or a combination of all three.

That's not always easy to do. It goes against the grain. It can be seen as subversive – destabilising the 'thought glue' that holds a company together. And it can be unsettling. Many of the defensive reactions on both sides (outlined in Chapter 11) have their roots in a fear of taking on board and engaging with a different way of thinking.

The importance of stepping out of taken-for-granted mindsets has run through every chapter – from the earliest of planning stages through to implementation.

- Checking the urge to acquire – particularly when set against a veritable industry encouraging merger activity.

- Probing the assumptions about how value will be delivered. Historically, many of the value assumptions that drove the merger waves in North America – and swelled the statistics on underperformance – were culture-specific and highly dubious. Out of this analysis, twelve common ways of destroying value were identified.

- Ensuring the tight coupling of acquisition strategy to implementation. That included the fine-tuning of organisational integration around acquisition strategy. And developing an acquisition-specific HR strategy to encourage managers to think and act in ways more likely to realise *acquisition* goals.

- Selecting interface managers (from either side) on the basis of their ability to engage productively with the thinking of their opposite numbers. It is an essential quality in integration managers and their teams in *any* acquisition. The chapters on culture and on global integration managers indicated the depth of what is required to develop the capability at international and global levels.

Integration Managers

Finally, strategic integration requires every acquisition to have two managers – a business manager (focusing on markets) and an integration manager (focusing on hierarchies). The two need to work closely from the earliest days of acquisition planning. But their ways of thinking are different.

One is thinking *business* like a typical board or CEO (strategy, finance, markets, competition). The other is thinking *process* (organisation, people, structure, culture, cooperation). Between them, they straddle the two themes in strategic integration – market competition and organisational cooperation. But the skills of integration managers are more elusive. Business managers can be recruited. Integration managers with *firm-specific* process capabilities require to be grown.

And arguably their skills are more important, certainly during the first couple of years. The integration manager is the business manager's right hand. He or she has to create the internal organisational conditions across both companies to sustain and grow and develop the enlarged market. That's absolutely vital for ensuring that value doesn't slip away.

These are the main points of the book. A lot of ground has been covered in a limited number of pages and obviously there are omissions. And as with any toolkit, some tools will prove more useful than others, and some will get used for purposes not intended. However, three groups of readers should find at least some of the chapters of immediate practical use.

- *Acquiring firms* should be able to plan implementation and integration in more detail. The frameworks when tailored to each situation should provide a shared map of how integration is to proceed – what is to happen and what is not, and *why* – and identify areas of potential conflict or concern. That should maintain the desired focus and momentum and allow tighter control over the process. There should be fewer instances of managers down the line trying to hijack the implementation agenda and redirect integration efforts.

- *Target firms* who traditionally have a backseat in integration planning should be able to take more of an initiative. They can use the frameworks to check out in detail what is to happen to their organisation. They can use them to probe the organisational rationale and the value assumptions behind the deal – and whether to go ahead. They will have a shared map to prepare key managers for what is to happen and to prepare them for areas of difficulty. And if acquirers have not done their integration planning, sensible targets will resist. There is an armoury of material here to help them to negotiate an acceptable agenda *before* a deal is struck.

- *Academics* interested in the dynamics of integration or looking for research ideas should find plenty to stretch their minds and get their teeth into. There are many hypotheses waiting for empirical testing. There has also been deliberate dovetailing into related disciplines and that should open up new avenues of enquiry. Given the annual spend on M&A and given the dearth of research into implementation, building up the knowledge base is long overdue.

Whatever your purpose or interest, best of luck!

Notes

Chapter 1

1. In popular usage the terms acquisition, merger, merger and acquisition (M&A) and takeover are used loosely and interchangeably, although there are very precise definitions of an acquisition and a merger for legal and accounting purposes. An acquisition or takeover is the act of buying more than 50% of a vendor's equity after which the vendor's assets are incorporated into those of the acquiring company. The vendor as a legal entity disappears. A merger is when two companies agree to merge or combine their assets to create an entirely new company. Both companies then cease to exist as separate legal entities.

    A merger can also be defined in its **organisational** sense, and it relates to the subsequent merging, or integration, of the different structures, cultures, technologies, systems and personnel from each side. An acquisition or merger in a legal or financial sense does not in itself imply that any organisational merging has happened, or indeed that it should happen. See Chapter 10 for further discussion.

Chapter 4

1. Rumelt (1974) tells us that in 1959, only about 7% of the 500 largest US firms could be classified as conglomerate (i.e. earning most of their income from unrelated businesses). By 1969, the figure had almost tripled but only to a modest 19%. In the UK the pace was even slower – by 1969 only about 5% of the top 100 UK firms could be classified as unrelated conglomerates (Channon, 1973).
2. For an excellent and highly readable analysis of the financial background to conglomeration in the 1960s, see Blair (1972, pp. 293–300).
3. At around the same time, General Electric developed its more sophisticated 'Market Attractiveness – Business Strength' matrix which used multiple criteria for evaluating investment decisions. This captured better the complexity of capital allocation decisions yet it remained less popular – perhaps because it was not simple and visual; perhaps because it could not be slickly marketed.
4. Hostile bids in the UK seldom have exceeded about 5% of all acquisitions in any year but note that there are wide variations across time and between countries.

In the US during the 1970s and early 1980s, nearly a quarter of all large bids were hostile. Across much of mainland Europe, the hostile bid is still comparatively rare.

Chapter 8

1. Very familiar examples could include Just-In-Time (JIT) Management, Total Quality Management (TQM) and even simple Quality Circles. These have delivered very patchy performance improvements in different parts of the world. Even in individual countries, the performance spread between firms has been considerable (see, for example, Oliver and Wilkinson, 1992; Delbridge and Turnbull, 1992).

Chapter 10

1. Hence the sometimes puzzling phrase in systems textbooks: To survive, organisations need to acquire *negative entropy* (i.e. they need to acquire 'negative disorder' or 'negative decay') in order to survive.

Chapter 11

1. Readers familiar with the HR literature may wonder why Beer's four HR goals have not been chosen here (i.e. the four Cs – commitment, congruence, competence and cost-effectiveness). The reason is that Guest's HR goals offer more dimensions, are more measurable and lend themselves better to an acquisition context.

Chapter 12

1. See, for example, Ogbonna (1992) or Storey (1992).

Chapter 14

1. In social science terms, culture is a massive reification of a diversity of social processes – many of them operating at barely conscious and unconscious levels.
2. For example, NASA (in theory) could joint-venture with a bunch of Parmesan engineers who believed the moon was made of blue cheese and ruled by giant mice gods. Apart from some raised eyebrows, provided the engineers were skilled and liaison was smooth and the final product arrived on time to the

correct specifications, maybe it doesn't matter too much what each side believes in.

3. Here I am indebted to a few long-forgotten sociologists such as Eubank (1932) whose thinking was influential in shaping social anthropology in its early days.

Chapter 15

1. Peters and Waterman tell the story of a scientist at Foxboro rushing into the president's office late one evening with a brilliant solution to an urgent problem. The president was delighted and wanted to show his appreciation in an immediate and tangible way – but he had nothing appropriate to give. So he leaned into his drawer, pulled out a banana, and said: 'Here!' Ever since then, the small 'golden banana' pin has been the highest accolade for scientific achievement at Foxboro (Peters and Waterman, 1982, pp. 70–1).

2. This is Handy's (1986) well-known classification of structures-as-cultures.

3. Appraisal systems are typically devalued and underutilised and seen as embarrassing rituals of judgement. Or seen as another channel of control for browbeating managers into signing up to targets superiors want to happen. Or they are simply dismissed as paper-based exercises of little consequence.

   These attitudes indicate misuse of appraisal systems. When used properly, appraisal systems should allow both parties to explore and understand the difficulties and concerns each side has in delivering performance. In a post-merger situation, the process of exploration between one manager and another is far more important than any target-setting. That depends a lot on whether appraisals emphasise process or outcomes. There is evidence (e.g. Randell, 1989) that appraisals in the UK are based more around principles and process; in the US more around outcomes and targets and 'ticking boxes'.

Chapter 16

1. An earlier version of this model was presented in April 1996 at the Conference on HRM in Transition Economies, Alma-Ata Management School, Almaty, Kazakhstan.

2. Quoted by Nancy J. Adler in the Preface to Lane et al. (1997).

3. For further discussion see Hofstede (2001), pp. 166–70.

References

Agrawal, A., Jaffe, J.F. and Mandelker, G.N. (1992) 'The Post-Merger Performance of Acquiring Firms: A Re-Examination of an Anomoly', *Journal of Finance*, 47, pp. 1605–22.

Argyris, C. and Schön, D. (1978) *Organizational Learning*, Reading, MA: Addison-Wesley.

Ashkenas, R.N., DeMonaco, L.J. and Francis, S.C. (1998) 'Making the Deal Real: How GE Capital Integrates Acquisitions', *Harvard Business Review* (January–February), pp. 165–78.

Beer, M., Spector, B., Lawrence, P.R., Mills, D.Q. and Walton, R.E. (1984) *Managing Human Assets*, New York: Free Press.

Belbin, R.M. (1981) *Management Teams: Why They Succeed or Fail*, London: Heinemann.

Beman, L. (1973) 'What We Learned From the Great Merger Frenzy', *Fortune* (April), p. 70.

Black, J.S. and Gregersen, H.R. (1991) 'When Yankee Comes Home: Factors Related to Expatriate and Spouse Repatriation Adjustment', *Journal of International Business Studies*, 22(4), pp. 671–94.

Black, J.S. and Mendenhall, M. (1990) 'Cross-Cultural Training Effectiveness: A Review and a Theoretical Framework for Future Research', *Academy of Management Review*, 15, pp. 113–36.

Black, J.S. and Stephens, G.K. (1989) 'The Influence of the Spouse on American Expatriate Adjustment and Intent to Stay in Pacific Rim Overseas Assignments', *Journal of Management*, 15(4), pp. 529–44.

Blair, J.M. (1972) *Economic Concentration*, New York: Harcourt, Brace Jovanovich.

Bradley, M., Desai, A. and Kim, H. (1988) 'Synergistic Gains from Corporate Acquisitions and their Division Between the Stockholders of Target and Acquiring Firms', *Journal of Financial Economics*, 21(1), pp. 3–40.

Buono, A.F., Bowditch, J.L. and Lewis, J.W. (1985) 'When Cultures Collide: The Anatomy of a Merger', *Human Relations*, 38, pp. 477–500.

Burns, T. and Stalker, G.M. (1961) *The Management of Innovation*, London: Tavistock.

Business Week (1981) 'For Executives of the 1980s, A Stress on Return' (1 June) p. 88.

Buzzell, R.D. and Gale, B.T. (1987) *The PIMS Principles*, New York: Free Press.

Caplow, T. (1964) *Principles of Organisation*, New York: Harcourt, Brace & World.

Chandler, A.D. (1977) *The Visible Hand: The Managerial Revolution in American Business*, Cambridge, MA: Harvard University Press.

Channon, D. (1973) *The Strategy and Structure of British Enterprise*, Cambridge, MA: Harvard University Press.

Cherns, A. (1976) 'The Principles of Sociotechnical Design', *Human Relations*, 29(8), pp. 783–92.

Cherns, A. (1987) 'Principles of Sociotechnical Design Revisited', *Human Relations*, 40(3), pp. 153–62.

Child, J. (1981) 'Culture, Contingency and Capitalism in the Cross-National Study of Organisations', in Staw, B.M. and Cummings, L.L. (eds), *Research in Organisational Behaviour*, Volume 3, Greenwich, CT: JAI Press.

Cyert, R. and March, J. (1963) *A Behavioural Theory of the Firm*, Englewood Cliffs, NJ: Prentice-Hall.

Davidson, K.M. (1985) *Megamergers*, Cambridge, MA: Ballinger.

Deal, T. and Kennedy, A. (1982) *Corporate Cultures*, Reading, MA: Addison-Wesley.

Dellbridge, R. and Turnbull, P. (1992) 'Human Resource Maximisation: The Management of Labour Under Just-In-Time Manufacturing Systems', in Blyton, P. and Turnbull, P. (eds), *Reassessing Human Resource Management*, London: Sage.

Eubank, E.E. (1932) *The Concepts of Sociology*, New York.

Firth, M. (1980) 'Takeovers, Shareholders' Return and the Theory of the Firm', *Quarterly Journal of Economics*, 94 (March), pp. 225–49.

Fombrun, C.J., Tichy, N.M. and Devanna, M.A. (1984) *Strategic Human Resource Management*, New York: Wiley.

Franks, J. and Harris, R. (1989) 'Shareholder Wealth Effects of Corporate Takeovers: The UK Experience 1955–85', *Journal of Financial Economics*, 23, pp. 225–49.

Gregory, A. (1997) 'An Examination of the Long Run Performance of UK Acquiring Firms', *Journal of Business Finance and Accounting*, 24(7–8) (September), pp. 971–1002.

Gregory, K. (1983) 'Native View Paradigms: Multiple Cultures and Culture Conflicts in Organizations', *Administrative Science Quarterly*, 28(3), pp. 359–76.

Guest, D.E. (1987) 'Human Resource Management and Industrial Relations', *Journal of Management Studies*, 24, pp. 503–21.

Guest, D.E. (1997) 'Human Resource Management and Performance: A Review and Research Agenda', *International Journal of Human Resource Management*, 8(3) (June), 1997.

Hamel, G. and Prahalad, C.K. (1989) 'Strategic Intent', *Harvard Business Review*, (May–June), pp. 63–76.

Handy, C.B. (1986) *Understanding Organisations*, London: Penguin Books.

Hansen, R.G. (1987) 'A Theory for the Choice of Exchange Medium in Mergers and Acquisitions', *Journal of Business*, 60, pp. 75–95.

Henderson, B.D. (1979) *Henderson on Corporate Strategy*, Cambridge, MA: Belknap Press.

Henzler, H.A. (1992) 'The New Era of Eurocapitalism', *Harvard Business Review*, 70(4), pp. 57–68.

Hofstede, G. (1980) *Culture's Consequences: International Differences in Work-Related Values*, Beverly Hills, CA: Sage.

Hofstede, G. (1983) 'Cultural Constraints in Management Theories', *Academy of Management Executive*, 7(1), pp. 81–94.

Hofstede, G. (2001) *Culture's Consequences: Comparing Values, Behaviours, Institutions and Organisations Across Nations*, London: Sage.

Hogarty, T.F. (1970) 'Profits from Mergers: The Evidence of Fifty Years', *St John's Law Review*, 44 (special edition) (Spring), pp. 378–91.

Holl, P. and Pickering, J.F. (1988) 'The Determinants and Effects of Actual, Abandoned and Contested Mergers', *Managerial and Decision Economics*, 9.

Hunt, J.W. (1990) 'Changing Pattern of Acquisition Behaviour in Takeovers and Consequences for Acquisition Processes', *Strategic Management Journal*, 11, pp. 69–77.

Hunt, J.W. and Lees, S. (1987) 'Hidden Extras – How People Get Overlooked in Takeovers', *Personnel Management* (July), pp. 24–8.

Hunt, J.W., Lees, S., Grumbar, J. and Vivian, P. (1987) *Acquisitions – The Human Factor*, London: London Business School/ Egon Zehnder International.

Jaques, E. (1976) *A General Theory of Bureaucracy*, London: Heinemann.

Jemison, D.B. and Sitkin, S.B. (1986) 'Corporate Acquisitions: A Process Perspective', *Academy of Management Review*, 11(1), pp. 145–63.

Jensen, M.C. and Ruback, R.S. (1983) 'The Market for Corporate Control: The Scientific Evidence', *Journal of Financial Economics*, 11, pp. 5–50.

Jung, C.J. (1964) *Man and his Symbols*, London: Aldus Books.

Kaplan, S.N. (1989) 'The Effects of Management Buyouts on Operating Performance and Value', *Journal of Financial Economics*, 24, pp. 217–54.

Katz, D. and Khan, R.L. (1966) *The Social Psychology of Organizations*, New York: Wiley.

Klein, B.H. (1977) *Dynamic Economics*, Cambridge, MA: Harvard University Press.

Kluckholn, F.R. and Strodtbeck, F.L. (1961) *Variations in Value Orientations*, Westport, CT: Greenwood Press.

Kobrin, S.J. (1988) 'Expatriate Reduction and Strategic Control in American Multinational Corporations', *Human Resource Management*, 27(1), pp. 63–75.

Lane, H.W., Distefano, J.J. and Maznevski, M.L. (1997) *International Management Behaviour*, Oxford and Cambridge, MA: Blackwell.

Lawrence, P.R. and Lorsch, J.W. (1967) *Organisation and Environment*, Cambridge, MA: Harvard University Press.

Lees, S. (1992) 'Auditing Mergers and Acquisitions – Caveat Emptor', *Management Auditing Journal*, 7(4), pp. 6–11.

Lees, S. (1996) 'Strategic HRM in Transition Economies', *Proceedings of the Conference: Human Resource Management – Strategy and Practice* [in Russian], Almaty, Kazakhstan: Alma-Ata Management School.

Leibenstein, H. (1976) *Beyond Economic Man: A New Foundation for Microeconomics*, Cambridge, MA: Harvard University Press.

Linnows, R.G. (1993) 'The Japanese Manager's Traumatic Entry into the United States: Understanding the American-Japanese Cultural Divide', *Academy of Management Executive*, 7(4), pp. 21–40.

Louis, A. (1982) 'The Bottom Line on Ten Big Mergers', *Fortune* (3 May), pp. 84–9.

McKinsey & Company Inc. (1985) 'The Role of the Corporate Centre' (October).

McKinsey & Company Inc. (1988) 'Shareholder Value Creation in Major Acquisition Programmes' (March).

Malatesta, P. (1983) 'The Wealth Effects of Merger Activity and the Objective Function of Merging Firms', *Journal of Financial Economics*, 11, pp. 155–81.

Mandelker, G. (1974) 'Risk and Return: The Case of Emerging Firms', *Journal of Financial Economics*, 1 (December), pp. 303–35.

Manne, H. (1965) 'Mergers and the Market for Corporate Control', *Journal of Political Economy*, 73 (April), pp. 110–20.

March, J. and Simon, H. (1958) *Organisations*, New York: Wiley.

Marks, M.L. and Mirvis, P.M. (1986) 'The Merger Syndrome', *Psychology Today*, 20, pp. 36–42.

Marris, R. (1963) 'A Model of the "Managerial" Enterprise', *Quarterly Journal of Economics*, 77 (May), pp. 185–98.

Marris, R. (1964) *The Economic Theory of 'Managerial' Capitalism*, Cambridge, MA: Free Press of Glencoe.

Mendenhall, M.E., Dunbar, E. and Oddou, G.R. (1987) 'Expatriate Selection, Training, and Career Pathing: A Review and Critique', *Human Resource Management*, 26(3), pp. 331–45.

Meyer, J.W. and Rowan, B. (1977) 'Institutionalised Organisations: Formal Structure as Myth and Ceremony', *American Journal of Sociology*, 83, pp. 340–63.

Miller, E.J. and Rice, A.K. (1967) *Systems of Organisation*, London: Tavistock.

Morck, R., Schleifer, A. and Vishnir, W. (1990) 'Do Managerial Objectives Drive Bad Acquisitions?', *Journal of Finance*, 45(1), pp. 31–48.

Mueller, D.C. (ed.) (1980) *The Determinants and Effects of Mergers: An International Comparison*, Cambridge: Oelgeschlager, Gunn and Hain.

Mueller, D.C. (1986) *The Modern Corporation*, Brighton: Harvester Press.

Nahavandi, A. and Malekzadeh, A.R. (1988) 'Acculturation in Mergers and Acquisitions', *Academy of Management Review*, 13, 79–90.

Ogbonna, E. (1992) 'Organisation Culture and Human Resource Management: Dilemmas and Contradictions', in Blyton, P. and Turnbull, P. (eds), *Reassessing Human Resource Management*, London: Sage.

Oliver, N. and Wilkinson, B. (1992) *The Japanization of British Industry: New Developments in the 1990s*, Oxford: Blackwell.

Pascale, R.T. (1991) *Managing on the Edge*, New York: Simon & Schuster.

Payne, A.F. (1987) 'Approaching Acquisitions Strategically', *Journal of General Management*, 13(2) (Winter), pp. 5–27.

Peters, T. and Waterman, R. (1982) *In Search of Excellence*, New York: Harper & Row.

Pettigrew, A.M. (1985) *The Awakening Giant: Continuity and Change at ICI*, Oxford: Blackwell.

Pfeffer, J. (1995) *Competitive Advantage through People*. Boston, MA: Harvard Business Press.

Porter, M.E. (1985) *Competitive Advantage*, New York: Free Press.

Porter, M.E. (1987) 'From Competitive Strategy to Corporate Strategy', *Harvard Business Review* (May–June), pp. 47–59.

Prahalad, C.K. and Bettis, R. (1986) 'The Dominant Logic: A New Linkage Between Diversity and Performance', *Strategic Management Journal*, 7(6), pp. 485–501.

Puffer, S. M. (1994) 'Understanding the Bear: A Portrait of Russian Business Leaders', *Academy of Management Executive*, 8(1), pp. 41–61.

Pugh, P. (1987) *Is Guinness Good for You?*, London: Financial Training.

Randell, G. (1989) 'Employee Appraisal' in Sisson, K. (ed.), *Personnel Management in Britain* (first edition), Oxford: Blackwell.

Ravenscraft, D.J. and Scherer, F.M. (1987a) *Mergers, Sell-Offs and Economic Efficiency*, Washington, DC: Brookings Institution.

Ravenscraft, D.J. and Scherer, F.M. (1987b) 'Life After Takeover', *Journal of Industrial Economics*, 36 (December), pp. 147–56.

Rice, A.K. (1965) *Learning for Leadership*, London: Tavistock.

Robino, D. and DeMeuse, K. (1985) 'Corporate Mergers and Acquisitions: Their Impact on HRM', *Personnel Administrator* (November), pp. 33–44.

Rumelt, R.P. (1974) *Strategy, Structure and Economic Performance*, Cambridge, MA: Harvard University Press.

Schein, E.H. (1985) *Organizational Culture and Leadership*, San Francisco: Jossey-Bass.

Schweiger, D.M. and Denisi, A.S. (1991) 'Communicating with Employees Following a Merger: A Longitudinal Field Experiment', *Academy of Management Journal*, 34(1), pp. 110–35.

Singh, A. (1975) 'Take-Overs, Economic Natural Selection, and the Theory of the Firm', *Economic Journal*, 85, pp. 497–515.

Smircich, L. (1983) 'Concepts of Culture and Organisational Analysis', *Administrative Science Quarterly*, 28, pp. 339–58.

Smith, K.W. and Hershman, S.E. (1996) 'Making Mergers Work for Profitable Growth', *Mercer Management Consultancy Commentary*.

Starkey, K. and McKinlay, A. (1990) 'Realigning Internal and External Environments: Organisational Change at Pilkington', in Wilson, D.C. and Rosenfeld, R. (eds), *Managing Organisations: Text, Readings and Cases,* London: McGraw-Hill.

Storey, J. (1992) *Developments in the Management of Human Resources*, Oxford: Blackwell.

Treacy, M. and Wiersema, F. (1995) *Discipline of Market Leaders*, Reading, MA: Addison-Wesley.

Trompenaars, F. (1993) *Riding the Waves of Culture*, London: Economist Books.

Tung, R.L. (1982) 'Selection and Training Procedures of US, European and Japanese Multinationals', *California Management Review*, 25(1), pp. 57–71.

Tung, R.L. (1994) 'Strategic Management Thought in East Asia', *Organisational Dynamics* (Spring), pp. 55–65.

Vaara, E. (1999) *Towards a Rediscovery of Organisational Politics*, Helsinki: Helsinki School of Economics and Business Administration.

Weick, K.E. (1979) *The Social Psychology of Organising*, Reading, MA: Addison-Wesley.

Weick, K.E. (1995) *Sensemaking in Organisations*, London: Sage.

Weston, J.F. and Mansinghka, S.K. (1971) 'Tests of the Efficiency Performance of Conglomerate Firms', *Journal of Finance*, 26 (September), pp. 919–36.

Williamson, O.E. (1975) *Markets and Hierarchies: Analysis and Antitrust Implications*, New York: Free Press.

General Index

Corporate Index